D1564899

Merchants and Migrants in Nineteenth-Century Beirut

Harvard Middle Eastern Studies, 18

Merchants and Migrants in Nineteenth-Century Beirut

Leila Tarazi Fawaz

Harvard University Press
Cambridge, Massachusetts
London, England   1983

Library of Congress Cataloging in Publication Data

Fawaz, Leila Tarazi
  Merchants and migrants in nineteenth-century Beirut.

  (Harvard Middle Eastern studies ; 18)
  Bibliography: p.
  Includes index.
  1. Beirut (Lebanon) — Commerce — History.   2. Beirut
(Lebanon) — History.   3. Merchants — Lebanon — Beirut.
4. Migration, Internal — Lebanon — History.   I. Title.
II. Series.
HF3759.Z9B443   1983   307.7′64′095692   83–4396
ISBN 0-674-56925-3

To Karim

Preface

The spectacular growth of Beirut in the nineteenth century has never been dealt with in a satisfactory manner, in spite of the ample and excellent work already done on other aspects of Middle Eastern urban history, most notably on Cairo and some of the major North African towns. This neglect of Beirut is not owing to a lack of documentation. An abundance of material is available, though much of it has never been assembled systematically, and no one really knows how much exists. A great deal of this material is in Beirut itself—in the archives of the National Museum and in private archives of families, companies, and institutions—and has only to be found and put together slowly and patiently, a task now made virtually impossible by the war in Lebanon. I was fortunate to have completed my research before the outbreak of hostilities in 1975 and to have benefited from the help of many people who put material at my disposal.

A good deal of documentation is also available in government and other archives outside Lebanon. In Egypt, for example, there is a plethora of information, particularly for the years 1831–1840, when the Egyptians ruled over the Syrian region. For the whole of the nineteenth century, however, the most comprehensive archives outside Lebanon are British and French. For the history of the Syrian coast and Mount Lebanon, the British material has not been as thoroughly exploited as the French.

My use of the terms "Syria" and "Mount Lebanon" (or "the Mountain") must be defined. "Syria" has had four different meanings in this century. Until the end of World War I, the area stretching from the Taurus Mountains in the north to the Sinai peninsula in the south, and from the Mediterranean on the west to the Syrian desert on the east, was under Ottoman rule. After the war, it was divided in two, with the southern part turned into Palestine and Transjordan, both under the British Mandate, and a northern area placed under the French Mandate known as Syria. Between 1925 and 1936, this northern area was further subdivided into four areas known collectively as the Levant states. They were the states of Syria and Greater Lebanon (which together constitute the present-day Syrian and Lebanese republics); the government of Latakia (at first called the state of the 'Alawis); and the government of Jebel (Mount) Druze. Latakia and Jebel Druze were annexed as provinces to the state of Syria in 1936. Thus Syria was used to mean both the state of Syria excluding Latakia and Jebel Druze before 1936 and the state that included them after 1936. For my purposes the terms "Syria" and the "Syrian region" will be used to designate only the area comprising present-day Syria and Lebanon — that is, the original northern, or French-mandated, territories — and unless otherwise specified, the terms "Lebanon" and "the Mountain" will be restricted to the old territory of Mount Lebanon and not to the present republic of the same name.

The term "Mount Lebanon" has been used since the late eighteenth century to refer to both the northern and the southern districts of the Lebanon range. The Lebanon range is the highest of the massifs of the Levant, with its highest point — Qarnet al-Sauda (east-southeast of Tripoli) — reaching 3,038 meters, and its second highest — Mount Sannin (east-northeast of Beirut) — reaching 2,548 meters. The northern regions include the districts of Bsharri, Batrun, Jubayl, and Kisrawan. The southern district, beyond Kisrawan and separated from it by the Beirut–Damascus road, is the region known as the Shuf or Jebel Druze.

A word on transliteration: Names of people and places commonly found in Western literature have been anglicized (such as "Beirut," not "Bayrut"), and personal names are as the individuals and families chose to spell them. Other Arabic names and words have been simplified, with diacritical marks eliminated.

Early research on this book was made possible by generous funding from the Center for Middle Eastern Studies at Harvard University, the Radcliffe Institute, and the American Research Center in Egypt. I have since received a grant from the Joint Committee of the American Council of Learned Societies and the Social Science Research Council to document the civil war of 1860 in Mount Lebanon and the Syrian interior. Some of that material is also incorporated here.

I am indebted to Jafet Library at the American University of Beirut and to Yusif Khuri, the head of its Arabic division, and to the German Oriental Insititute, particularly its then director, Peter Bachman, and its administrator, Walter Tülp, for putting their excellent libraries at my disposal. Thanks are also due to Maurice Chehab and his assistant, Hassan Hichi, for the use of the Museum of National Antiquities; Dar al-Awqaf and al-Mahkama al-Sunniyya al-Shar'iyya for their kindness and cooperation; the Greek Orthodox archdiocese and Archbishop Ilyas and Gofrail Salibi; the Compagnie de Gestion et d'Exploitation du Port, des Quais et Entrepôts de Beyrouth, the director Philip Tawile, Antoine Bechara, and Alfred Saghbini, Nazem Rahal, and Antoine Sakr of its archives; the Public Record Office in London; the Archives du Ministère des Affaires Etrangères in Paris; Widener Library and its ever-obliging staff at Harvard University; Dar al-Watha'iq and Dar al-Kutub in Cairo, and Mahmud al-Shaniti, then head of archives, and Sawsan 'Abd al-Fata, Muhammad Kamil Shata, Itrahim Fathallah, and Hashim al-Adhim of Dar al-Wata'iq.

Photographs of nineteenth-century Beirut were put at my disposal by Fuad Debbas and by Carney Gavin, Elizabeth Carella, and Ingeborg O'Reilly of the Harvard Semitic Museum. The map detail of Beirut reproduced in the book was kindly provided by Eugen Wirth.

A great many others have also given generously of their time and assistance, including Afif and Jamil Bayhum, Nicolas de Bustros, Yvonne Lady Cochrane, Antoine, Selim, and Fuad Debbas, John Joly, Samia Nassar, Hassan Tamim, and all those listed under "Interviews" in the bibliography.

A number of people helped me formulate my ideas at various stages of my research. Muhsin Mahdi read parts of my manuscript and was very supportive; Joseph Fletcher, Jr., Charles Issawi, Abdul-Karim Rafeq, Kamal Salibi, and François Vigier taught me more than they realize; Richard W. Bulliet was extremely helpful throughout my research; and H. A. Hanham inspired and encouraged me all along.

Samir Khalaf first pointed out to me the need for a social history of Beirut and generously put at my disposal all the material gathered from a project that he and Per Kongstad of Copenhagen University were undertaking on the urbanization of the Hamra quarter in Beirut. Dominique Chevallier also put some primary material at my disposal and helped me in many ways.

My warmest gratitude goes to David Landes and Albert Hourani, who provided inspiration and encouragement in special degree. My debt to them cannot be repaid.

The friendliness of my colleagues and students at Tufts University should not be left unnoted. I am also very grateful to Odile Hourani, Sonia Landes, Mary Russell, Nadim Tarazi, and especially Marilyn Edling, Barbro Ek, Axel Havemann, Hoda Saddi, and Nakhle Tarazi. My thanks to Margaret Sevcenko, who edited my manuscript and made invaluable comments, to Elizabeth Suttell, Aida Donald, and Joyce Backman of Harvard University Press, and Brenda Sens and Mary Towle, who helped me in many ways. The family of Claire and Nagib Tarazi, the family of Salwa and Adib Fawaz, and all my friends were in the unenviable position of being used as testing grounds for my ideas. But none has been called upon to provide the patience and encouragement that Karim Fawaz has so willingly given through it all.

Contents

Merchants and Migrants
in Nineteenth-Century Beirut

1876 plan of Beirut, dedicated to Sultan Abdul Hamid II by the Danish consul; photograph (detail) by Eugen Wirth. The shaded area (I) near the harbor is the old city with its bazaars, central mosques, churches, official buildings, including the Ottoman bank (3) and telegraph and postal service (4), and various consulates. Beyond this are newer areas, with mulberry plantations and gardens, private homes, businesses (39 is the Beirut-Damascus Road Company), the military barracks (6), the new seraglio (2), and other public buildings.

1 Introduction

Until recently, most people in Beirut would have been astonished if someone called them "Beirutis." One could ask person after person where they came from and receive for an answer the names of countless villages and towns in the various areas in and around Lebanon. Even if it had been their grandparents or great-grandparents who had first settled in the city, people still regarded themselves as belonging to the ancestral village, however long ago they might have left it. This is partly because many came from places so nearby that they could continue to visit back and forth, and in that way preserve their feelings of identification. More likely, however, it simply reflects the fact that their families had moved to Beirut within a few generations and still maintained the attitudes of an immigrant population.

Beirut achieved its present size in very recent times. The first stages of its modern growth go back to the nineteenth century. Although one of the eastern Mediterranean's oldest settlements, it remained throughout most of its long history a comparatively small and insignificant port town, with only brief moments of greater glory. At the beginning of the nineteenth century it comprised only about 6,000 people and a quarter of a square mile in area. By the end of the same century, however, it had been transformed into a major seaport and the most important city of greater Syria, with a population of 120,000 souls. The center of the Syrian population and economy had moved from the interior to Beirut, from Mount Lebanon to Beirut, and from other seaports to Beirut.

This demographic and economic explosion, while remarkable in itself, reflected an even more profound political transformation. For Beirut did not replace, much less increase, its population by a surplus of births over deaths, but almost entirely by immigration. A series of international, regional, and local developments combined to attract vast numbers to Beirut and set into motion a series of consequences whose repercussions are still being felt today.

The subject of this book is the relationship between migration and urbanization as it was manifested in Beirut's social transformation in the nineteenth century. In barely seventy-five years the city grew from a town of 6,000 to a metropolis of 120,000 and from a community where Muslims and Christians lived side by side to a city where new sectarian tensions reflected fundamental changes in the socioeconomic and political balance between communities. These changes shaped nineteenth-century Beirut and account for much of the stress in modern Lebanon.

Although urbanism is one of the most dynamic and best studies of the Middle Eastern disciplines, with rare exceptions the literature that has so far resulted concerns itself solely with particular cities at particular times without attempting to draw any theoretical conclusions. One of the few studies that does assess broader issues discerns alternating periods of urban development between coastal and inland cities in the history of the Middle East.[1] The nineteenth century is identified as a period of coastal revival, owing to the growth of trade with Europe following the industrial revolution and the development of steam navigation. That observation was the point of departure for my inquiry into the reasons behind the startling growth of Beirut in the nineteenth century.

As my inquiry progressed it soon became apparent that Beirut's growth bore out this theory, for it demonstrated in many ways the series of socioeconomic and political changes that typically accompanied the entry of the Middle East into the international network of power and trade. Technological revolution, the ascendancy of Western Europe, its growing influence over large parts of the globe, and the subsequent domination of world markets by a Western-dominated economic system all acted as catalysts for change in those parts of the world brought into the European orbit. Obviously the growth of trade with Europe in an age of steam navigation would work to the advantage of seaports, and to that extent Beirut's emergence as an international trade and commercial center was indeed simply one manifestation of a more general trend.

But why did all coastal cities not benefit to the same degree? In particular, why did not the more famous ports on the eastern Mediterranean—Acre, Tyre, or Sidon—prosper as Beirut did? The answer to that question lies not with the Western-instigated economic transformation of the period, but with the regional and local shifts in power that accompanied it. If the West accounted for the growth of seaports generally, regional and local realities determined which among them benefited in particular. However great the influence of the West, regional and local influences still determined the degree and forms that influence took. Beirut's success cannot be explained away simply by pointing to the city's position in the world market. Its site on the Mediterranean may explain its growth, but the particulars of that growth lie in its links with the Syrian hinterland.

How much change to attribute to outside influences and how much to the internal social dynamics is an important question in the study of any area. In dealing with the non-Western world, social scientists, formed by Western schools of thought and preoccupied with modernization, have until recently neglected the role the internal dynamics of a society play in its evolution. Outside influences were undeniably important, but to focus on them to the exclusion of local conditions can only end in a distortion of the picture. A comparable distortion is already common among urbanists who apply criteria relevant solely in the West to cities in the rest of the world. For example, the coupling of industrialization and urbanization leads to the labeling of vast areas of North America and Australia, however sparsely populated, as "highly urbanized," and the densely populated regions of the less-developed countries as "underurbanized" or "overurbanized." That distinction also carries a value judgment with it: becoming a modern industrial city is clearly a goal to be actively pursued. One result has been endlessly to analyze nonindustrial cities in order to determine what it is they lack. For Beirut and any other city whose function has been mainly commercial as distinct from industrial, that attitude also seems to belittle the role they have played in shaping their societies.[2]

Commercial and trading centers, like all cities, show differences in social organization that result in different social and economic development. Beirut and Alexandria, for example, both benefited in the nineteenth century from the growth of sea trade, but whereas the main export of Alexandria, cotton, dominated the Egyptian economy, silk, the major export of Beirut, only played a part in the Syrian situation. Alexandria's affluence was based on the importance of cotton in the world economy, an importance that the silk trade never achieved. As a result Alexandria, a city of merchants, bankers, and cotton brokers, grew far more than Beirut did so long as cotton reigned. Beirut grew less, but remained diversified in its economy; it was a political, educational, and even cultural center. So in the twentieth century, when both cotton and sea trade lost ground, Alexandria languished, while Beirut, though suffering a comparable decline in the silk and sea trade, continued to thrive. Its greatest period of prosperity did not even occur until after World War II, when it continued unabated until the outbreak of civil war in 1975. The diversity of Beirut's functions allowed it to serve both its own hinterland and the world at large.

Another reason behind these very different histories was the more marked involvement of the European countries in Alexandria than in Beirut. Although both cities owed a great deal to European capitalism and entrepreneurship in the nineteenth century, European investment in Alexandria was so great that the city remained for a long time under the control of Europeans. In Beirut, in contrast, the local population played an active role in the city's economy, and a new class of Beiruti merchants was formed upon which the city could later rely. In Alexandria, as in North Africa generally, foreigners filled mercantile roles and, when they finally left, it took time to fill the vacuum. In Beirut, local merchants continued to run the economy as they always had. Alexandria and Beirut also had very different relations to the rest of their countries. Beirut was never dominated by Damascus as Alexandria was by Cairo, and its ties with Mount Lebanon were far closer than those of Alexandria to its hinterland.[3]

If there were any city in the Middle East where the conditions appeared to be ripe to produce a population divided along socioeconomic lines, it was Beirut. But because Beirut prospered, it was also a natural destination for emigrants from Mount Lebanon in times of stress, and the circumstances compelling their migration meant that they brought with them allegiances based on clan, communal, and regional ties. Determining why people migrate can tell a great deal about them once they are established in a new milieu, but too often scholarly analysis ignores this human element. Migration involves not just abstract situations but acute disruptions in the lives of individuals, both those who move and those who stay behind. Ties are severed in the family, the clan, the quarter, the neighborhood, the whole village, especially when there is no time to plan because of the circumstances that surround hasty but often permanent departures.

In addition, although traveling was less complicated than it is today in terms of bureaucratic obstacles — passports, visas, and the like were practically unknown, at least in the Ottoman empire — the worst enemy of traveling was not man but nature. The traveler, however rich, still had to face the elements, climb mountains, cross deserts, and suffer a whole range of discomforts in food, lodging, and transport. Some glimpse into the hardship involved can be gleaned from travel accounts or the reminiscences of family elders about traveling in their youth, whether Armenians through the Fertile Crescent, Syrians seeking jobs in the Sudan or Egypt, or practically anyone crossing the seas to America. Small wonder, then, that whatever the original intention, the emigrating population rarely returned to the homeplace.

Why did so many people pull up stakes so often? In the Middle East migrations have been a recurrent theme throughout history, whether of invaders, refugees, merchants, or missionaries, nomads or town dwellers. Clearly, whatever the hardships, either the rewards of moving or the perils of staying behind were still greater. Both glory and fear have moved people — literally as well as figuratively — in the Middle East just as they have done elsewhere.

People came to Beirut for many reasons. There was the real, if intanible, appeal of city life as well as the search for new opportunities. In Beirut those opportunities could include an education or a career in government service, but were most apt to be in commerce or trade. The migrations that had the most profound effect on the city's social relations were those inspired by political crises and internecine strife. Political crises probably did not affect the majority of immigrants to Beirut in the nineteenth century, but it did affect the most influential of them.

Political migrations, as distinct from economically induced ones, almost invariably involve middle-class and wealthy people who would otherwise not migrate at all. That is why political crises often deprive the troubled area of craftsmen, entrepreneurs, professionals, and other productive groups to the benefit of the communities in which they settle. The areas these people abandon are, of course, affected, as the social balance of the village, town, province, or nation is changed by the departure of the dissatisfied, defeated, persecuted, or frightened. Their departure may bring its own problems, but it can also remove sources of tension and eliminate civil unrest.

The opposite can be true for the areas that receive the migrants, who bring with them the attitudes acquired in another time and place that restrict their ability to change and to adapt to a new environment. That resistance to change has its impact on their new habitat. The persistance or reinforcement of earlier social attitudes is, of course, not exclusive to migrants of political crises. Exposure to new groups does not necessarily induce assimilation, whatever the circumstances, and it often has the opposite effect: it is not uncommon for migrants to cling more tenaciously to their native attitudes and customs than they ever did before they emigrated. Allegiance to a particular local family or leader may be left behind but, partly because of that, other traditions are correspondingly strengthened.[4]

In Beirut, the migrant population driven to the city became a divisive force. As political emigrés, they brought with them prejudices against all members of whatever group had occasioned their departure, and they handed their feelings down to their children and others who had neither experienced nor participated in the original disputes. The impact of a migrant population's attitude varies in every case, but it is always present. In the Middle East today, Jews have carried memories of persecution to Israel that still influence their choice of political options. The children of Palestinian refugees fight for the liberation of a land they know only from accounts handed down to them by their elders; however settled they actually are, they perceive themselves as transients, and that conviction influences their behavior. Iraqi, Syrian, and other political leaders who left their countries in the fifties, sixties, and seventies to settle elsewhere cling to an identity that contains a lost social status. Refugees of the 1975 war in Lebanon settle wherever they can and perpetuate memories and attitudes that shape their outlooks.

Migrants are also forced to rely more than others on members of their own religious or ethnic community. Of the traditional allegiances of family, community, and region, community is the least apt to be weakened by the move and, as a result, takes on a decisive role in the new milieu. From a simple awareness that a group of people comprise a distinct community to the conviction that the community survives in the face of opposition from others is a line often crossed in times of stress.

The role of migrants in the growth of sectarianism in parts of the Ottoman empire in the nineteenth and early twentieth century is undeniable. Although studies so far have seen it as a consequence of the frustration of traditionally privileged groups – Sunni Muslims in particular – which arose from the reforms that benefited Christians,[5] this theory ignores the fact that most of the Beirut migrants belonged to Christian sects and that they, too, played a role in the changing social relations. Cities are not necessarily melting pots; they can just as easily perpetuate, reinforce, and reshape traditional ties. As a general rule, however, the greater the opportunities provided to a migrant group, the more likely it is to merge into the mainstream. In the absence of any national pulls at a time when centralized government, rapid communication, and homogenized education did not yet exist, the opportunities generated by economic growth did serve to break down the lines of traditional affiliation and to replace them by socio-economic ties. In nineteenth-century Beirut, however, conditions existed that encouraged both the creation of new social classes that cut across communities and the reinforcement of old alliances and prejudices. Which of them dominated, and who took advantage of them?

2 The Legacy of the Past

Beirut is located on the northern end of a hilly site bordered to the north and west by the Mediterranean and to the south and east by the Mount Lebanon chain. The site falls sharply to the northwest, west, and east, more gently to the north, where Beirut is situated, and is level to the south. The city slopes northward toward the harbor in the bay of Saint Georges. To the west the promontory of Ras-Beirut juts into the sea.[1]

It was a site with notable geographic advantages. One was that the narrow coastal plain on which the city was located was widest near Beirut; another was that its harbor in the bay of Saint Georges was protected from the prevailing southwest winds by the headland of Ras-Beirut, an unusual east–west projection in an otherwise north–south coast.[2] Geography probably accounts for the remarkable continuity of the town's history since the fourteenth century B.C. and for the town's survival through so many ups and downs as a seaport between Roman and modern times. The Mediterranean played its most important role in the Middle East under Rome and again after the advent of the industrial revolution, which shifted the patterns of trade toward Europe. Between these two periods it was less important, for the Arab conquest had moved the urban focus of the Middle East to the interior.

The arriving traveler of two centuries ago was greeted by a prospect of houses and gardens on low ground flanked by hilly green suburbs, the Mediterranean below, the slopes of Mount Lebanon in the background. The best approach was by sea, but any high point overlooking the town afforded a pleasant sight. Traveler after traveler admired the prettiness of Beirut's environs and the harmony of the landscape.

One traveler was so carried away that he compared the town to "a lovely sultana leaning her elbow on a green cushion and gazing dreamily and indolently at the waves." Another saw "a coquette going to the seashore to see it reflecting her fineries and to gaze at herself in the blue waters." Yet another wrote of the "Beautiful Gate of Syria": "The world must be very rich in beauty if there exists half a dozen places on its surface much more beautiful than Beyrout; but I for one cannot believe that there are: its loveliness is of many kinds, and though different pictures may combine to represent its beauties, no one will contain them all.[3]

On closer contact, however, the early-nineteenth-century traveler's enthusiasm was apt to fade. Landing was already enough to sober most. There was barely what could be called a harbor, only an open roadstead, and no mole to disbark on. "Boats landing from ships anchored outside would strike bottom before reaching the beach, and the passengers, men and women, were then borne by brawny boatmen and dumped on the land." Men, women, children and luggage were thrown on a quay, which remained until well into the nineteenth century "small, dirty, fishbespattered." After 1830, travelers sometimes also had to put up with quarantine in a lazaretto too crowded and small for comfort or health. Even if they were fortunate enough to be spared the quarantine, nothing could spare them the misery of customs and, afterwards, of being assaulted by an intensely curious and excited crowd forcing their services upon the exhausted travelers. One irritated traveler had to push "through a complete mass of bipeds, quadrupeds and bales of goods, along the rotten wooden and stone quay" in order to find sanctuary at one of the two European hotels. Beirut did not even acquire those accommodations until some time in the early nineteenth century.[4]

Despite its drawbacks, however, this smelly, ugly, poorly equipped, and poorly maintained harbor was in many respects still the most important part of town, its window on the sea, guarded by two castles. A belt of thick walls interrupted by six gates, all but one of which was locked at night, girded the town and gave it the aspect of a stronghold. Beirut's fortifications, dating back at least to the tenth century, had been destroyed and restored on several occasions, but they were gradually eliminated in the course of the nineteenth century, beginning in the 1830s, when Beirut and the surrounding region was occupied by the Egyptians. In 1840 the Ottoman Turks, who had ruled the area before the Egyptians, and their European allies sought to liberate the town from Egyptian rule. In the process, the British naval squadron sent to bombard Beirut destroyed most of the fortifications that remained. Although remnants of the walls could still be found into the twentieth century, by then the town had long since ceased to be a stronghold.[5]

To our early-nineteenth-century traveler, though, the town would still have looked fortress-like, and as he left the port area and wandered deeper and deeper into the town, the atmosphere would have become more and more oppressive. He first crossed a relatively new and pleasant part of town just outside the port area. The only two good streets of Beirut were to be found there, lined with the largest stone houses of the town. Just beyond was the street inhabited by bankers and moneychangers, and beyond that the Greek quarter, with its coffeehouses and cabarets.[6]

The traveler then approached the center of town, where the streets were narrow and winding and badly paved, if paved at all. They were also filthy, with animal hides and offal heaped along the roadway. Traffic was a mixture of people and camels, horses, and donkeys. Even in the daytime, the streets were dark, with arches or mats covering many of them and the thick walls of the abutting stone houses cutting out the remaining light. The walls were high; the few openings covered by shutters or compact wooden trellises — glass was not yet in use. Behind the walls, the houses were built in a series of constructions facing a middle, open space or courtyard, which was spacious, cool, and cheerful. But the passerby could not have seen over the walls, and from the street the city held a gloomy and unfriendly aspect. "I have never seen anything as bizarre, irregular, and extraordinary as the construction of the Arab town of Bayruth," wrote the French man-of-letters Jean Joseph François Poujoulat in *Correspondance d'Orient* (which records in seven volumes his travels to the east with his friend, the historian, poet, and member of the French Academy, Joseph Michaud, in 1830–31). "The houses built in stone, are higher than those of any other town in Syria; arches, secret paths (*issues*), dark passages, narrow and tortuous streets inspire at first a kind of fright in the traveler who wants to visit the town; each house constitutes a huge, inaccessible dungeon."[7]

Houses were crammed together so that their flat-roofed terraces communicated with one another. This closeness added to the liveliness and friendliness within, for the flat-roofed terraces were used for laundry, sleeping on hot nights, and conversing with neighbors. But to the traveler they could only be seen as strange and confusing.

The pedestrian passed on until he reached the bazaar in the center of

1841 gravure from a daguerreotype by Lerebours. Courtesy Fuad Debbas

the city, and here there was also confusion, but at least it was merry and lively. The bazaar was the heart of old Beirut, where all activities converged. The narrow and covered streets, each with its own specialty, all packed with small shops composed of raised booths and topped with single-story dwellings, crisscrossed each other. A few neglected public fountains, numerous inns (khans), and coffeehouses added to its picturesqueness.[8]

A number of other buildings could be spotted in the center of town. Five or six were mosques, the most notable the Jami' al-'Umari al-Kabir, originally the church of Saint John built by Crusaders. The town also had at least three churches. The largest of them was the Greek Orthodox church of Saint George; the others included a Maronite church and a Catholic church run by Capucin monks. Another church of Saint George was located near the Dog River outside the walls of the city. But all these religious buildings of Beirut were architecturally rather ordinary, and certainly no match for their counterparts in Damascus, Istanbul, or the other Eastern capitals.

The administrative buildings of old Beirut were equally ordinary. The seraglio at the eastern end of town was an unimpressive remnant of what once had been a famous palace during the reign of the Druze Emir Fakhr al-Din II al-Ma'ni, prince of Mount Lebanon from 1590 to 1635, when the power of the mountain princes had reached its peak and extended from Antioch in Syria to Safad in Palestine. It was flanked by two prisons. The seraglio and the house of the local judge sheltered the entire administrative apparatus of old Beirut, and their modesty reflected the insignificance of the town's administrative role before the second quarter of the nineteenth century. The rest of Beirut's public buildings included two or three baths and hotels, all adequate but again not particularly interesting. One of the public baths was located near the seraglio; one hotel was on the harbor and another on the western edge of town.[9]

It did not take long to cross Beirut on foot. The whole of the fortified town covered no more than 570 meters from the harbor to its southern gate and 370 meters from its eastern to its western portals. Beyond those limits, on all sides except the shore, the traveler could see stretching in the distance cemeteries, sand dunes, gardens, and sprinkled among them a few houses. The sand dunes extended southwest of town, and the imaginative believed that they had been blown there by winds from Egypt. West of town on the seafront was the Pigeon Rock area; south, the pine forest; eastward, the hill of Saint Dimitri and, farther ahead, the Dog River (Nahr al-Kalb) and its ancient ruins, all favorite spots for riding horses.[10]

The town seemed isolated because of its fortified walls and its almost deserted suburbs. A belt of hills and mountains stretched beyond, adding natural fortifications on the southeast of town, though also, as the French writer Volney, visiting Beirut in 1784, pointed out, limiting Beirut on its southeast side. He even concluded that the hills combined with the limited supply of water within the city would prevent it from ever acquiring any prominence.[11] He was correct, for a time. Beirut's double barrier of mountain ranges, the Lebanon and the Anti-Lebanon, isolated it from the hinterland and, more crucially, from Damascus, the major city of the interior.

Easy communication with the interior was essential to Beirut's development because, of all the subregions of Syria, two — Mount Lebanon and Damascus — were most dependent on Beirut. It served as the trading outlet for the Mountain as well as the port for the Damascene caravan trade. Theoretically, then, Beirut's situation was promising because the prosperity of any port depends upon its services to a major city and a populated area, and Beirut had both. The intervening mountains, however, kept it relatively isolated until an adequate transportation and communication system linked it with both areas in the nineteenth century. But even before that, Beirut's natural economic links to the rest of the area were evident in the fact that the city's destinies had always to some extent been influenced by what happened elsewhere in Syria.

For centuries Beirut's history was tied to the destinies of the great empires that succeeded one another in the Middle East. Syria's location made it a crossroad for armies, tribes, and peoples coming from all over the Mediterranean basin or from the Arabian peninsula, Mesopotamia, or Central Asia. Syria's earliest known history dates back to the late fourth and third millennium, when it was inhabited by Semitic peoples, Mediterranean with some mixture of other stocks, speaking in old Canaanite tongue. The Canaanite area was subsequently divided up among the tribes of Israel in southern Syria, the Aramaeans farther north and in the interior, and the Phoenicians on the coast. They remained there for centuries, until other foreign invaders came. The Hittites, the Assyrians, the Neo-Babylonians, the Persians, the Macedonian Greeks led by Alexander the Great, the Ptolemies and the Seleucids, the Romans, and then the Byzantines, all ruled parts or all of Syria at various times. Finally Syria was taken over by the Arab Muslim conquerors in the seventh century A.D.[12]

Exactly when in that time Beirut was built is uncertain. We know only that it is a very ancient city, one of the oldest on the eastern Mediterranean. There is also no certainty concerning the etymology of its ancient name, Biruta, which became Berytus in classical times and Beirut since (also spelled Bairut, Bayrut, Beyrut). But it is now generally accepted that the name is derived from the Semitic word for "well" or "pit," Akkadian *burtu*, Hebrew *be'er*, Arabic *bi'r*, suggesting that the city's supply was ensured by an abundance of water from wells, the only means of maintaining the local water supply, at least until Roman times.

There is archeological evidence that Beirut existed before the fourteenth century B.C., but the earliest known reference to it so far dates from that time. It is found in the Tell el-Amarna tablets, a unique source of information discovered in Egypt in 1887, which record correspondence from rulers in western Asia to the Egyptian king. Beirut is mentioned as being on an equal footing with other powerful city-states of the period in Syria and Palestine.

From the collapse of the Egyptian empire in the early twelfth century B.C. to the foundation of the Persian empire of Cyrus the Great in the sixth century B.C., Beirut's history is unknown. Perhaps the city was destroyed, as many coastal cities were, by new invaders. It is possible, too, that Beirut became incorporated into a political district headed by another, better-known sister city on the coast — Sidon to its south and Byblos to its north were both more prominent by that time. If so, it was simply not mentioned because new conquerors — the Assyrians and Neo-Babylonians — would only have been concerned with the leading cities. But whatever its fate after the twelfth century B.C., we do know that it had been rebuilt by the sixth. Classical sources refer to it, though still in ways that suggest it was secondary in importance to Sidon and, farther south, Tyre.

With the end of the Persian empire (550–330) and Alexander the Great's conquest of the Syrian coast in 332 B.C., Beirut became part of the Hellenistic world. This period and especially the Roman period that began in the first century before the Christian era seem to have constituted the high point of Beirut's early history, although this impression may simply be a result of the better documentation available in Roman times. Around 200 B.C., Beirut was annexed by Alexander the Great's successor Seleucid state and renamed Laodicea in Phoenicia. Under Seleucid rule it prospered as a commerical link between East and West, one of the earliest instances of the economic race that was later to ensure Beirut's prosperity.

Then a war of succession in 140 B.C. led to the city's destruction. When it emerged again, it was to live its most glorious period first under Roman and then under Byzantine rule (64 B.C.–A.D. 635). It was colonized by veteran Roman legionnaires, elevated around 14 B.C. to the rank of a Roman colony, and called Colonia Julia Augusta Felix Berytus. Berytus rapidly acquired important administrative and commercial functions. It became famous for its school of law, which drew students from all over the Roman world and rivaled the schools of Athens, Alexandria, and Caesarea. With prosperity and fame came an increase of population that led to new public buildings: theaters, baths, a hippodrome, and an elaborate aqueduct system supplying the city with its first canals.

By the mid-fourth century, most of Beirut's population had adopted the new religion of Christianity, and the city was the seat of a bishop. In particular, its law students converted to Christianity in great numbers, and many were martyred during the Christian persecutions that began in 303 and lasted until 313. One of these martyrs was Saint George, whose legend was spread in Europe by the Crusaders and who became the patron saint of England in the fourteenth century. According to the version of the legend popular in Beirut, George was a soldier under Diocletian who slayed the dragon near the mouth of the Beirut River, where the church of Saint George was subsequently erected.

As Christianity spread, so did differences on matters of doctrine (such as the human and divine nature of Christ), ritual (leavened or unleavened bread), and discipline (celibacy of priests). These schisms and controversies reverberated in Syria, where they eventually resulted in the establishment of a whole range of Christian denominations, some larger and more influential than others. In Beirut and Lebanon these included the Melchites, who accepted the doctrine of the two natures—human and divine—in the one person of Christ formulated by the Council of Chalcedon in 451, and the Monophysites and Nestorians, who did not. "Melchites" comes from *Malikiyun* or royalists, a name given to them by Christian rivals who reproached them for adopting the orthodox Byzantine line. When the schism between the churches of Rome and Constantinople occurred in 1054, the Melchites followed Constantinople and thereby became heretics in the eyes of Rome. In the late seventeenth and early eighteenth centuries, however, a group of Syrian Melchites joined Rome, thereby becoming one of the "Uniate" churches who in that period recognized papal supremacy and in return were allowed to retain their own customs and ritual. After uniting with Rome and organizing a church of their own, these Uniate Melchites became known as Greek Catholics and the non-Uniates as Greek Orthodox. The word "Greek" implies here not that they were Greeks by origin or ancestry — in fact, their clergy as well as their membership in Arabic-speaking lands were and remain Arab — but that they continued to use the Byzantine rite in their liturgy.

The Monophysites like the Nestorians rejected the decrees of the Council of Chalcedon, and instead believed in the union between the divine nature of Christ and the human nature of Jesus. They became dominant in parts of Syria, where they belonged either to the Jacobite, or Syrian Orthodox, church or to the Armenian, or Gregorian, church. For the modern history of Lebanon, however, they are less important than another Monophysite offshoot, who proclaimed the Monothelete doctrine of the two natures of Christ but one divine will. This group assumed the name of their patron saint Maron, who died around 410, and became known as "Maronites." In the twelfth century, they recognized papal supremacy, but retained their own liturgy and priesthood. Over the centuries still other churches were established in Syria including, in addition to the Greek Catholics, other Uniate groups such as the Syrian Catholics, Armenian Catholics, and Chaldaean Catholics, as well as Roman Catholics of the western or Latin rite. The last to arrive on the scene were the various Protestant denominations, mainly the result of Western missionary activity in the nineteenth century. In Syria Protestants were generally Presbyterian and, in Palestine, Anglican.

In July 551, a violent earthquake and tidal wave destroyed Beirut and reduced its population to a few thousand. Efforts to restore the town were unsuccessful, mainly because of political instability. Byzantine territories were lost to the Persians only to be reconquered and then again lost to the latest and most effective threat to both Byzantine and Persian imperial power. In the name of Islam, which was revealed by God to his prophet Muhammad (ca. 570–632), the Arabs from the Arabian peninsula began in 633 a conquest that was rapid, lasting, and all-inclusive, spreading Arab domination from North Africa to Central Asia. Beirut was easily taken in 635, the year Damascus was conquered only after a six-month siege. From then until 1110, it remained under Muslim Arab rule.

Beirut's fortunes fluctuated in rhythm with the fortunes of the two dynasties that governed this Arab empire, the Umayyads (661–750) and the Abbasids (750–1258). The Umayyads used Damascus as their capital, and its proximity to Beirut benefited the latter, which was incorporated into the Damascus district, one of the five military districts into which Syria was divided. At the same time, Beirut's population underwent some change, as Arabs replaced Byzantines and Byzantine sympathizers who left or were expelled after the Arab conquest. In addition, colonists from Persia were settled in Beirut and other coastal cities, partly as a preventive measure in case of Byzantine naval attack.[13]

These changes in Beirut's population increased the number of local Muslims, although until the late thirteenth century a vast proportion of the Syrian population was still Christian.[14] Most of the Muslims in Beirut belonged to what later became known as Sunni ("orthodox") Islam, professed by the Arab rulers and the majority of Muslims in their lands. They held that Muhammad's successors ("caliphs") should be chosen by acclamation. The other branch of Islam, the Shi'i ("partisan"), believed that Muhammad's successors should belong to the family of the Prophet's cousin and son-in-law, 'Ali. As Sunnis became dominant in Beirut, they gained renown as learned men. The most famous of these was a jurist known as al-Awza'i, who lived in Beirut until his death in 774.

Muslims tolerated both Christianity and Judaism but, as the Muslims moved in, many Christian families left the coastal cities for Mount Lebanon, which thus slowly established itself as a haven for religious minorities and independent groups. Beirut, however, continued to be inhabited by Christians, and probably too by Jews and others.

In the mid-eighth century, the Abbasids replaced the Umayyads and moved their capital to Baghdad. This ended Syria's preeminence, and under the Abbasids the area remained dissatisfied and prone to invasion, including a series of incursions in the late tenth century by Byzantines, who sacked Beirut in the process. Syria also suffered from being caught between two main rival centers in the Arab world, Baghdad, the capital of the Abbasids, and Cairo, where a new Shi'i dynasty, the Fatimids, built an empire that stretched from Tunisia to parts of Syria and western Arabia. By the time of the First Crusade, Syria was weak, divided, and under the control of various local leaders, a situation that affected Beirut as well as other Syrian towns. The weakness of the Arab empire in its later years provides at least one explanation for the fortifications that were constructed by the coastal cities. The first references to fortifications in Beirut date to the tenth century.

The Crusades were launched from the West in 1097, in response to

Pope Urban II's appeal in 1095 for the delivery of the Holy Sepulchre from Muslim hands. The first contact Beirut had with the Crusaders occurred in May 1099, when they came from the north to provision themselves and spent a night there. After they captured Jerusalem, they returned, and this time launched a three-month siege that ended with the city's capitulation in May 1110. The first attempt by the Arabs to regain Beirut in 1183 was unsuccessful. It was launched by Salah al-Din ibn Ayyub, known in the West as Saladin, the Sunni military hero who assumed control in Egypt and used it as a base from which to extend his sway over Syria and to build up sufficient power to repel the Latin conquerors. By the time of his death in 1193 he had reduced the Crusader-held territory to a few coastal towns between Acre and Jaffa.

Soon after Salah al-Din's death, however, the Latins reconquered the territories they had lost. In October 1197 Beirut was retaken without bloodshed, partly because the local garrison had fled and partly because, at least according to tradition, a Christian carpenter had opened the gates of the main tower to the conquerors.[15] Most of the other fortifications of Beirut were destroyed by Salah al-Din to weaken the city's defenses in the event that it might again pass into enemy hands and have to be recaptured. Whether a Christian carpenter of Beirut actually betrayed the city or not, the very existence of the story suggests that the sympathies of the Christian population in the city, whether Crusader or not, were understood to lie with the Latins.

The Crusader period had put the local Christians at an advantage. Although divisions between various Christian denominations persisted — the Orthodox, for example, reportedly being less in sympathy with the Crusaders than Roman Catholics — on the whole, Christians of all persuasions suffered from the fall of the Latin kingdom in the late thirteenth century. In Syria, Christians constituted the large majority of the population until the late thirteenth century; in the Crusader-held areas their proportions were made even larger by the emigration of many Muslims.

In all likelihood, Christians remained in the majority in Beirut too, with the rest of the population made up of Muslims, a small Jewish community, and others.[16] One sign of Christian preponderance in Beirut in that period was the construction of churches. In 1110, the Hospitallers (Knights of Saint John of Jerusalem) built a church on the model of Latin churches and named it the Church of Saint John the Baptist. Another church dedicated to Saint Nicolas was probably built during Frankish rule. Foreign merchant communities also had their churches, either using structures already in existence when they came or building their own. Beirut also had a convent with an adjacent sanctuary renowned in those days for a miracle.

If the Crusaders are associated with the construction of churches, they are even more clearly associated with the building of military fortifications. The Ibelins who governed Beirut restored its walls and added new towers. Frankish rule also brought commercial prosperity to the city. It never equaled in status and wealth the most prosperous coastal towns — Acre, Tyre — but it was revived as a center of exchange and for the manufacture of sugar and iron. Its foreign merchant colony grew. The Venetians, who enjoyed special privileges in all Frankish cities, probably had the same rights in Beirut. The Genoese participated in the government of the town and in the 1220s made it their main depot.[17]

Beirut changed hands once more when the Mamluks, who took over in Egypt in 1250, gradually extended their control over Syria. Beirut was among the last Crusader possessions to be taken, capitulating to the Mamluks in July 1291, and it remained under their control until 1517. After an initial period of decline and anarchy caused by the military and political changes of the period, the Mamluks divided Syria into a number of provinces. Beirut was made part of the Damascus province, but the city was in effect under the military protection of chieftans of southern Lebanon, the Buhturids of the Gharb.

These Buhturids were neither Sunni nor Christian, but Druze, the name given to the descendants of the followers of the Fatimid Caliph al-Hakim (996–1021), who formed their own religious sect in the early eleventh century and named it after one of the sect's founders, Muhammad ibn Isma'il al-Darazi. It is nonproselytizing and secret; it has two classes of believers, the initiates who lead the masses and the noninitiates or followers. The Druzes remained relatively independent of central control, partly because they were concentrated in the Shuf, or southern, district of Mount Lebanon and partly because they had won the confidence of the Sunni Mamluks by fighting the Crusaders.

Despite brief periods of prosperity, Beirut declined during the Mamluk period. The economic fortunes of the city fluctuated with shifts in Mediterranean trade relations: it suffered from the decline of Syria as an important commercial center at the end of the thirteenth century, and then benefited in the late fourteenth century from the revival of trade between Syria and the Venetians, Catalans, and Genoese, only to suffer again from the rivalries of Western merchants, from the imposition in the fifteenth century of a tax on all merchandise imported into Beirut, and from the decline of Syria's trade with the West following the discovery of the sea route to the Indies.[18]

Some improvements were made in Beirut by the Buhturids who ruled the city in the name of the Mamluks, but they were modest. The fortifications, destroyed by the Mamluks when they first took Syria as a preventive measure against new European encroachments on the Syrian coast, were partially restored, especially along the coast from which raids were always feared, and two towers were built. In addition, some buildings were constructed, including a mosque, a bath, a khan, and palaces, and canals and aqueducts were built or repaired.

Not much is known about Beirut's population in the Mamluk period. Population estimates for Beirut before the twentieth century are both unreliable and incomplete, but it probably declined, partly as a result of plagues in 1491–92.[19] The composition of the population also began to change, as it did in all of Syria, becoming more Muslim as the Mamluks fought against, or drove away, anyone suspected of having supported the Crusaders. The Church of Saint John in Beirut became a mosque, the convent a stable. Yet one church was restored by Western merchants with the permission of the central authority,[20] and Christians, Jews, and others continued to live in Beirut. In the 1420s Ghillebert de Lannoy, a Burgundian courtier who surveyed the Holy Land for the English king Henry V with an eye toward launching another crusade, tells us that Beirut was inhabited "by a great number of Saracens, by Christian merchants like Venetians, by Genoese, Greeks and others."[21]

The decline of Beirut in Mamluk times was also in part attributable to its rule by the Druze mountain lords whose main power base lay in the Shuf district far to the south. The Buhturids fully appreciated Beirut's usefulness to them, since their district of the Gharb was adjacent to it and control of the city brought in the revenues of the harbor and resources such as wood and iron. The advantages of controlling Beirut were channeled not to the benefit of the city but to the strengthening of the Buhturids' position as lords of the Gharb.[22] The usefullness of an outlet on the sea was not, however, lost to the mountain lords who succeeded the Buhturids. The political connection between Beirut and Mount Lebanon was revived again when the Ottomans replaced the Mamluks, and remained a central theme of Beirut's history into the nineteenth century. There was a difference, however: instead of the mountain extending its control over the city, gradually but irreversibly the city gained control over the mountain.

3 The Mountain and the City

The Mamluks had fought successfully against Crusaders, Mongols, and other invaders, but proved to be no match for the Ottoman Turks, a Turkic people, originally from Central Asia, who had converted to Sunni Islam and moved into Anatolia to create the last great empire in the Middle East. Syria was part of that Ottoman empire from 1516 to its final demise at the end of World War I.

After the Ottomans had conquered Syria, they divided it into three provinces (called *eyalets, vilayets,* or *pashaliks*): Aleppo, Damascus, and Tripoli. In 1660 a fourth vilayet of Sidon was created, and now and then the vilayet of Tripoli was absorbed into one of its bordering vilayets, Damascus or Sidon. The northern region of modern Lebanon formed part of the vilayet of Tripoli (which included also parts of today's republic of Syria), and a southern region formed part of the vilayet of Sidon (which included parts of today's Israel). The Biqa', also now part of the republic, was separated from these two regions and made part of the vilayet of Damascus.

In the nineteenth century, the Ottomans made a number of administrative changes. In 1840, the vilayet of Sidon was enlarged and Beirut made its capital. In 1864, a vilayet of Syria was formed out of the vilayets of Sidon and Damascus and subdivided into five *sanjaks* (a subdivision of a province): Beirut, Acre, Tripoli, Latakia, and Nablus. In 1888, a vilayet of Beirut was formed from the vilayet of Syria, and the city of Beirut became the administrative capital of the vilayet carrying its name.[1]

No political or administrative entity distinct from the Syrian administration existed in Mount Lebanon before the nineteenth century. After its conquest, the Ottomans established little in the way of adminstrative apparatus in Syria, and life there, especially in isolated areas under its domination, changed little. This loose structure allowed a number of local dynasties to become virtually autonomous. In Mount Lebanon, two successive dynasties controlled the area. In the sixteenth and seventeenth centuries, the south was dominated by the Druze princes or emirs of Lebanon who followed the Buhturids. The greatest of this Ma'n dynasty was Fakhr al-Din (1586–1635), who extended his territories beyond Lebanon and even established relations with European powers. After him, however, the Ma'n rulers were weak, and eventually they were replaced. In 1697 the Shihabs, Sunni Muslims, some of whom converted to Maronite Christianity in the late eighteenth century, took over and extended their rule farther north. They remained in control until the nineteenth century.

Although officially independent from Mount Lebanon, Beirut maintained its close political ties with that area. Twice it was effectively controlled by the Mountain, when strong princes managed to extend their sway. Fakhr al-Din brought Beirut under his control. In 1749 it again fell under the control of a mountain prince, this time the Shihab emir Mulhim (1732–1754), and it remained the winter residence of the Shihabs until al-Jazzar in 1775 became governor of the vilayet of Sidon and brought it back under direct Ottoman control.

The reign of the Shihab dynasty was not peaceful. One source of the unrest was the upsetting of the sectarian balance in the Mountain. Before Ottoman rule, Shi'i Muslims had dominated, except in the northern district of Bsharri, Batrun, and Jubayl, which were under Maronite control. Then sometime in the early eleventh century, the inhabitants of Wadi al-Taym and probably the Shuf converted to Druzism, and by the end of the century the regions of the Shuf and the Wadi al-Taym in southern Lebanon were entirely Druze territory. The Shi'is had dominated that region until after the Crusades, but then began to disappear, partly a result of the ascendancy of Sunni dynasties in Syria, especially the Mamluks, who fought against them. Maronites replaced Shi'is in the north and Druzes in the south. On the Syrian coast, Sunnis dominated pockets of Christians, most of them Greek Orthodox.

In the seventeenth century, the Druzes allied themselves with the Maronites who moved into the Druze districts in the south, beginning a "veritable Maronite colonization" of Lebanon. Maronites were until the nineteenth century the most widespread community in Mount Lebanon, as the Maronite peasantry from northern Lebanon moved into southern districts previously inhabited by other Christians and by the Druzes. In the meantime the Druzes were further weakened by factionalism and feuding among their leading families. Those who lost out emigrated from Lebanon to Jebel Druze, the hilly area beyond the Hawran plain, further shifting the balance to the Maronites. In the late eighteenth century the Shihabs themselves converted to Maronite Christianity.[2]

The most famous of the Shihabs was Bashir II (1788–1840). Under his rule the Egyptians occupied Syria (1831–1840), and Bashir II supported the invaders against the Ottomans. When the latter regained control in 1840, they replaced Bashir with a weak Shihab, who was unable to maintain control. In 1841 the first of a series of Maronite-Druze clashes erupted. To halt them the Ottomans reorganized their administration of the Mountain. They deposed the last Shihab prince in 1842 and divided Mount Lebanon into a northern district under a Maronite and a southern district under a Druze governor, both appointed by the Ottomans. The administrative autonomy of the Mountain was guaranteed, but the new system otherwise worked poorly, since the governors were weak and local tensions ran deep. In 1845, war again broke out between the two rival sects and in 1857, when in north Lebanon impoverished and overtaxed Maronite peasants revolted against their Maronite lords. The revolt spread to the southern districts where the peasants were Maronites and the lords were Druzes, leading in 1860 to the most serious civil war Syria suffered in the nineteenth century.

By then, the Druzes inhabited parts of the districts of Matn and Jazzin of Mount Lebanon, though they were still most heavily concentrated in the southern district of the Shuf. All these districts included Christians as well. Pockets of Christians, mostly in towns and villages, lived amid the Druze-dominated mixed districts of the south. When agitation began in early May 1860, whole Christian families deserted their villages for Christian strongholds, especially the predominantly Maronite towns of Dayr al-Qamar and Jazzin and the predominantly Greek Catholic town of Zahle, where Christians of the district of 'Arqub, most of whom were Maronites, soon joined them. As May drew to a close, Druze victories in the district of Matn and the burning of B'abda and surrounding villages drove them to depart for Beirut. The Christian population of Matn was Maronite with some Greek Orthodox; the Christian population of the B'abda area numbered Greek Catholics among them as well.[3]

Early in June, the Druzes attacked Jazzin and drove its Christian inhabitants toward Sidon, though many were captured before reaching it. But soon Sidon was no longer safe, and Beirut, farther north on the seashore, became their destination.

Agitation soon spread to Wadi al-Taym in the Anti-Lebanon, a mixed district with Greek Orthodox constituting most of the Christian population. The refugees from Wadi al-Taym fled to the town of Hasbayya, which was itself soon attacked, together with the town of Rashayya. The Christians of both towns, again mostly Greek Orthodox, retreated to Damascus and to the coastal cities. In mid-June, Druze attacks on the towns of Zahle and Dayr al-Qamar provoked yet another flight. Some had left earlier, but most waited until it was too late and then crowded into neighboring villages and the coastal cities.[4]

In less than four weeks in May and June of 1860, about 11,000 Christians were killed, 4,000 more died of hardship, and about 100,000 became refugees. To these figures can be added those resulting from the disturbances in Damascus on July 9, 1860, and on the following days, where estimates varied "from 8,000 to 500 to 5,000," as one observer put it.[5] Some 5,000 may have died out of a population of about 10,000 to 12,000 males, including 2,000 to 5,000 refugees from the surrounding country. Most of those who survived sought refuge in the castle of Damascus and departed later for Beirut.

When the civil war ended, Mount Lebanon was once again reorganized. The French government sent an expedition to Lebanon, ostensibly to help the Ottomans reestablish order. It remained there for nine months. An international commission with representatives from France, Britain, Russia, Austria, and Prussia, headed by Fuad Pasha, met first in Beirut and then in Istanbul to draw up an agreement that would recognize the privileged and semiautonomous state of Lebanon from Mount Lebanon to the sea, but excluding Beirut, Tripoli, and Sidon. It was promulgated in 1861 and ratified in 1864. Under its terms Lebanon became a *mutasarrifate*, that is, a subdivision of a vilayet governed by a *mutasarrif*, who was given special powers. Until 1915 the mutasarrif was a Christian appointed by the Ottoman government and directly responsible to it. By the terms of the agreement he could not be from Mount Lebanon. A locally elected administrative council and a local gendarmerie assisted the mutasarrif. On the whole, this regime was able to maintain order, and for a time the area was both stable and prosperous.[6]

The abolition of the princedom of Mount Lebanon in 1842 had already allowed the Ottoman government in Beirut and Damascus more control over Mount Lebanon than it had in the past, and during the mutasarrifate it became in effect the political as well as the economic, educational, and social capital of the entire area, as the city was transformed from a small provincial port into the most important political and economic center on the Syrian coast.

There were several practical reasons for Beirut's revival as a port. One was its security. Napoleon's occupation of Egypt and his advance northward to Acre had demonstrated the vulnerability of the other coastal towns. Another was that, thanks to the proximity of strong rulers in the Mountain, it was a handy refuge from the corrupt rule of the Ottoman governors, a role it had already begun to play when Ahmad al-Jazzar ("the Butcher") Pasha came to power in 1775. Al-Jazzar, a Christian Bosnian by birth, was appointed to the vilayet of Sidon. He established his seat in Acre, but some of that time ruled over Damascus as well. He also tried repeatedly to bring the Lebanese emirate under his control so that he could include Beirut in his administration and use it as a base from which to check the power of the mountain princes. In 1799 he stopped Napoleon's advance in Acre, but that did not mollify the population under his tyrannical rule, and both Sidon and Acre lost prominence as both local and foreign traders moved their businesses to more hospitable surroundings.

When al-Jazzar died, Sulayman Pasha was appointed governor, after a brief struggle among a number of contenders. He tried to collaborate with the Lebanese Bashir II, the most powerful of the Shihab princes, and succeeded to the point that Bashir II sent troops to defend Damascus against the Wahhabis of Arabia, Sunni fundamentalists who had invaded Syria in 1810. Expelled by the Ottomans and Bashir II, they retreated into Arabia, where they remained until the governor of Egypt, Muhammad 'Ali Pasha, defeated them in 1818.

Sulayman Pasha died in 1819 and was succeeded by 'Abdallah Pasha, who was also unpopular, especially among the Christians, because when rebellion had broken out in Greece against Ottoman rule, a Greek raid on Beirut led 'Abdallah to reprisals against the local Christians whom he suspected of collaboration. 'Abdallah's rule was ended by the Egyptian occupation of Syria and Palestine in 1831. Muhammad 'Ali of Egypt (1805–1849), the strongest vassal of the Ottomans, who had tried to keep Greece in the Ottoman empire, was given Crete for his efforts, a prize he considered too modest. He demanded Syria instead and, when the sultan refused, decided to take both Palestine and Syria anyway. He sent his son Ibrahim Pasha to conquer them. Tyre, Sidon, Beirut, and Tripoli soon fell under Egyptian control, and by July 1831 all of Syria. Acre was besieged by the Egyptians in November 1831 and taken in May 1832. The Egyptians remained until 1840 when British, Russians, Austrians and Prussians decided to come to the Ottoman's aid; they did not want Muhammad 'Ali to destroy the Ottoman empire, which they considered essential to Europe's balance of power.

Throughout all of this, Beirut remained comparatively peaceful, thanks to the watchful eye of Bashir II, who protected it from the turmoil in Sidon and other coastal cities and villages. Traders moved to Beirut where they could conduct business without interruption. When Muhammad 'Ali finally took the whole area (1831–1840), he too moved the political center of the coast northward to Beirut. Once he had made Beirut the provincial capital, European consulates began to locate there. The first of them, including the French and the British, were established in the 1820s but only became permanent in 1833, when the French established a consulate of the first rank. Some of these consulates were new; others were merely moved to Beirut from other places. In 1832 there was an American consular representative in Beirut and after 1836 an American consul; the French consulate was officially transferred from Acre to Beirut in 1837, and the French consulate at Tripoli was reduced to an agent and the consulate itself moved to Beirut. By the 1840s, a number of European consulates in Beirut had been upgraded, and by mid-century France, England, Russia, and Austria had consulates-general there. Others, including Prussia, Sardinia, Tuscany, Spain, Naples, Holland, and Greece, soon joined them.[7]

This shift of administrative center also secured the economic ascendancy Beirut had gained over other ports as a result of wars and upheaval. Sidon had lost its place under al-Jazzar. Acre had withstood Bonaparte's siege in 1799 but was unable to resist that of Ibrahim Pasha in 1831, and under the Egyptians (1831–1840) permanently lost its political and administrative preeminence. Those were all misfortunes that benefited Beirut. Henri Guys, the French consul in Beirut in 1808, 1810, and 1824–1838, believed that precisely between 1824 and 1838 economic development and prosperity came to the city. Certainly by the 1830s it was considered both the capital and the chief port of Damascus and, for that matter, all of Syria. In the 1840s, a French consular report noted that Tripoli, "like all the other ports of Syria," had lost out to Beirut, which had monopolized the trade of the whole coast. By 1855, Sidon, which half a century earlier had dominated Beirut, was described as "crushed" by that city.[8]

Beirut's growth was also undeniably linked to the new international trade routes that had grown out of the industrial revolution. Techno-logical revolution in Europe, the growth of the Mediterranean trade, the advent of steamships and improved communications with the West, all promoted the growth of seaports. Beirut became the center of a new trading network, but it was only one of the many growing centers all over the Eastern world. This was of course one reason why so many European consulates-general were established there. Their presence in the town and the European economic and political inter-ests they represented allowed Western influence to penetrate deeper in Beirut than anywhere else in Syria.

4 Population Growth

Estimating population for Beirut in the nineteenth century when reliable statistical methods did not exist is a precarious undertaking. Although regular and reliable censuses were taken in the Ottoman empire from its earliest times, their quality in the later period of the empire varied with time and place. In many cases they were rarely and incompletely done, partly because their purposes, military service and taxation, were unpopular and people did their best to avoid them. No general censuses at all were taken in Syria in the nineteenth century, and no records were kept of births and deaths so that the natural rate of population increase could be determined. Information on migration is also lacking, even for exceptional years: in 1860, for example, information on refugee movements was kept, but in a rather haphazard fashion. As the century progressed, government censuses became more regular, but even the Ottoman authorities themselves admitted that their figures were approximate. Unofficial estimates varied widely, quoted one another, and were often based on ignorance or bias. Those failings are by no means peculiar to Middle Eastern history, but they do require that sources be used with caution.[1] (See Table 1 at the back of the book.)

In the sources, plans for taking the census are mentioned but seem actually to have been carried out only in the late nineteenth century. The figures from them are found either in Ottoman yearbooks or second-hand, through contemporaries who quoted official estimates. Among the latter are Butros al-Bustani, who published the *Arab Encyclopedia*; the British diplomat David Urquhart, who was close to Ottoman circles and who visited Lebanon in the middle of the century; contributors to the Baedeker guides for various years; and Vital Cuinet, author in 1896 of a human geography of Syria and Palestine. Other sources apparently also rely on official estimates, though they do not always say so. They include Amin Khuri's *Directory for Beirut* in 1899 and reports by Western consuls and other officials.

Reliance on governmental figures had its perils. Most of the figures are too low for the very reason that many people wished not to be counted. In Bustani's *Arab Encyclopedia*, for example, figures based on "old government registers" are given alongside more realistic estimates because, as Bustani explains, many of the inhabitants of Beirut had remained technically foreigners, especially those who came from Mount Lebanon and preferred to be considered, and to be taxed, as inhabitants of the Mountain. The Baedeker for 1876 also provides a figure of its own for the population of Beirut and notes that the official figure is much lower.[2]

But even government figures tended now and again to be too high, as in 1850, when Urquhart's figures for Beirut taken from an official Ottoman house census are significantly higher than anyone else's.[3] No one's statistical reliability can be established with certainty for that period, but it is still difficult to disregard Urquhart or his sources, especially since he is one of the few who explains where he got his figures. Here as elsewhere one can only avoid being misled by seeing how his figures fit a population curve.

Some sources apparently do not rely on governmental figures at all. A few try to come up with their own estimates, but do not establish them with enough certainty to be usable.[4] Others appear to rely on private records — missionaries, for example, on missionary archives or their predecessors — but those estimates also suffer from contradictions and dubious conclusions.[5] Finally, some authors give no hint as to how they arrived at the estimates they quote. Much of the travel literature falls into this category, but so do people with better credentials, who were familiar with the area and even lived there for some time. However familiar they may have been, one cannot assume accuracy for any figure they fail to justify.[6]

Unreliability is further complicated by the inclusion by some authors into Beirut's figures of the surrounding suburbs; others do not specify whether or not they included them. Four of the sources from the 1830s included the suburbs; earlier authors may not have, but so few people lived outside the walls then that the totals would not have been much affected by adding or omitting them. In the 1840s, another source, named "Wilson," explicitly excluded the suburbs in his population count, and it was two to seven thousand people lower than the other estimates for the same period which do not specify whether they include the suburbs or not. In any case, the problem vanishes by the end of the century, when the city expanded so far beyond its original limits that the distinction between the city and suburbs had all but disappeared.

The unreliability of figures is also aggravated at times by authors who quote unsubstantiated numbers for periods prior to the years about which they are writing. When accuracy is not always established for the latter, it diminishes even further the reliability of earlier figures. On the other hand, they are not always far off the mark. In the 1920s, for example, a report by British Naval Intelligence mentioned that Beirut had probably doubled in population since 1880.[7] We can infer from this an 1880s figure that seems slightly high but not utterly improbable, since it agrees roughly with most of the figures available for that time.

Henri Harris Jessup, an American Presbyterian missionary who lived in Syria for fifty-three years, first in Tripoli in 1856, then after 1860 in Beirut as acting pastor of the Protestant church and superintendent of its school, also quotes figures for years before his arrival. His estimates for 1840 accords with others, as do his estimates for the 1820s, though he does give two different figures, 6,000 people in 1823 and 8,000 in 1825. It was probably an error, although conceivably one figure could have excluded and the other included the suburbs. But the point is that, in most cases, hearsay and error are by and large correctable because the other estimates available for the population of Beirut in that period are sufficient to provide a standard against which to measure.

For periods when the population of Beirut poses more of a problem, however, differences in numbers can cause confusion, especially for the 1850s, when estimates range all the way from 20,000 to 50,000. The problem was probably caused by authors' quoting estimates for the 1850s to provide a contrast to the post-1860 period and to emphasize the increase in population; to make the contrast dramatic, they probably underestimated the numbers for the pre-1860 period. Contemporary estimates for the population of Beirut in the 1850s range between 40,000 and 50,000; estimates by later authors around 20,000. The Baedeker of 1876, for example, estimated the population of Beirut at 20,000 around 1850, while the edition of 1894 quoted the same figure for a period more generally described as "before 1860." Jessup said that Beirut had 22,000 people in 1856; Jules Hoche, a Frenchman who visited Beirut and wrote a semipopular work on the "Crusaders'

Lands," stated in the early 1880s that in 1860, before the civil war, it had a population of 20,000.

Despite the shortcomings of the sources, the figures are remarkably consistent if we look at them for trends rather than accurate statistics. Very few figures are so off the mark that they have to be separately accounted for. In general, it seems safe to conclude that between 1830 and 1850 the population of Beirut roughly quadrupled. Until the 1820s the population remained small.[8] It began gradually to grow after 1830, and then more rapidly, especially after 1845. Immediately after 1860, it more than doubled again. A consistent rise resulted in another doubling of the population between 1865 and about 1920. Natural increase played little part in this growth. Information on natural increase is practically nonexistent, so there is no way of denying significant change in the birth and death rates. But there is no reason to assume it either, since immigration remains the most likely and logical explanation.

So, though 1860 is most often citied as the high point of Beirut's growth, we should not forget that much of it really took place earlier.

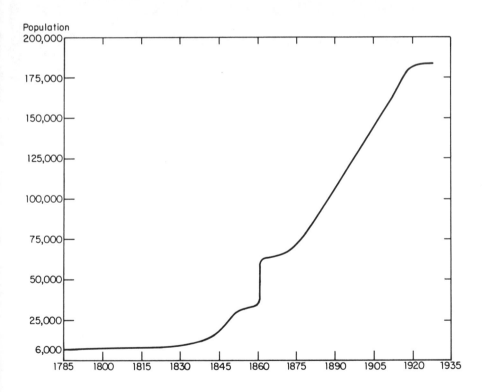

View of Beirut from the American College, ca. 1870
Photo by Bonfils. Courtesy Harvard Semitic Museum

By 1860 the population of Beirut had already nearly quadrupled. The significant increase in population before the 1860s was also reflected in the town's physical expansion. Although Beirut still had most of its walls until 1840, it had already begun to extend beyond them. Early in the century only a few scattered houses could be found outside, and according to Guys, who probably wrote in the 1840s, even those had been erected only some thirty years earlier. But by the late 1830s another contemporary observer estimated that about half the population of Beirut lived in the countryside. Drawings and observations by others suggest that this was an exaggeration: the number dwelling outside the city was still not lårge, but one must assume from the statement that it had at least increased.[9] For one thing, even in the

1830s the demand for building stones, masons, and builders exceeded the supply. For another, the sources agree that by 1850 the country-side was heavily populated. Urquhart, who played down the number of houses outside the walls in 1840, mentioned that in 1850 the countryside was wholly built up. In 1851–52 a marine lieutenant turned missionary, C. W. M. Van de Velde, and in the same decade Gregory Wortabet, first Armenian Protestant convert in Syria, both refer to the extensive and even crowded suburbs. In 1857, the missionary W. M. Thomson, who lived in the area for twenty-five years and who traveled a good deal through it, noted in his celebrated *The Land and the Book* that fifty years earlier scarcely a house could be found outside the walls; now two thirds of the population lived there and, he added with only slight exaggeration, this was the most rapid expansion anywhere in the Ottoman empire.[10]

It is also to this less noticed and numerically less impressive immigration to Beirut before 1860 that the roots of the later immigration can be traced. The earlier immigration set the tone and pattern for the later one in important ways and influenced the long-term development of the city. Its importance can be better appreciated when one considers the several local factors that might have kept people away. The city was not only small, crowded, and inadequately provided with municipal services, but subject to diseases, taxes, occasional political convulsions, and economic recessions.

The role of improved sanitation in the growth of Beirut has been mentioned by a number of authors, who in particular point to its special privilege of possessing the only quarantine center in Syria, established in 1834 by a board of health set up under the Egyptian regime (1831–1840). Some contemporary observers and one historian have even singled this out as one of the major causes for Beirut's expansion. Beirut, together with other urban centers of the area, did adopt a number of sanitary measures, including smallpox vaccination, introduced by the Egyptians and carried out afterwards by rival French, English, and American missionaries, in their free clinics and by their itinerant medical crews. Beirut, "the healthiest place in Syria" in the first half of the nineteenth century, remained so and improved later when French and American medical schools were established.[11]

But the effect of these developments on population growth was probably in fact limited. Sanitary conditions in Beirut were no better than they were in any of the preindustrial and early industrial cities of Europe. The quarantine center was perhaps less significant in improving the health of Beirut than it was in improving the economy, since it made the city the necessary stop of every ship in the area. By the second half of the century, there were so many problems with the lazaretto, or quarantine center, that the Ottoman authorities considered relocating it near the town of Tripoli: the expansion of Beirut had brought is so close to the lazaretto as to threaten the town with infection.[12] It had also become too small; in times of political crisis people were piled into it and sometimes died of neglect. In 1860, when thousands of refugees were brought to Beirut, many were quartered in the lazaretto where they died from exposure and malnutrition. During epidemics people were jammed in. In one such instance, two thousand people were said to have been confined in a space "barely sufficient to accommodate in any degree of comfort so many hundreds." The result was that the lazaretto had become a "pest hole" that probably often did more to spread disease than to prevent it.[13]

Conditions outside the quarantine center were little better. Hospitals were miserable in both Syria and Palestine, and in Beirut there were none at all, until an Ottoman military hospital was established in 1846, with American, French, Prussian, and local hospitals still later.[14] These facilities may have helped to reduce mortality rates toward the end of the century, but it is unlikely that they had much effect on population growth before 1860. The nineteenth century may have witnessed fewer epidemics than previous eras, but it certainly had plenty to cope with. Diseases spread from one corner of the region to the other; a major epidemic in Beirut was usually symptomatic of a more general phenomenon. The quarantine center rarely stopped an epidemic, though it may well have reduced its scale and virulence.[15]

Fevers were so common in Beirut early in the nineteenth century that, according to legend, Ibrahim Pasha had trees planted in the pine forest on the outskirts of Beirut in order to purify the air and prevent their occurrence. Smallpox was reported in "all cities and countries" in the Middle East in 1810. An epidemic of plague (the sources do not specify whether it was bubonic plague) occurred in 1813, 1816, perhaps sometime in the early 1820s, then again in 1826, 1827, 1829, and 1831.[16] After the creation of the quarantine center, three cases of cholera were reported in August 1835, and more in September. In 1836, the plague appeared in the suburbs of Beirut, introduced by overland pilgrims from Jerusalem, but it was stopped. The year after, the plague broke out again but was confined to the lazaretto and did not spread into the town. Cholera returned in 1838, and so did the plague in June of that year; it was avoided in 1840, when it hit Damascus, but reappeared in 1841, carried from Acre, and in 1842.[17] In 1848 and 1851 cholera also reappeared. After cholera was reported in Egypt in 1865, it spread to Beirut and its environs in July of that year, and throughout the summer resulted in the death of about three thousand people.[18]

In 1861, "all classes" of the local and foreign population suffered from a less defined epidemic, which caused few deaths but which testified to the lack of sanitation, conditions having perhaps deteriorated as a result of rapid urbanization. The causes of that epidemic were attributed to "the malaria [meaning, most likely, foul or bad air] generated by the unclean state of the town and surrounding country from accumulation of animal and decomposing vegetable matter left by the French Army of occupation and the crowds of refugees who flocked to this place after the recent outbreak." From descriptions, the disease seems to be the first reported instance of *abu rikab* (father of knees) or dengue fever, an epidemic that recurred later in the century. Its main symptoms were fever, pain in the limbs, and nausea. It was very contagious and painful, and it often followed a cholera epidemic, perhaps because of the deterioration in urban and sanitary conditions that usually resulted. When the cholera had abated in October 1865, the fever broke out and "hardly a man, woman, or child escaped, though it was not fatal." In September 1874, Jessup wrote to a friend that the summer had been one of "unprecedented sickness . . . I suppose it would be safe to say that tens of thousands of people are now lying sick of various fevers, from Gaza on the south to Aleppo on the north." Cholera returned to Syria in June 1875 and reached Beirut in August.[19]

The next outbreak of cholera occurred in Beirut in August 1883, brought by people fleeing Egypt, where the disease had appeared earlier. In Beirut it was less severe, but again dengue fever followed and returned again in the fall of 1888, when thousands of cases were reported. In 1891, cholera broke out in northern Syria, except for Latakia and Alexandretta, but it did not spread elsewhere. In May 1896, scarlet fever turned up for the first time (carried, it was believed, by emigrants returning from America), and many children died.[20] In the fall, typhoid, smallpox, and rabies spread by dogs were reported in Beirut, and "scores died of the small pox." In 1897, Syria experienced cholera and cattle plague; in 1899 one case of plague occurred on a steamer in Beirut, but no others were reported. In 1900 a few cases of plague were reported in the city; another case was mentioned in 1902.[21] Occurrences were only sporadic by the turn of the century, probably reflecting some further improvement in sanitary conditions. More improvement had to come, however, before epidemics would subside altogether.

Whether epidemics represented serious threats to public health, contemporaries believed they did, and their effects on the population of Beirut were immediate. They not only discouraged people from coming into or remaining in Beirut, but thousands left the city every time an epidemic was expected or declared. In 1831, plague drove a number of inhabitants to Mount Lebanon. In 1848 cholera provoked flight to the country of the "terror-stricken" population of the suburbs. In 1865, news that the cholera was in Egypt brought "frightful panic" to Beirut; "no less than 20,000 people left the city in a week.[22] By August, after cholera had reached Beirut, the French consul-general estimated that three fourths of the city's population had left. In 1875, he estimated that cholera caused about 40,000 to leave the city for the mountains. Jessup, describing the same exodus, gave a lower figure of 20,000, suggesting that contemporary accounts may not be entirely accurate in their statistical estimates, though they do convey the extent of the fear and disruption that accompanied epidemics.[23]

In 1883, "large numbers" again left for the Mountain in anticipation of cholera, and despite the cordon established between the Mountain and Beirut in an effort to prevent the spread of the disease, thousands more followed. The controversy between those for and against the cordon illustrates both the urge of the frightened Beirutis to leave and the interests of the authorities in the interior of Syria to prevent it, but such was the determination to flee that the cordon was often trespassed. In 1900 " a continual flight" from Beirut to the Mountain followed the announcement of the plague. People believed that the Mountain constituted "the best prophylactic measure it is possible to adopt as experience of past cholera epidemics have amply proved.[24]

But not everyone left. According to the sources, different religious communities reacted differently to epidemics. The Christians fled, the Muslims stayed. The terror-stricken people who had fled their suburb because of cholera in 1848 were reported to have been Christians. Visiting what was probably the same suburb, Ras-Beirut, where cholera was most serious that year, the British consul-general had to hire a Muslim to attend to a Christian woman dying of cholera because her husband had run away and her parents refused to go near her. In 1865, most of the victims of cholera were reported to have been Muslims. "The Moslims being fatalists will not flee nor take medicines," wrote Jessup. The same point was echoed by French consul Henri

Guys, who characteristically criticized any Muslim habits or beliefs he did not share.[25]

Many did not leave simply because they could not afford to. The British consul-general had "seldom seen such filth and misery" as he saw in the Christian home where the woman sick with cholera lay abandoned. This may have been due to the neglect engendered by disease, but other evidence is more categorical. The consul-general in that year is said to have visited "wretched huts of poor and others attacked by the malady." In 1875, the poor and the handicapped were among those left behind in Beirut. In 1891, Dr. John Wortabet, son of the Armenian convert Gregory Wortabet, noted: "At every visitation of Cholera the rich inhabitants of infected towns seek refuge in the villages of the Lebanon," while "the poorer population . . . are left behind." In 1900, "those who could go" again fled to the Mountain.[26]

The rich, regardless of religious affiliation, were the ones who left. Many Muslims of the "new school" were quick to adjust their doctrines to circumstances in 1865 and follow "a great exodus of Moslems from Beirut to the Lebanon."[27] It is likely that few of the poor left; if most victims were Muslims that year, it was partly because more Muslims than Christians were poor and partly because, time and time again, Beirut failed to quarantine refugees from neighboring regions that were predominantly Muslim.

Epidemics affected Beirut economically; trade stagnated. As a result of cholera in 1848, shops and bazaars were deserted. In 1865, "all business ceased," and the combination of cholera, local disasters, and a commercial crisis brought heavy losses and innumerable failures to the local and foreign merchant community over the next eight months. Epidemics and cordons caused prices to go up, food to disappear from the market, and fears of famine and of riots to set in. In 1865, "the labouring classes were on the verge of starvation." In 1883, vegetables and dairy products supplied to Beirut by the surrounding villages stopped coming in, and the stock of flour and fodder for horses began to run short. The quality of food declined, and its price shot up "far beyond the means of the poorer classes," provoking fears of famine and unrest among the population.[28]

On occasion, epidemics were aggravated by natural disasters. Plagues of locusts destroyed crops in 1865, in whole districts already burdened with cholera. Winters severe enough to be recorded in memoirs and chronicles are mentioned in 1854 when the "poorer and labouring classes" suffered unusual distress from the disruption of the grain supply to Beirut, which caused a bread shortage and an increase

increase in food costs. In 1870 a poor harvest affected merchants. Jessup remarked, "There has hardly been a year since I came to Syria when some one or more of these plagues have not visited the land."[29]

To natural adversities were added the effects of man-made disasters, as the increasing ties of the area with the rest of the world had its repercussions on local life. International and regional conflicts and economic recessions brought stress and hunger. The rebellion against Egyptian rule in Syria resulted in local conflict, the destruction of crops, and a blockade of the coast that led to a scarcity of grain and a specter of famine in Beirut and Lebanon.[30]

The panic that followed the British bombardment on September 11, 1840, was described in the memoirs of Assaad Kayat (As'ad Ya'qub al-Khayyat), a successful Greek Orthodox trader from Beirut who became a Protestant and British subject. It caused Europeans to flee the country and the local inhabitants to depart for Mount Lebanon. Most of them left on foot and had to abandon all their possessions; they traveled day and night, suffering thirst and overcrowding in the outlying villages. Unrest abroad also translated itself on the local scene into rumors that spread at the slightest opportunity and left behind economic stagnation and social tension.[31]

Internal policies could have the same effect. Little is known about taxation policies in Beirut or the effects on the population, but more is known about the effects of Ottoman efforts to levy troops. It constituted one of the surest ways of frightening people away from recruitment centers such as Beirut. In 1840, when the war against the Egyptians exacerbated the usual fears and tensions, the very arrival in Beirut of the pasha of the district was enough to convince the population that he had come to levy troops. As a result, "the bazaars and the city are now almost deserted and commerce is quite at a stand."[32] Throughout the century, the very threat of conscription could provoke the same reactions, as did the presence in Beirut of recruits from other parts of Syria, even when they stayed in the city only long enough to embark for other areas of the empire.[33]

Beirut shared most of these problems with other cities, and to desert one's native habitat for Beirut was not to leave any of them behind. What was it, then, that encouraged such a massive immigration, especially when one considers that most of it came from rural Mount Lebanon, which was spared much of the cholera that visited Beirut and also provided an easier escape from conscription?

One factor was growth of the population in the Middle East in general, especially in the Syrian interior and those areas of Mount Lebanon from which Beirut drew most of its immigrants. Estimates for Syria remained unreliable until the first comprehensive censuses were carried out in the 1930s, but even these tentative estimates suggest a population explosion that was checked only by occasional bouts of emigration between the 1860s and 1914.[34] In Mount Lebanon, the area most dependent on Beirut, both natural and cultural factors worked in favor of demographic saturation by 1830 or 1840.[35] Most of the increase seems to have been among the Christians; in any case they soon outnumbered the Druzes. The resulting sectarian imbalance meant that the excess of population and hence the source of emigrants were mostly Christian. Everywhere in the Middle East, population pressure in the countryside lay at the source of the growth in urban centers like Beirut, while the combination of proximity, economic opportunity, and political insecurity encouraged the movement.

Economic opportunities in particular were expanding rapidly. By the 1820s Beirut had become the commercial center of Syria and Mount Lebanon, its prosperity based largely on the silk industry. As the cultivation of silk expanded, so did Beirut's economy, for it was the closest to the area that produced "the most silk and of the best quality." It became a center for silk traders, producers, and entrepreneurs. The cultivation of mulberry trees, begun in the seventeenth century in the gardens surrounding Beirut, was further developed in the nineteenth. It was probably, as Guys observed, to cultivate silkworms that a few huts were first built in the areas surrounding Beirut, and the houses that travelers began to notice outside the walled city were no doubt mostly located amid mulberry plantations. This cultivation of silkworms also tied the city more closely to the nearby countryside and to Mount Lebanon. Peasants came down to the suburbs of Beirut to harvest the crop, and mountain merchants came to Beirut to conduct business. Silk was the most lucrative of the enterprises that tied Beirut and Mount Lebanon together.[36]

But the silk trade cannot wholly explain the movement of population to Beirut, if only because it was already active in the first three decades of the nineteenth century, when the population of the city did not grow very much. A variety of factors still discouraged permanent settlement in that period, and by and large the transactions between Beirut and people from adjoining areas involved a transient population — peasants came for the silk harvest and then went home again. The Druzes never stayed long. They were essentially rural people and, in addition, not at ease in a town ruled by Ottomans. After Beirut's separation from Mount Lebanon in the late eighteenth century, the

Druzes had joined forces with the Shihab emirs of Mount Lebanon from whom Beirut had been repossessed by the Ottomans; for that and other reasons, the Beirut Druzes remained relatively few.[37]

Christian merchants were also reluctant to stay in Beirut for any length of time. The only thing that encouraged them to trade in Beirut at all was the refuge offered by Mount Lebanon and the protection extended in the jurisdiction of Emir Bashir II, which started at the gates of the city. This refuge and protection had already been crucial to Beirut's prosperity in the late eighteenth century, when other centers on the coast had been destroyed or could not provide the handy political refuge that Mount Lebanon afforded. But the very fact that Christians needed a refuge testifies to the precariousness of permanent settlement in Beirut. Information about individual merchants suggests that some kept away from Beirut altogether in the period of al-Jazzar (1775–1804), when it was neither safe enough nor important enough to lure many merchants.[38] The few who did live or do business there were also compelled to flee occasionally. The Bustros family papers, for example, tell how the family left Beirut seeking refuge at al-Khraybi near Shuwayfat in Mount Lebanon during Bonaparte's siege of Acre in 1799 and that others did the same, because they feared Ottoman retaliation on local Christians suspected of sympathizing with Europeans.[39]

French merchants driven out of the territories of al-Jazzar did not dare settle in Beirut and did not return to the city until the relatively peaceful administration of Sulayman Pasha (1805–1819).[40] It is fair to assume that local Christian merchants did the same. Although, unlike the French, they still conducted business in Beirut under al-Jazzar, no doubt they found it easier under Sulayman, whom they often praised, in contrast to the hostility they expressed toward his predecessor. Under his rule, the sons of Antun Bustros built a house in Tabaris on a piece of land inherited by him and his brother. The family had owned the land at least as early as 1796, but they did not build their elaborate house on it until sometime between 1809 and 1820. Other merchants followed, among them the Medawars, the Sursocks, and the Naccaches. The Pharaon family had been there earlier, as had a number of important Muslim merchant families such as the Bayhums. The secure period of Sulayman Pasha also encouraged the arrival of more humble refugees from elsewhere when Wahhabi pressure in the interior of Syria led many to leave.[41]

Later, however, politics once again checked the movement to Beirut and drove out those who were in the city. Under the troubled administration of 'Abdallah Pasha (1819–1832), merchants once more took to coming into Beirut only briefly, and the role of Mount Lebanon as a refuge was once more revived. A few, though, had no other alternatives but to remain behind. In 1821, early in the reign of 'Abdallah, political pressure in Acre drove the well-to-do merchants of that city to Mount Lebanon and Beirut, and when trouble began they had no place else to go. The Bustros soon had to abandon their newly built house; Greek incursions in the early 1820s aroused fears of Ottoman retaliation against them as Greek Orthodox Christians, and they fled once again to Mount Lebanon. This time they went to Ba'bda, under the rule of Emir Bashir II, where they remained for twelve years, "coming down to Beirut sometimes one at a time and sometimes all together." Every minute in the city brought danger, and they stayed only long enough to conduct essential business. Other merchants fled from the city after a Greek raid of 1826, which resulted in the confiscation of their goods and their arrest when they returned to Beirut at the command of the authorities. The confiscated goods amounted to about a fourth of what they possessed and were worth about 300,000 piastres. Obviously it was profitable to do business in Beirut, but more security was needed before many would be willing to risk it very often.[42]

Then in the 1830s Beirut gradually began to be a safer place for Christians than the Mountain, as in the last decade of Emir Bashir II's rule, Egyptian exactions of one sort or another oppressed the already impoverished peasantry and increased political tensions. In the 1840s and 1850s, when civil war broke out and spread throughout the Mountain, the centralization of the administration undertaken by the Egyptians and consolidated by the Ottomans in Beirut ensured safety — wherever the seat of government was, security was apt to be maintained. Although Beirut was less prosperous in the 1830s and 1840s than it had been or was later to become, relative political security and stability began to have its effects on population growth.[43] The flight from Beirut after the bombing of the city in 1840 during the Ottoman war against Muhammad 'Ali proved temporary. Assaad Kayat, who vividly described the stream of people who left Beirut, included himself and his family in the multitude, but he was also quick to return.[44] Security was not really an issue in Beirut. The foreign powers waging war against the Egyptian presence in Syria at one point decided to bombard Beirut to achieve their ends, but the security of its Christian population was never really in question.

Besides, the alternatives were worse. Mount Lebanon had been a refuge in times of war and cholera, but the growing interdependence with Beirut that had begun in the 1830s was never interrupted long enough to check Beirut's demographic growth. Merchants who earlier came to the city only to transact business soon began to settle there permanently as the city became safe for longer and longer stretches of time. Exactly when this trend began is difficult to say, but by the 1830s, when French traders were debating where to resettle after the Egyptian invasion, they decided to establish themselves in Beirut, "because if other ports include a few local merchants, Beirut has a greater number of them and among the richest.[45]

Beirut's prosperity also attracted some of the destitute, as Egyptian taxation and other exactions brought hardship to the peasants in Mount Lebanon, and many migrated to Beirut along with other coastal towns. Thus it was mentioned by the inhabitants of the district of Kisrawan and others in Mount Lebanon that the poor of Lebanon were "scattered among the cities and villages of Syria." Many left their villages in the region of Sidon, between Tripoli and Hama, and in the province of Akkar to seek refuge in the cities of the coast and elsewhere.[46] Nor was their departure always voluntary, as the Egyptians forceably recruited labor for their projects along the coast. Peasants were made to work in the mines a few hours away from Beirut; masons and builders were levied to build Egyptian fortifications; sometimes even the youth in Beirut itself were picked up to work on the coast.[47]

Beginning in the 1830s, then, Beirut began for the first time to outstrip the populations of neighboring cities along the coast. In addition to Christian merchants and peasants, various delegations and political groups of all sorts came to Beirut from the Mountain when it became an administrative center, and the political power and stability in the city after 1830 allowed it to sustain its role as an asylum, though only after the civil war of 1860 did a great many of these refugees remain permanently. Its role as a refuge diminished in the tranquil decades that followed, but never quite disappeared. Syrian residents in Egypt in 1882 (the Greeks also tried to come but were stopped); Armenians beginning around 1900; and in recent decades, Palestinians and other Arabs have intermittently revived that function in the decades since.

Throughout the nineteenth century, immigration and emigration were simultaneous phenomena in the city, but the people involved changed with times and political circumstances. In Beirut the common incentive and discernible pattern in the composition of the incoming population was security and the opportunities in Beirut's thriving economy. The common denominator was religion. Since Christians needed protection more than Muslims did, more Christians than Muslims sought refuge in Beirut and, in so doing, changed the balance of the religious communities in the city.

5 Population Change

The 1876 edition of Baedeker's guidebook informs travelers that in Beirut "the Muslim element is gradually being displaced by the Christian." By the 1912 edition, the passage reads: "The Muslim element of the population is in every way less important than the Christian." Through immigration, the city's religious composition had been transformed. Christians had migrated to the city in such numbers that they gradually superseded the Muslims as the city's dominant community.[1]

To assess the changes in Beirut's religious composition, one has first to challenge the commonly held assumption that in the nineteenth century Beirut's population, like that of other coastal cities on the Syrian coast, was overwhelmingly Muslim to begin with. Etienne de Vaumas, for example, writes that Beirut "until the time when it started to develop at the end of the nineteenth century, was a city which was basically Sunni and with a Greek Orthodox minority." Said Chehabe-Ed-Dine repeats that the population of Beirut in 1860 was for the most part Sunni. Gabriel Baer writes that the creation of Greater Lebanon in the twentieth century resulted in the annexation of the Sunni regions of Beirut and Tripoli to Mount Lebanon. The generally accepted opinion is that Beirut's population remained predominantly Sunni even up to the French Mandate.[2]

A minority, but more correct, opinion is that the Christian population of Beirut had already begun to increase in the first half of the nineteenth century. Even Shaykh Taha al-Wali, otherwise a proponent of Sunni predominance — who remarked that, in the period of al-Jazzar, Christians of all denominations were so few in Beirut that they could all pray in the same church — also notes that after the death of al-Jazzar, and particularly after the Egyptian occupation, their number increased. By the time Guys was writing in the 1830s and 1840s, the Christian population had increased so markedly that it had become the largest Christian colony on the otherwise Sunni-dominated coast.[3]

It is doubtful, then, that the large number of Christians in Beirut by the 1830s was a new phenomenon. The composition of Beirut's population was probably already very different from that of other coastal cities. Even in the seventeenth and eighteenth centuries Christians were numerous there. Even seventeenth-century travelers noted how mixed the population was — that Christians and Jews, as well as Turks and Arabs, formed the population of the city. Western travelers may exaggerate the Christian presence in Beirut because of their natural attraction to coreligionists, but they would have carried their biases to all the places they visited, and still they remarked on the difference.[4]

The mixture itself may not have been uncommon; what was unusual was the suggestion that Beirut had a Christian majority. Laurent d'Arvieux, son of the French consul in Sidon, who lived in the commercial ports of the Levant between 1653 and 1665 and later became emissary of the French king to Tunis and Constantinople and consul in Algiers, Aleppo, and Tripoli, visited Beirut in 1660. While there he wrote: "The great majority of its inhabitants were Greek and Maronite Christians, while the rest were Moors [most likely meaning Arab Muslims], Turks and Jews." We have no way of substantiating his estimate and it may well be an exaggeration, but even if it is, Christians must still have been numerous enough to make the comment possible. If they were not in the majority, they were clearly more numerous in Beirut than in the neighboring cities. Forty years later Nicholas Poiresson, superior of the Jesuit missions to Syria and Persia in the mid-seventeenth century, claimed that Beirut had "more Maronites, i.e., Catholics, at least in relation to its size, than any other city in Syria."[5]

In the eighteenth century, Christians were still numerous, perhaps even more so than in the seventeenth. A bishop from Ireland, Richard Pococke, visited Beirut in the 1730s and wrote: "The town is under the influence of the Maronites and Druzes, as many other places are under the Arabs [most likely meaning Muslims]." Another traveler who visited Beirut in 1797 noted that the suburbs of Beirut were almost as large as the city and that prior to al-Jazzar's rule, the gardens in these suburbs belonged to Christians.[6]

To explain the large number of Christians in Beirut, one has first to determine the period in which the Christian population began to increase. Although information is scanty, evidence suggests that under the Mamluks (1291–1516) Beirut recovered from the Crusader era and became predominantly Muslim. After the Ottoman takeover (1516), the population changed once again. Christians became more numerous in Beirut than in other cities. Why more Christians than Druzes took advantage of the link of city and mountain we do not know, except that Christians were more apt to be involved in mercantile activities; but the fact remains that the Christian population increased in Beirut just at a time when the new administrative structure placed Beirut, alone of the coastal cities, in direct relationship with the Mountain.

Against this background, the small Christian population in al-Jazzar's time is clearly an anomaly. The drastic reduction in Christian numbers under his rule obscures the fact that Beirut had otherwise almost always had a large Christian population, and probably explains why so many have assumed that Beirut was as Sunni-dominated as the other coastal cities until the late nineteenth century. The exceptional reduction of the Christian population under al-Jazzar was temporary. In 1784, the French writer Volney noted that, although the Pasha had taken Beirut away from the jurisdiction of Mount Lebanon and although the Druzes no longer dared live on the coast any longer, Beirut continued to be the "warehouse of Maronites and Druzes." Baron François de Tott, the French diplomat who helped reorganize the Ottoman army and navy in Istanbul and became inspector-general of the French consulates in the commercial ports of the Levant in 1776–1778, visited Beirut and mentioned that traders who had left Beirut for Mount Lebanon during the period of al-Jazzar were simply "awaiting the end of the Pasha."[7]

As soon as al-Jazzar's rule ended, Christians returned once again, and by 1826 were at least strong enough — or appeared to be enough of a threat — to be accused of collaborating in the Greek attack on Beirut. Certainly by the 1830s Christians once more represented a substantial part of the population, and their numbers were still rising. When Ibrahim Pasha appointed an advisory council in Beirut in the 1830s, the council was composed of an equal number of Muslims and Christians.[8] One might argue that this balance was politically motivated and did not necessarily reflect their proportions in the city. It could well be that councils set up by the Egyptians elsewhere in Syria and Palestine carried the same proportionate representation, regardless of the actual composition of these areas. In the case of Beirut, however, the assumption gains credence when we discover that, even after the Egyptians departed, representation on the committees of Beirut remained unchanged.

Western observers corroborate the assumption as well. Some refer to the various sects without offering any numbers. But they still manage to give some sense of their relative importance and to suggest that no one of them could claim a clear-cut majority, either by qualifying their comments or by mentioning the smaller communities as being few. Jessup writes, for example, that in the days of the missionary Pliny Fisk (1823–1825), one of the pioneers of American missions to Syria and Palestine, the population consisted of "Mohammedans, Greeks, Maronites and a few Druzes and Jews"; Poujoulat wrote in 1831 that it was composed "of Maronites, of Catholic Greeks and Muslim Arabs." Austen Henri Layard, British archeologist, traveler, and attaché at the embassy in Istanbul, visited Beirut and wrote in 1840 that it was "Mussulman, Arab, Christian and European," but that the European community was very small.[9]

Some travelers exaggerate the numbers of Christians. Delaroière claims that Maronites formed the bulk of the population of Beirut, to which had to be added Greek Orthodox, Greek Catholics, Syriacs, a few Turks, and a fairly large group of "Franks." In 1838, Edouard Blondel, a French trader who visited Syria three times between 1837 and 1839, claimed that if one counted the Maronites, Armenians, Greek Catholics, and Greek Orthodox, Christians would "certainly" constitute three fourths of the population, in addition to which Jews could be found in great numbers; Muslims were in the minority. Delaroière's comments on the population, like his comments on other facts concerning Beirut, were probably influenced by earlier authors; and his and Blondel's exaggerations of the number of Maronites in Beirut were probably affected by their particular interests. Still the statements are significant because they could not possibly have been made about other cities of Syria in that period. We know that in the 1830s Christians were in fact almost as numerous as Muslims: of the 15,500 people Guys counted in Beirut in the 1830s, the proportions were about half and half.[10] There were also more Christian religious services in Beirut than in any other city of Syria. In contrast to the days of al-Jazzar, when Christians of all denominations could fit in one church, in the 1830s:

Beirut has another and eminent advantage over the other towns of Syria, in its religious services and privileges; many ministers of

many lands reside here in villas, where are to be met, occasionally, learned men from the monasteries of the mountain, bishops,
priests, savans of the Maronites, Greeks, and Catholics. The Sab-
bath does not here, as throughout most of the East, oblige the
stranger to feel himself in a strange land.[11]

As the pace of growth of the population quickened in the 1840s and
1850s, immigration kept the equal proportions of Muslims and Christians reached in the 1830s. Guys in the 1840s gives a slightly higher
number of Christians, but the Ottoman census quoted by Urquhart
for 1850 suggests that Muslims were slightly more numerous.[12]

The more or less equal proportions of Muslims and Christians cited
by Guys and Urquhart concur with observations by contemporaries.
Laorty-Hadji, a Frenchman who visited Syria, and Baron Isidor Justin
Severin Taylor, a French man-of-letters who was appointed inspector-
general of fine arts and who traveled to the east in connection with his
occupation, wrote in the 1850s that Beirut was a half-Muslim, half-
Christian city; the historian of Mount Lebanon, Tannus al-Shidyaq,
also said that most of the inhabitants of Beirut were either Muslim or
Christian. Only the British consul-general claimed in 1853 that Christians were "vastly in the majority in Beirut," which is doubtful, as are
the similar statements by d'Arvieux and Blondel, but again they do
confirm at least how different Beirut was; about its neighboring cities
such an exaggeration would never have been made.[13]

The numerical equality of Muslims and Christians, in any case,
came to an end after 1860. Between 1840 and 1865 the number of Muslims in Beirut doubled; the number of Christians tripled. After 1860
Muslims constituted just over a third of the population, Christians just
under two thirds. This changed numerical distribution is substantiated
in an Ottoman estimate in the *salname* (yearbook) of 1874 which
counted a greater number of "non-Muslim" than Muslim males, the
only Ottoman estimate to do so.[14] Druzes, Jews, and foreigners may
have been added to Christians under the term "non-Muslim," but as
their numbers remained small throughout the century, the increase in
the non-Muslim category most likely reflected the large number of
Christians. By 1873, a British observer in Beirut found Muslims in the
minority in both Beirut and Mount Lebanon and, unlike the same
claim made by the British consul-general in the 1850s, this time it
agrees with other available evidence. The exception is a comment by
Louis Lortet, dean of the faculty of medicine at the University of Lyon
who traveled to Syria and Palestine in 1875–1880, that about half the
population was Muslim and the rest were "Christians, Maronites,
Greeks, Druzes, Italians, etc."[15]

Christians retained their majority for the rest of the century. Estimates are relatively numerous for its last two decades and, despite variations in absolute numbers of Beirut's population, their proportions are consistent. The Christian population tripled in Beirut between the 1840s and the 1860s, and almost tripled again between 1861 and the end of the century; the Muslim population barely doubled. Between 1861 and the end of the century, Muslims lost about one fourth of the proportion reached by 1861, while Christians remained about two thirds of the population. The Christian majority is corroborated by Jules Hoche; by the 1886 edition of W. M. Thomson's *The Land and the Book*; by the Ukrainian Orientalist and traveler, Krimsky, who wrote in 1896 that "most of the inhabitants of Beirut were not Muslims but Christians"; and by an anonymous author who wrote about 1900 that more than two thirds of the population was Christian.[16]

In the early twentieth century, the proportion did not alter significantly. As we have seen, the 1912 Baedeker gave Muslims about a third of the population, the Christians half. In 1913 a source quoted by British Naval Intelligence gave Christians two thirds of the population. The only exception is the Ottoman estimate in the *salname* of 1908 which reduces the population total and divides the population almost equally between Muslims and Christians. This estimate is the only one, however, that distinguishes between Beirut's inhabit-

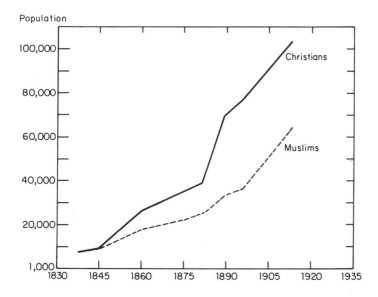

ants (included in this census by denomination) and Lebanese and foreigners residing in Beirut.

World War I had its effects on the total population but not on proportions of Christians and Muslims; Muslims remained at a third and
Christians at about two thirds. The first major change in the makeup
of the population was recorded in the official estimates of the French
mandatory authorities in 1922. There Muslims had increased slightly,
to 39 percent; Christians have moved back to about the level of the
1840s, from about 60 percent to about 45 percent. Greater equality in
numbers between Christians and Muslims in Beirut remains a trend in
the twentieth century.[18] (See Table 2.)

That Muslims declined in their proportion of the population should
not be allowed to obscure their growth in absolute numbers. Although
they declined from about one half to about one third over the course
of the nineteenth century, their numbers increased by 58,000 in about
seventy-five years, and that increase, like the Christian one, is attributable largely to migration.

Most of the Muslims in Beirut continued to be Sunnis. The number
of Shi'is remained so small that many sources do not even mention
them. Those that do report that in 1895 there were 80 Shi'is as against
36,000 Sunnis; and in 1920, 1,500 Metualis (or Shi'is) as against 45,000
Sunnis. The Shi'is had no mosque in the city until the 1940s, when a
slow growth in their numbers began. Their substantial presence now
constitutes one of the major new developments in the society of modern Lebanon.[19]

The Christians, in contrast to the Muslims, were subdivided into a
large number of sects. (See Table 3.) The result was that, even when the
Muslims became a minority, the Sunnis continued to constitute the single largest religious sect in the population. Until the 1920s, however, the
margin between Sunnis and the next most numerous sect, Greek Orthodox, continued to shrink, and at times it almost disappeared.

The Greek Orthodox were the largest Christian sect in the city, and
they maintained that numerical superiority throughout the nineteenth
century, constituting between 23 and 29 percent of the total population and reflecting the sizable Greek Orthodox immigration into Beirut in the nineteenth century.

The Maronites followed close behind the Greek Orthodox and
moved closer and closer as the century wore on. From constituting
about 10 percent of the population in the 1830s, they more than doubled their proportion by 1860–61 to 21 percent, and increased it again
between 1861 and the 1920s to between 21 and 26 percent. Only the

numerous Greek Orthodox migration to Beirut in the same period maintained them as the largest Christian sect.

Greek Catholics were in fourth place and remained steady at about 7 or 8 percent of the population. Though much smaller in numbers than Sunnis, Greek Orthodox, or Maronites, the fact that the percentage was sustained at a time when the population of Beirut was growing so fast and so much indicates that Greek Catholic immigration into Beirut was also high.

The remaining Christians were Roman, Syrian, Armenian Catholics, Armenian Orthodox, and Protestants. Estimates are rough, since the sources rarely provide any information about them. But generally they appear to have fluctuated somewhere between 1 and 4 percent of Beirut's population. The balance of the population of Beirut was made up of Druzes, Jews, and "foreigners." There were few Druzes in Beirut partly because there were not very many of them in Mount Lebanon, partly because, although the Druzes were as mobile as larger groups (an often neglected point), they preferred to move inland, particularly to the Hawran, perhaps because they were an agricultural rather than a commercial people.[20] Jews fluctuated between 1 and 3 percent of the total, representing numbers that, though low, must still have been considerably higher than in previous centuries. There was no synagogue in Beirut in the seventeenth century; there was both a synagogue and a Jewish school in the nineteenth.[21]

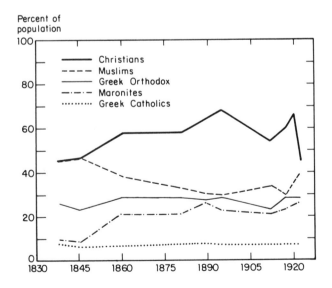

The impact of Druzes and Jews on the growth of Beirut varied but was minor for the most part. Both groups remained small — the migration to and the population of Beirut remained preponderantly Muslim or Christian.

"Foreigners" were always listed in the sources as a separate category in a series otherwise religiously defined. Sometimes Turks were counted as foreigners, but most often Europeans were meant. In any case, the number of Europeans in Beirut was small, and the number of Turks even smaller. Until the French Mandate, foreigners constituted only 1 to 3 percent of the population of Beirut, in contrast to other parts of the Middle East where their numbers were much larger. Under the mandate, the proportion of foreigners in Beirut grew from 1 to 3 percent to 15 percent in 1922, no doubt as a result of the French presence.

The heavy migration to Beirut of Sunnis, Greek Catholics, Greek Orthodox, and Maronites was drawn from Mount Lebanon, the Syrian interior, and other coastal cities, all of which were heavily populated by other religious communities. Sources are silent about the extent of the Muslim migration. Most of the local and foreign sources available happen to be Christian and paid more attention to developments among Christian groups. Sources are also most apt to report on population movements in times of crisis; Muslim immigration seems to have been distributed more or less steadily throughout the nineteenth century and to depend on administrative and economic developments more than on civil strife. As a result, Muslim migration to Beirut has to be deduced from statistics, physical changes, and oral tradition. All point to a growth in the Muslim population. The number of mosques grew throughout the nineteenth century, from about six in 1800 to thirty-one after 1900.[22] Tradition in many Muslim families traces their settlement in the city back to the nineteenth century. No substantial information tells us where they came from, and at this stage we can only infer that they must have come from such Sunni-populated areas as the interior of Syria, the Syrian coast, and parts of the Biqa' in Lebanon.

Christian migration to Beirut is better documented, especially when it results from political crises that attracted attention to the religious affiliation of immigrants and dramatically transformed the sectarian composition of the city. In the early nineteenth century, some Christian families left the vilayets of Damascus and Aleppo, as a result of the Wahhabi advance on Damascus in 1810, and took refuge in Beirut and Lebanon, but on the whole their number must have been few and their migration limited.[23] The deterioration of the political situation in

Mount Lebanon in the 1840s had a more direct and significant impact, causing a wave of Christian migration to Beirut. For example, the exodus of Christians from Dayr al-Qamar was so marked after the clashes between Maronites and Druzes of 1840–41 that the son of its joint governor came to Beirut in December 1841 to ask the Sar'askar (Ottoman commander-in-chief) Salim Pasha to send back "immediately" all the Christians from Dayr al-Qamar, but consular intervention suspended the order.[24]

In the same decade Christians from other troubled or unsafe areas moved to Beirut, sometimes moved by pressure from official authorities, more often by hostility at home. In 1845, a "large number" of the Christian inhabitants of 'Abay were brought to Beirut under Ottoman and foreign supervision to protect them from Druze animosity. Probably as many as seven hundred Christians left 'Abay for Beirut at that time. Other Christians left because of animosity from other Christian sects. In the 1840s, Protestant missionaries from Beirut opened a mission in the district of Hasbayya, which, together with the district of Rashayya, stretched southward from the foot of Mount Hermon to what became after World War I the frontier between Greater Lebanon and mandated Palestine. The mission converted about a hundred and fifty Greek Orthodox to the Anglican Church, which subsequently led to their persecution and exile. It is probable that a number went to Beirut, where they would have the protection of the English consul and English and American missionaries. Another wave of Christians moved to Beirut in 1850, this time as a result of clashes between Christian and Muslim communities of Aleppo.[25]

Many of these Christians were well off; they included traders and skilled artisans, people who would never have left had it not been for persecution. At the time of the disturbances of 1841 in Dayr al-Qamar, "all the trading and many of the middling classes of Christians" left the town. Among them was a Mr. Souza, one of its leading merchants, who said:

> Himself and twenty or thirty other principal merchants constituting the body of Merchants of Deir el Kamar alive to the precarious state of Christians who lived amongst the Druzes had resolved not to go back there no matter what the form of government of Deir el Kamar was but that when things were quieter they intended to collect their debts, sell their property and then settle in Beyrout, Sidon and elsewhere.[26]

Many of the Christians who left Aleppo in 1850 must also have been prosperous, since the population of this city was known to be "the wealthiest" in Syria. When disturbances occurred, most of the Christians who could afford to planned to migrate.[27]

The largest group of Christian migrants came to Beirut in 1860, when Christians of all denominations and all socioeconomic levels fled troubled areas in Mount Lebanon and Syria, wandering from one region to another before moving on to the coastal districts. Although many failed to reach their destination, many more succeeded and Beirut's population almost tripled in the number of Christians. Information on refugees in Beirut in 1860 can be found in a number of contemporary accounts, including chronicles, memoirs, consular reports, reports by the Anglo-American Relief Committee formed in Beirut in July 1860, and other official papers. This vast but unsystematic information conveys the impression that throughout 1860 Beirut continued to receive refugees. A list found on "The Maronite Refugees in the City of Beirut" dated 1860 is unusual in that it was drawn up by local authorities (whether secular or religious is unclear) and identifies exactly the refugees' place of origin, in contrast to Western sources that mention only region. The list provides family names and number of persons per family under the name of the village or town from which they came.[28]

Number of Maronite refugees in Beirut	Place of origin	District
178	Hasbayya	Hasbayya (Wadi al-Taym)
100	Zahle	Shuf Bayyadi (Baqa' Gharbi)
47	Zahle area	Shuf Bayyadi (Baqa' Gharbi)
10	'Aytanit	
47	Khirba	
52	'Ayn Zibde	
125	Sighbin	Iqlim al-Jazzin
61	Jazzin and Wadi Jazzin	Iqlim al-Jazzin
42	Mazra'at al-Shuf wa Sumqaniyya	Shuf
77	Bkasin	Iqlim al-Jazzin
33	'Azur	
19	Mashmusha, Midan, Bjannin, mazra' Sabbah	Iqlim al-Jazzin
85	Qaytuli	Iqlim al-Jazzin
10	al-Qub'	
17	Dibbiyya	Iqlim al-Kharrub

Number of Maronite refugees in Beirut	Place of origin	District
24	mazari 'al- Dibbiya	Iqlim al-Kharrub
18	Other places in Iqlim Kharrub	
69	Scattered	
1,220	Dayr al-Qamar	Manasif
292	Bayt al-Din	Manasif
2,526		

All the Maronites listed came from the mixed Druze districts of south Lebanon, often from areas where Maronites constituted a majority of the Christian population, such as al-Jazzin, Bayt al-Din, Dayr al-Qamar, and Iqlim al-Kharrub. Some came from areas where other Christians sects predominated, such as Hasbayya and Zahle were, respectively, Greek Orthodox and Green Catholics were in the majority. The largest number came from the largest towns, Dayr al-Qamar, Bayt al-Din, Jazzin, Zahle and Hasbayya, but many also came from villages so small that they do not appear on any standard map of the region.

Maronites were the most numerous among the refugees that the Anglo-American Relief Committee took care of. The number of refugees in Beirut rose from 10,000 in the middle of August 1860 to over 20,000 by the end of the month, and was still growing. Of that 20,000, about 7,000 received daily aid from the Anglo-American Relief Committee. Of these 7,000 the vast majority were Maronites; next came Greek Catholics; a considerable number were Orthodox; only about a hundred were Protestants. The proportions among those receiving relief does not necessarily reflect the actual religious composition of the refugees in Beirut. Though the relief committee claimed that it was "wholly unsectarian" in its charitable endeavors, only Christians were mentioned in their circulars because only Christians had asked for help; "not a Druze, Mohammedan, or Jew has applied for assistance." It is safe to assume that Jews and particularly Muslims or Druzes would not have felt it advisable to apply for help from an institution that called itself the Anglo-American Relief Committee.[29]

Although Maronites constituted the largest group supported by the committee, it is unlikely they were the largest group of refugees to remain. The people who came from areas close to Beirut were no doubt most numerous and most apt to be Maronites, but they were also more likely to be transients than were the people who came from the Syrian interior, who would find it both more difficult and more dangerous to return home. Among those who stayed, the Greek Orthodox from Hasbayya, Rashayya, and Damascus were probably most numerous, though that surmise is only tentative. Lack of research and the silence of the sources leave us only with oral tradition, which must be taken somewhat skeptically. Still, if more Maronites and Greek Catholics than Greek Orthodox are found on the lists of the Anglo-American Relief Committee, it is at least likely that the committee had refugees for the most part from Mount Lebanon on its hands; the report even mentions that the thousands of refugees supported by the committee had fled to Beirut "from the Mountain."

Many Greek Orthodox also found relief elsewhere. Thousands of them were assisted by the Ottoman government. Relief was also extended to refugees by the Greek government and other European powers, by the Muslims and Christians of Beirut, and by Catholic missionaries.[30] The greatest influx of Greek Orthodox occurred after the disturbances of July 1860 in Damascus. The Christian population of Damascus had been almost entirely Greek Orthodox, and refugees from Hasbayya and Rashayya had since been added.[31] After the incidents of July, thousands left for Beirut. Along the Damascus road processions of men, women, and children on horses, mules, camels, and on foot formed long caravans that blocked both the road and the streets of the city. In one month about 11,000 were said to have come, more than 3,000 of them in a single day.[32]

Local and foreign authorities in both Damascus and Beirut did their utmost to convince them to stay in Damascus, but they were unable either to calm their fears or to outweigh the enticements of those Damascenes who had already settled in Beirut. Despite official pressure and an improvement in the situation at Damascus, throughout the summer Christians continued "to leave for Beirut daily, selling their bedding, cooking utensils, and anything they possess, to procure the means of hiring an animal for the journey." In October, in one day, 1,400 left for Beirut, and every day brought "fresh drafts" of refugees. In November it was reported that "the exodus from Damascus still goes on," and over 1,000 refugees had arrived the day before; if the stream of emigration from Damascus persisted, soon "none but the scanty dregs of the Christian population" would remain there.[33]

We have the memoirs of one of these Damascene refugees, a member of a Greek Orthodox family named Debbas. He was Dimitri, son of Youssef, son of Gerji Debbas; his memoirs cover forty-four manuscript pages, written in a mixture of colloquial and classical Arabic, several decades after the event; Dimitri Debbas had in the meantime become a prominent notable of Beirut. The lapse of years between the events of July 1860 and the time Dimitri recorded them seemed to affect the author's recollections only in minor ways, however, and no official report conveys as these memoirs do what the movement of these thousands was like.[34]

Dimitri was born into an old and respected family. Their notability is reflected in their ancient house, where inscriptions testified to the three archbishops the family had produced: Athanasius III (1611–1619), Patriarch Kerillos III in 1620, and Patriarch Athanasius IV (1720–1724), himself the son of a priest.[35] Another proof of the distinction the family possessed are four imperial *berats* (certificates) engraved on leather. Three of them relate to the patriarchs of the family and the fourth to Gerji Debbas, who was either Dimitri's grandfather or perhaps the grandfather of Dimitri's father Youssef (the text simply says "our" grandfather). Gerji had held the position of chief engineer of Damascus around 1750 and had been asked by no less than 'Abadallah, Pasha of Acre, himself to go to Acre to cast copper. He was the only one the pasha allowed to cast large caldrons. At the age of fourteen Dimitri was taught by his father to run silk and cotton looms, and he built a business of his own between 1851 and 1860.

The civil war of 1860 destroyed Dimitri's business and the social position his family had established over the centuries. The war had started in Mount Lebanon, and tension was already building in Damascus. On the afternoon of Monday, July 9, Dimitri, then twenty-three years old, was near Bab al-Barid when trouble started in the city.[36] He rushed to his shop in a khan near Bab Tuma and locked himself in; from his hiding place he heard and saw fighting in the street.[37]

Dimitri sought refuge in the houses of various prominent notables of the city, to each of whom he offered credit for the help extended. When night fell, he found his way to the house of the agha (warden) of the quarter, 'Abdallah Shurbagi, where "thousands" of other Christians had gathered. In the course of the night security reinforcements arrived, but the agha still sent the Christians to other quarters of the city, asserting that Bab Tuma was not safe. He entrusted them to some Muslims, who took them to the house of another Muslim notable, 'Abdallah Afandi al-Ma'adi, where a crowd of other Christians had already gathered. On Tuesday morning, they went on to the house of a prominent Damascene notable, Shaykh 'Abdallah al-Halabi. The streets and intersections through which they passed were blocked by refugees from the surrounding villages who had crowded into the city that morning. As they were crossing a street, Dimitri noticed another Muslim notable, 'Abduh Afandi Khayr, opening his house to Christian notables who worked in the seraglio. Dimitri followed them. 'Abduh Afandi Khayr led them through two palaces into a third, where thirty or forty Christians had already assembled. Among them was Dimitri's nephew Esber Yazigi, who remained with his uncle from then on. On Wednesday, the Christians who were under Muslim protection were taken to the house of Shaykh al-Halabi. Dimitri made it into that house, where a large, excited, and frightened crowd of Christians was assembled, and bread was distributed.[38]

The following morning, the Sar'askar summoned the Muslim notables to the seraglio and demanded that they hand over the Christians under their charge. They adamantly refused, however, but compromised by agreeing to send them for the protection to the Citadel of Damascus. The Christians in Shaykh al-Halabi's house anxiously awaited their return, and when they found out they were to go to the Citadel they feared a repetition of the massacres that had gone on in Hasbayya, Rashayya, and Dayr al-Qamar. Dimitri Debbas at first shared these fears but was somewhat reassured when an elderly Muslim, Hajj al-Bakri, who used to export cloth to Aleppo for Dimitri's father, told him he would be safe there. Dimitri joined the procession of Christians going to the Citadel escorted by friendly Muslims.

Thousands of men, women, and children had already gathered in the Citadel when Dimitri and his companions arrived.[39] Their condition "would have made a rock weep," says Dimitri, and neither their apprehensions nor their misery was alleviated when two days later the women were separated from the men in the midst of lamentations. Hashim Agha comforted them like a caring father, however, and Dimitri warmly praises his humanity. Later, when the Druzes threatened to attack the Citadel, Hashim Agha closed the gate and directed its cannons toward Damascus. According to Dimitri, the Christians owed their survival solely to Hashim Agha; the renowned Algerian Emir 'Abdal-Qadir; and the Muslim notables of the Maydan.[40] Dimitri invariably distinguished the attitude of the Muslim notables from that of the angry mob.[41]

Dimitri had been in the Citadel for eight days before negotiations began between religious leaders, foreign consuls, and the Sar'askar in Damascus to send the Christians in the Citadel to Beirut. The Sar'askar agreed to send about 300 North Africans with a leader and 14 Druzes to escort the first caravan of about 840 people. Many were on horses, but a good number—including Dimitri—were on foot.

At al-Dimas the caravan was approached by a large band of Kurds; this threw panic into the hearts of the refugees, but nothing happened. The first night no one slept. Back on the road the next day, when the caravan reached the Wadi al-Qurn, shooting could be heard in the distance, and a group of Druze fighters appeared. The head of the Druze bodyguard ordered the caravan to stop and rode to the Druze soldiers to negotiate, while the refugees left behind appealed to their priests — 'Abdallah Tawwa and Ni'mi al-Farra — for a blessing. But the head of the bodyguard soon returned, and they advanced without further delay, studiously avoiding the direction of the other Druzes. The caravan reached Khan al-Marj in a state of exhaustion, but there was no time for rest; again 500 Druzes surrounded the terrified people. The Druzes guarding the caravan discussed the situation with the consuls, then went to negotiate. They returned to report that the price of free passage was 5,000 liras in gold. The consuls wrote up a promissory note for the amount needed to be paid by the English consul in Beirut, and the hostile Druzes sent a messenger to Beirut to check on its validity. As the caravan awaited his return in a state of great apprehension, the Kurds arrived and food was prepared. About nightfall, the messenger returned. The note had been accepted, and muleteers, bodyguards, and refugees were put back on the road without further delay. The distance from Khan al-Marj to Beirut was covered with no further stops.

When they arrived in Beirut, the refugees were put in quarantine just outside the city. Members of the Bustros family in Beirut went to the mutasarrif and talked him into allowing the refugees to enter the town, and Beirutis of other religious communities followed suit. By that time the refugees were so exhausted that they almost had to be carried into the town.

Dimitri and about thirty other Greek Orthodox were lodged by the Greek Orthodox school, the Madrasat Thalathat Aqmar.[42] A couple of days later, Christians came with bread and melons, and other food and supplies followed. Eight days later, another caravan arrived from Damascus, and the school became so jammed that a number were moved by the Sursock family to the cellars of Khalil Sursock's house. Families slept inside the cellars; young single men, including Dimitri, slept in the open.[43]

Beirut was filled with refugees. Every public space, quarantine center, school, religious headquarters, cemetery, and garden was filled with people. The government rented khans and houses to lodge still more. Even the ships in the harbor sheltered refugees. Families also had to accommodate relatives and friends from Mount Lebanon and elsewhere in Syria streaming into Beirut, adding still further to the overcrowding. Sanitary conditions deteriorated as the flood of people kept pouring in.[44]

But the arrival of refugees was paralleled by a steady and more discreet departure of the rich, just as at other troubled times. During epidemics, they simply moved to the surrounding countryside. In 1860, however, the environs were worse off than Beirut itself, so they left Syria altogether on chartered vessels and steamers for Alexandria, Smyrna, Athens.[45] No one knows exactly how many left. One author spoke of the daily departure of "thousands"; even if this is exaggerated, there were at least enough to attract attention and inspire hyperbole.[46] The sources also say that most were Christians, but it is possible that there were many Muslim refugees. There is no information on how many eventually returned, but it is likely that many came back to the city where their economic interests were, once things had settled down. Many of the refugees probably also left Beirut to return home when peace came; certainly, there was strong Ottoman and consular pressure on the refugees to do so.[47] The towns of Mount Lebanon continued to grow in the last decades of the nineteenth century, which suggests that many complied, though research is limited and the growth might well be explained by natural increase alone.

In any case, the majority settled permanently in the city, and emigration from Damascus to Beirut was still continuing in 1867.[48] The drastic physical changes Beirut underwent immediately after 1860 reflected the city's population growth, and the rise of the growth curve of Beirut's Christian population after 1860 confirms that the refugees of 1860 account for a considerable part of it.

Beirut's economic opportunities made all of this possible, and because the immigrants were Christians, more Christians than Muslims benefited. In this way, Beirut's changing religious composition became associated with changes in the distribution of wealth. Christians not only outnumbered Muslims, but soon outdistanced them in social and economic position.

6 The Foreign Entrepreneurs

In the course of the nineteenth century, Beirut grew to become Syria's leading port and a center for European trade. Aside from a few Europeans who came to invest in the new markets, the chief beneficiaries of the prosperity were the Beiruti Christian merchants, primarily because, as coreligionists, in their dealings with the West they had advantages over the Muslims.

Beirut emerged as the leading port on the eastern Mediterranean just as sea trade was given a substantial boost by the advent of steam navigation. The wooden-paddle steamer began to carry mail, passengers, and freight in the 1830s. Its capacity did not exceed 1,500 tons, however, so the revolution in maritime transport did not really take hold until the introduction of iron steamships driven by screw propellers in the 1840s and 1850s. On the Syrian coast, a British line — soon replaced by a French one — and an Austrian line (the Austrian Lloyd) began to call regularly at Syrian ports in the 1830s and 1840s. Technical improvements and diminishing costs of steam navigation soon led to trade in a wider range of goods. After mid-century, the English had the greatest number of lines servicing the Mediterranean. Among the French lines, the most important was the Compagnie des Messageries Impériales (later called the Messageries Maritimes) created at the time of the reorganization of French navigation by Napoleon III. The Russian Steam Navigation Company joined in; English, French, Austrian, Greek, Italian, Belgian, Dutch, Spanish, Swedish, Norwegian, Turkish, and Egyptian ships also called at the port of Beirut. Total shipping entering the port grew from less than 50,000 tons a year in the 1830s to over 600,000 tons a year in 1886. By World War I, nine shipping companies served Syrian ports and called there regularly at intervals ranging from a week to a month; freighters from several other companies made more irregular calls. More ships called there than at any other port along the Syrian coast. While Turkey and Egypt accounted for about half of Syria's trade in the 1830s, they accounted for less than one third by 1910; the rest had shifted to Europe.[1]

Of the European countries involved in Beirut's economy, France and England were the most important. France had made trading contacts since at least the eighteenth century with the Syrian coast, where it established relations at certain key *échelles* or ports, and these trade relations were strengthened in the nineteenth century. England, on the other hand, had hitherto concentrated on the route to India, and Syria's importance to England hinged on the caravan routes crossing the Syrian interior, Iraq, and Iran. In the 1830s, British interests in India multiplied when the East India Company connected London to Bombay via Suez, and Syria's position as distributor of goods for the hinterland made it both a market for English manufactured goods and a supplier of raw materials.[2]

These different concerns accounted for the different roles the two countries played in Syria. France had the largest share of the export trade, ranging from 25 percent in 1833 to 32 percent in 1910. Its share in the imports of Syria was more modest: 15.9 percent in 1833 going down to 9.3 percent in 1910. England had the largest share of the import trade, ranging from 31.9 percent in 1833 to 35.3 percent in 1910.[3]

The nature of the trade between Syria and Europe also changed. In conformity with the mercantile system that governed trade between industrial Europe and the rest of the world, Syria's imports grew at a much faster rate than its exports, and this excess of imports entailed the purchase of manufactured goods in exchange for raw materials: precious metals, raw cotton, wool, silk, and other textiles, madder and other dyestuffs, oleaginous products and skins, grains, and other agricultural products.[4] The comparatively modest and still diminishing share of England in Syria's exports resulted from the fact that the British had little or no use for Syria's most important export, silk, whereas the French, with their large silk factories in Lyons, bought it in volume.[5]

The growth of Syria's trade with Europe was most visible in Beirut because, of the coastal ports, Beirut's trade was the least tied to Egypt and Turkey and the most active with Europe. That is also why its imports grew so much faster than its exports: from 19,747,158 francs to 54,240,640 francs, an increase of about 270 percent, in seventy years. Exports, on the other hand, increased only 36 percent, from

15,369,485 francs in 1841 to 20,727,000 francs in 1910. England's share in Beirut's imports was greater than its share in the overall imports of Syria, 43.35 percent as against 35.30 percent, a reflection of Beirut's preeminence as an import center. By 1910, Beirut imported 33.24 percent of Syria's total and exported 24.30 percent. It led in Syria's most important export staple, silk.[6]

Silk was essential to the economic life of the region and to the development of the port of Beirut. The growth of this silk trade changed the whole Syrian economy. Because it was all in raw silk, local textile manufacture declined to the point of ruin after 1880, and the export of silk fabrics was replaced by the export, first, of silk threads and, later, of cocoons. Until the mid-nineteenth century, silk fiber in various forms ranked second in Beirut's exports, after gold and silver objects, but after 1853 it became Beirut's first export, accounting in 1856 for one fourth the total value; with each decade the total increased. By the early twentieth century, perhaps 60 percent of the cultivated area of Mount Lebanon and parts of the coastal plains around Beirut, Tripoli, Sidon, and the Biqa' Valley and the Akkar were given over to mulberry trees. The silk industry represented an estimated 65 percent of all production in Mount Lebanon and 45 percent of the total value of exports from Syria, including Mount Lebanon. Other estimates give 62 percent for the whole Syrian region. Some 80 to 90 percent of it went through Beirut. In 1873, 40 percent went to France; after 1900, 90 percent.[7]

Raw silk had, of course, been cultivated in Mount Lebanon probably since the seventeenth century and was exported to France already in the early eighteenth century,[8] but in the nineteenth century new and better silkworm eggs were developed to fill the growing French demand for raw silk. The *baladi* ("local") silkworms were replaced after 1855 by eggs imported from Italy, France, and Egypt, and in the process various silkworm diseases were introduced as well, which destroyed the *baladi* breed sometime between the 1850s and the 1870s.

At first, the imported eggs met with only moderate success. Then, after 1863, Japanese eggs imported from Marseilles took hold. Though they were of inferior quality, they had the advantage of requiring shorter hatching periods and fewer mulberry leaves than other eggs. Introduced into Syria at a time when French sericulture was suffering from an epidemic of silkworm disease, the Japanese eggs themselves soon became a Syrian export to France and demand grew rapidly. In 1875, 250,000 ounces of eggs were produced in Syria, and 100,000 of them were exported to France.

Ultimately, the inferior quality of these eggs led to their replacement by eggs imported from Corsica and France and selected according to scientific methods. These new eggs produced yellow cocoons of good quality which competed successfully with those bred in the Far East and stimulated merchants from Lyons to invest in them. These French eggs became predominant in Syria, although others from Anatolia and Italy, or produced locally, were also available.

In the late 1870s and 1880s, Syria began to incorporate scientific methods into its own cultivation of silk. By 1912 the quality of local eggs and their share in local sericulture had improved, although French eggs continued to dominate the market. But by then, also, the silk industry had begun to suffer competition from rayons manufactured from cellulose. During the period that most concerns us, however, demand for Syrian raw silk rose steadily, since artificial silks did not begin to be commercially viable until long after the turn of the century.[9]

Most of the silk-reeling factories, where the cocoons were unwound and twisted into fiber strong enough to handle, were in rural areas close to the mulberry plantations; a few could be found in Beirut and its environs. They were owned both by local tradesmen and by Europeans, most often French merchants from Lyons and Marseilles, who both financed and introduced modern techniques into their factories.

The first silk-reeling factories were fueled by wood, and the silk was reeled in the traditional way. Probably the oldest of the French silk-reeling factories was established around 1810 in Qrayye, a village of the Matn district, along the Beirut-Damascus road between the villages of Bhamdun and Hammana. In 1851 this factory also had 64 spinning wheels that performed the next stage beyond reeling, the making of silk thread. Around 1840 two French noblemen, Comte de la Ferté and Vicomte de Lemont, established a factory with ten wheels in Beirut, but they encountered many difficulties and in 1847 forfeited the factory to an English firm to whom they had mortgaged it for collateral. The English firm increased the number of wheels to 80 and produced silk exclusively for their firm in London. Another unsuccessful French factory was started in the 1840s when a Frenchman bought a forty-wheel factory in Ghazir in Mount Lebanon from a French silk merchant, who was anxious to get rid of it because upkeep was so high. In his turn the new owner was forced to sell it to another French firm in 1862.[10]

The best known of the silk factories was established by the Portalis Brothers, French traders from the south of France who had settled in Alexandria. In 1838, Nicolas and Joseph Portalis founded, in association with a local Druze shaykh, a factory in Btatir, in the Shuf district of Mount Lebanon, near Bhamdun. In 1840, they gave the factory to their brother, Antoine Fortuné, who later acquired another French partner, a member of the firm of Pastré Frères of Marseilles and Alexandria, one of the oldest French companies in Egypt. Supported by a rich trader who had settled in Alexandria and, later, the new partner, this factory increased its capacity to eighty wheels from its original forty, used modern techniques of thread manufacture, promoted Syrian silk on the markets of Lyons, and became a model for future silk factories in the Syrian region.

Other silk factories were established in the 1840s and 1850s, some by local traders, among them the Maronite family of Asfar, who were involved in silk trade with the shaykhs of Mount Lebanon and the Greek Orthodox family of Sursock, who migrated from the Jubayl district and became one of the most notable merchant families of Beirut, involved in finance, trade, and real estate. Most factories, however, were owned by Europeans. An Englishman, John Gordon Scott, started one in the village of Shamlan in the Gharb district of Mount Lebanon. By 1846, it had sixty wheels. Of three French factories established in the 1840s and 1850s, one was equipped with steam power and a hydraulic press for cocoons. By 1852, five factories belonged to Frenchmen.[11]

In the early 1860s political upheavals disrupted manufacturing and even destroyed some of the factories. After the civil war, changes in the Syrian region, French military intervention, the administrative reorganization of Mount Lebanon, and political stability combined with a continuous decline of French silk production and an increase in world demand for silk to revitalize the industry. Expansion and modernization were undertaken, some of the old factories changed ownership, and new ones powered by steam were established. By 1867, 67 factories were under the jurisdiction of the French consulate-general in Beirut, using 728 basins employing 1,300 people. The number of factories rose from 105 in 1882 to 122 in 1887, to 150 in 1900, to about 193 in 1913. In 1887, they had 6,957 wheels and in 1912, about 8,669, of which 878 were in the vilayet of Beirut.[12]

Although the largest factories were owned by Europeans, an increasing number were in local hands. In 1867, there were ten French-owned factories, double the five in 1852. Of the 122 factories containing 6,957 wheels in 1837, the five largest (containing 1,800 wheels) belonged to Frenchmen, the rest to local people. By 1900, although the number of factories had jumped to 150, still only five belonged to

Frenchmen. By 1913, seven factories were French-owned; the remaining 188 belonged to local people.[13]

Between 1904 and 1910, 73 major exporters shipped out the silk from Beirut. Among the largest were local merchants with large business interests in Beirut — such as S. Bassoul and Sons, the representatives of merchant houses from Lyons; the Pharaons, whose business interests included banking, silk-reeling factories, and insurance; G. Habib and Company; and Elias Lahoud and Sons. They also included foreign companies — Veuve Guérin et Fils, a merchant house of Lyons dealing in silk production and banking, and owning one of the biggest reeling factories of Syria; Mourge d'Algue, which had a reeling factory in Syria, factories for silkworm eggs and soap in Marseilles, and insurance companies; Casimir Eynard, who was the major exporter of silk from Beirut, and, in addition, the owner of silk-reeling factories and insurance companies, as well as an importer of soap and silkworm eggs, and a commissioner and adviser for the French external trade.

This trade necessarily involved large-scale credit transactions, and major banks financing the silk export included some by now familiar names: Bassoul; the Pharaons; Veuve Guérin; Habib Sabbagh et Fils (exporters of wool and owners of a local bank, which later entered into partnership with the Banque d'Indochine); G. Trad et Compagnie, a local bank that later entered into partnership with the Credit Lyonnais; and the Imperial Ottoman Bank, which opened a branch in Beirut in 1856; and the Ottoman Bank, established with the backing of some of the largest financial houses in Europe as the bank of the Ottoman government and the trustee of the Ottoman public debt. In addition to financing the export of silk, banks helped pay for the silk-reeling factories.[14]

A whole range of brokers dealing mostly through or in Beirut also benefited from the silk industry, and as most of the silk was produced for the French market, much of the investment in silk came from import-export houses of Marseilles and Lyons. These houses advanced capital to the silk manufacturers either directly or through brokers in Beirut, most of whom were local merchants. A number of brokers also maintained their own business on the side, buying cocoons from the silk cultivators and selling them to the silk-reeling manufacturers or to commercial houses. They borrowed capital to buy the silk crop, sometimes gambling on futures at usurious rates that guaranteed the brokers a low price for the future crop. For example, brokers would borrow capital from European merchants at a rate of 6 percent and then lend it out to peasants at rates that varied between 20 percent and 100 percent, with the crop as collateral. Or they bought the cocoons in advance for, say, 12 piastres and resold the silk at harvest for 18 piastres.[15]

A whole range of successful silk entrepreneurs soon rose to the top of the economic and social ladder, which traditionally had been occupied by older, more established merchants, landowners, and notables. Since these members of the new merchant class acted as middlemen between the peasant and the market, they undermined the status and role of traditional feudal chieftains of Mount Lebanon. This initiated a social revolution not only in the urban milieu where the entrepreneurs flourished, but also in the nearby countryside.[16]

Transportation is essential to any economy, since the amounts involved as well as the price of goods to be traded depend in part on the transportation available and on its cost. The export price of silk included the cost of transporting it to Beirut. Imported goods often had to travel much farther than silk because Beirut imported for the hinterland. Trade was developed and exploited to the full only after the building of a new Beirut-Damascus road in 1859–1863.

The need for improving the road had become obvious early in the nineteenth century. Throughout the Middle East the roads used were still mainly those built by the Seleucids and the Romans, kept up by the Byzantines and the early Umayyads, and neglected by the 'Abbasids, the Mamluks, and the Ottomans. In the early nineteenth century all transport was still done by pack animals — mules in mountainous areas and camels in the desert — and travel was slow. It took three to four days and two to three nights for slow caravans and two days and a night for the well-equipped traveler to go the distance. The trip was also dangerous and expensive. One had first to cross the formidable chains of the Lebanon and the Anti-Lebanon, leaving Beirut by the pine forest on the edge of the city and following little torrents and wadis where both terrain and thieves made every step hazardous. Then one reached the Biqa' plain and crossed the western side of the Anti-Lebanon range, along the Wadi al-Harir, a narrow cut called the silk pass, reportedly because of the numerous caravans that had been stripped of their silk merchandise. Then came the Wadi al-Qurn, also famous for its thieves, this time of purses, followed by the plateau of Dimas and the valley of Barada. Then one had the choice of reaching Damascus by crossing Kalbat al-Mazza or the way through Dumar, Qasyun, and Salhiyya. Travelers reached Damascus perhaps wiser but surely not richer than they had been after leaving Beirut.[17]

A project to rebuild the road was undertaken in the 1850s. Initially, two schemes following different routes had been considered by a French enterpreneur, Comte Edmond de Perthuis, a former marine officer and an Orleanist who left France after the revolution of 1848 to settle in Syria, where he represented the Messageries Maritimes. The first scheme he considered followed the traditional route between Beirut and Damascus, leaving Beirut by the pine forest to cross the Lebanon range, the Biqa' plain to the southeast, entering the Anti-Lebanon from the Wadi al-Harir, and Damascus from the plateau of Dimas and the valley of Barada. The other scheme followed a longer but less steep path, leaving Beirut for Sidon and crossing the Biqa' plain from west to east. The second scheme had one danger, however, at least from the point of view of Beiruti inhabitants and entrepreneurs: it threatened to turn Sidon instead of Beirut into the port of Damascus. So the second scheme was shelved, since local entrepreneurs used their influence to turn foreign projects to the benefit of Beirut, and foreign entrepreneurs who invested in schemes such as the Beirut-Damascus road were equally interested in cooperating with local entrepreneurs to preserve Beirut's economic ascendancy.[18]

Construction on the Beirut-Damascus road began in 1857. The Ottoman government granted Perthuis a concession to build a carriage road between the two cities, and Perthuis formed a French company under Ottoman jurisdiction, with an office in Beirut and another in Paris. The company raised 3 million francs by distributing 6,000 shares at 500 francs each. The Compagnie des Chemins de Fer de Paris à Orléans and the Chemins de Fer de Paris-Lyons-Méditerranée of the Credit Lyonnais invested in the company. Construction started in January 1859, and passenger and freight transport began at once between Beirut and whatever point the road had reached. On January 1, 1863, the first convoy of goods reached Damascus, and soon after the road was opened for the transport of passengers. The completed road extended 110 kilometers from Beirut to Damascus.[19] In January 1863, a daily service of stagecoaches was started, taking thirteen hours between Beirut and Damascus. After February, two daily services were provided, one leaving from Damascus and one from Beirut.[20]

After some initial difficulties, the Beirut-Damascus road company began to show profits. There were problems with construction and thefts along the road, and after its completion, hard winter rains flooded the road and damaged it, making it difficult for the company to pay interest on its shares. From the beginning, however, demand was high for the road company's services, and in the summer season seats on stagecoaches had to be reserved in advance.

In 1863, the transport of travelers and goods used the services of 348 horses and mules, a stagecoach, 14 omnibuses, 10 light carts for tent, 104 haulage carriages, and 4 city wagons. Traffic was maintained for years afterward at around 11,000 travelers a year. Goods moved at a rate of 4,730 tons in 1863 and rose to 21,400 tons in 1890, making it possible for the company to pay out larger and larger dividends: 42 francs in 1872, 45 francs in 1874, 50 francs in 1875, 78 francs in 1881, 80 francs in 1882 and the years following. Although charges to transport goods and people were high, they were obviously not too high; the company was considered a model of good management and dependable service.[21]

The profits earned by the Beirut-Damascus road company are one clue to the importance of the road for the economic life of Beirut. Some historians consider it the most important single reason behind the establishment of Beirut as the main port on the eastern Mediterranean, and it certainly ensured the continued domination of Beirut as the main port of the Syrian region by facilitating trade between the port and the hinterland, making the latter increasingly dependent on Beirut. The road also inspired the establishment of related industries, as witnessed by the number of wheel- and harness-making workshops that sprang up in Beirut between 1863 and 1890.

The road, of course, also helped the economic development of the hinterland. Most of the silk-reeling factories established in Mount Lebanon after 1860 were located along the highway. This ended the relative isolation of Damascus, led to the opening of more European shops in that town, and promoted tourism and, in the process, a whole series of associated industries — antiques, leather work, furniture, and hotels. It also provided work for the people who came from villages and who, since the construction of the road, were closer in contact with Beirut. One consular report mentions that the majority of the drivers and wagoneers employed by the Beirut-Damascus road company were natives of the village of Hammana in the Matn district of Mount Lebanon.[22]

There were limits to the number of relays the road company could maintain. The shelter and food the company could provide in the 1880s sufficed for no more than about 1,000 horses and mules, and it refused to increase its facilities because the Ottoman government would not guarantee that the concession to maintain and operate the road would be extended.[23] Instead the company began to consider the possibility of turning the road into a railway. A British company was already planning to build a railway between Damascus and Haifa, a project that presented two dangers to the entrepreneurs in Beirut. To the French, a British railway would deal a deathblow to the Beirut-Damascus road company, not to mention French interests in Beirut and its vicinity, by diverting trade away from Beirut. To local entrepreneurs, it threatened to make Haifa the leading regional economic center.[24]

To avert these dangers, two groups holding separate concessions for railways in Syria merged to form a Beirut-Damascus railway company. In 1888, a Christian notable from Ba'labakk, Joseph Moutran, obtained permission from the Ottoman government to build a line running between Damascus and Muzayrib, a town in the district of Hawran, about 103 kilometers south of Damascus. Moutran then sold the concession to a newly created company called the Société des Tramways de Damas et Voies Ferrées Economiques de Syrie. In early 1891, the Beirut-Damascus road company created the Société de la Voie Ferrée Economique de Beyrouth à Damas and set out to examine possible routes for a railroad that would require the least time to build so as to forestall any shift of commercial activity to Haifa. In June 1891, Hassan Bayhum, a prominent Sunni notable of Beirut, was granted a concession to build a Beirut-Damascus railway along the route selected by the Société de la Voie Ferrée Economique.

At this point, to present a unified front against the threat of the British Damascus-Haifa railway, the Société des Tramways de Damas et Voies Ferrées Economique de Syrie and the Société Ottomane de la Voie Ferrée Economique de Beyrouth à Damas merged into a new company funded by French and Belgian capital, the Société des Chemins de Fer Ottomans Economiques de Beyrouth-Damas-Hauran en Syrie. The new company bought the concession obtained by Hassan Bayhum and started the construction of the railway. The construction of the Damascus-Muzayrib line had started in the meantime, in anticipation of the British line between Haifa and Damascus, and so hurriedly that the result was "a trunk without destination" of little use from the time of its opening in 1894 until the opening a year later of the Beirut-Damascus line.[25]

How effective the Beirut-Damascus railway was, in the end, in safeguarding Beirut's commercial preeminence is open to question. On the one hand, it did not directly play a major role in the city's economic development, though, on the other, whether the quick reaction of entrepreneurs in Beirut had much to do with it or not, the British line between Haifa and Damascus, begun in 1892, was abandoned temporarily in 1898 after only eight kilometers had been built. Nor was it a financial success. Although most of the goods traded between Beirut and Damascus traveled by railway once it was opened, the company lost money until World War I, partly because of problems in construction of its continual extensions and partly because of competition from other lines. The Beirut-Damascus-Muzayrib line lost money for years. In 1900, when it moved its offices from Beirut to Istanbul and was renamed Société Ottomane du Chemin de Fer Damas-Hamah et Prolongements, a former instructor at the Syrian Protestant College in Beirut commented that it "had less rolling stock than its lengthy name might lead one to expect."[26] The company's financial losses may also have come from mismanagement; travelers found schedules unreliable, the trip slow and uncomfortable. Just before World War I the company did begin to make profits, but then the war intervened. Only in the 1920s did the railroad finally begin to play a major role in Beirut's economy. Whether it did so before then is more questionable, but undoubtedly contemporaries thought it did, judging by the fierce competition that went on over the railway concessions and lines. Undoubtedly also the railroad did a more efficient job of tying the city to the interior, and this was obviously a prerequisite for Beirut's prosperity and continued growth.

Beirut's harbor underwent comparable improvements with the construction of modern facilities in 1890–1895. French initiative was again at the source. According to Baron Maxime de Dumast, an administrator of the Port company in the 1850s, the project originated when the same Comte de Perthuis who had inspired the Beirut-Damascus road suggested to the Messageries Maritimes that they investigate the idea of building a new port. An engineer of the Messageries Maritimes, a Mr. Stoecklin, was sent to Beirut in 1863. There he learned of a project for a new harbor conceived in 1860 by a French lieutenant, Guepratte, staff-chief of the naval division. Stoecklin wrote a report advocating the construction of a new harbor to the Messageries Maritimes, which endorsed it and sent it on to the Sublime Porte.

In the words of Dumast, however, "in the East, nothing is simple, and, especially, nothing is quick." Negotiations started between French parties and the Ottoman government ended twenty-five years later in the creation of a company sponsored jointly by the Beirut-Damascus road company, the Ottoman Bank, the Comptoir d'Escompte de Paris, the Banque de Paris et des Pays-Bas, and the Compagnie des Messageries Maritimes.[27] As with the other French-initiated projects, local entrepreneurs quickly stepped in. As soon as the French company was formed, in what Dumast called a "coup de théâtre," the

Ottomans gave the concession to Joseph Moutran and associates on June 19, 1887. Moutran, the same notable from Baʻlabakk who acquired the concession of the Damascus-Muzayrib railway, then turned around and passed it on to the French company in exchange for what Dumast referred to as some "personal advantages."[28]

With the concession in hand, the French company reconstituted itself under an Ottoman umbrella. On June 20, 1888, the Compagnie Impériale Ottomane du Port, des Quais et des Entrepôts de Beyrouth was established; it remained thus until 1926, when it became directly French; it became Lebanese in 1960. Based in Paris, with a permanent representative in Beirut, the company had capital of 5 million francs, gathered from banks, companies involved in the original group, and a number of local entrepreneurs. Its first president was Perthuis an Ottoman subject — a local Christian notable named Salim Malhama — was included on its administrative council. Its concession gave it exclusive rights to build and manage a harbor in Beirut until 1990. In May 1890, the company acquired from the customs of Beirut the concession of managing customs sheds and loading and unloading all goods imported and exported through them.[29]

The company started the construction of the new harbor without delay, using a design based on a plan drawn up in 1889 by Henri Garetta, Stoecklin's son-in-law. In place of the old harbor, which was 150 meters long, 100 meters wide, and 2 meters deep, by 1894 the new harbor consisted of a pier about 800 meters long, platforms 2–6 meters deep with wharf (filled land gained on the sea and forming a pier), a crossbar 350 meters long, a 60-meter ram, and, between the crossbar and the ram, a channel 150 meters long, leading to a dock area of 21 hectares. In addition, various buildings for customs, quarantine, port police, and the like were built. Ships anchored at the long pier, where goods were unloaded on motorized lighters and people on barges.[30]

After the new harbor opened, annual tonnage increased every subsequent year except 1897, 1912, and 1913, three years when maritime traffic between the Ottoman Empire and European countries suffered from international crises: Greek-Ottoman war in 1897; Italian-Ottoman war in 1912; Balkan war in 1913. Other local, regional, and international events occasionally caused fluctuations but not a net decline. After reaching a peak in 1891–92, imports and exports fell, particularly in 1895, when a limited silk crop, Armenian massacres, and bankruptcies following speculation in Transvaal gold all affected commerce. Recovery was interrupted again in 1897, but after that imports and exports through Beirut kept growing until 1913. (See Table 4.)

The new harbor and the growth in shipping were only two manifestations of the tremendous leap the city's economy had taken. There were others. Travelers agreed that Beirut was the most important commercial city on the coast, one of them claiming that with the possible exception of Damascus, Beirut was the most prosperous city in either Syria or Palestine.[31] Others commented on its well-stocked ships and bazaars; its rich commercial houses; its busy harbors, both old and new, its trade, and the people of many lands who crowded its disembarkation area, with their babal of languages and assortment of dress.[32]

Most striking was the obvious wealth of its population, and among the richest were the Europeans. European merchants had been among the first beneficiaries of Beirut's economic expansion, since the development of a world economy under Western hegemony in the age of imperialism and industrial revolution had brought Beirut its share of European investment—but they were by no means new to the area. They dated back at least to the days when the Syrian coast was under Frankish domination (1110–1187, 1197–1291), and the Italians especially had found an active trade in Beirut in indigo, wood, pearls, spices and incense, amber, musk, and textiles. Foreign merchants could also be found in the manufacture of sugar and iron, the production of lamps, bowls, jars, trays, ewers, cups, bottles, and other objects made of a paste of silicon clay covered with enamels.[33]

They continued to trade in Beirut during the Mamluk domination (1291–1517). Guillebert de Lannoy, as we have seen, found Venetians, Genoese, Greeks, and others there in 1422.[34] Among the others must have been French traders who began to follow the example of the Venetians and Genoese, in the thirteenth century, settling in Beirut and other ports in what one author called—a little prematurely—the beginning of "the hold of Marseilles over the eastern Mediterranean."[35] French merchants in this period did not yet constitute a serious threat to the commercial domination of the Italian city states.

After they conquered the Syrian coast in 1517, the Ottomans allowed European merchants to continue to operate in that area, but under a system known in the West as "capitulations," treaties arranged by *capita* or headings that recognized and codified their special status in the East. The capitulations were granted, first to French subjects and then all other Europeans in the empire, as concessions to trading communities that provided for commercial and judicial privileges within the empire. They remained in force until World War I, but their function changed during that period—privileges became rights as Western influence grew and Ottoman power declined. Commercial treaties between the empire and European countries in 1838 opened up the empire to European manufactured goods by regularizing customs duties on imported, exported, and transit goods, allowing European merchants to purchase goods anywhere in the empire and abolishing state monopolies current under the European domination. These treaties were detrimental to local manufactures and to centers of local production, but they benefited European interests and centers of trade with the West, such as Beirut. The capitulations also helped to transfer economic predominance from the Venetians and Genoese to the French. The fact that the first capitulations were signed with the French gave their trade on the Syrian coast leverage that proved to be the basis for later French economic influence in the Levant. Although the Italians, English, and others soon acquired the same privileges, the French had a head start. In the 1550s, French factories were established on the Syrian coast, and in Constantinople and Smyrna as well. In the seventeenth century, they practically monopolized the trade through Sidon. The coastal trade continued to expand in the eighteenth, while the trade of other Europeans with Syria — mostly Venetians and English — declined.[36]

But all this French commercial activity had little effect on Beirut before the nineteenth century. The cultivation of silk attracted some French merchants to the city and probably accounted for the appointment in 1655 of a deputy French consul in Beirut, still a subsidiary of Sidon, but generally speaking the French centered their mercantile activities elsewhere. In 1660, d'Arvieux counted only five French merchants in Beirut, all agents of French merchants in Sidon. In the eighteenth century, they were even fewer and there were none at all during the reign of al-Jazzar or Napoleon's invasion. When they finally came, they did so from a new position of strength. The commercial treaties of 1838 protected their economic interests as never before during Ottoman rule, and their privileged position gave them economic advantages over local merchants and guaranteed them a large share of the profits.[37]

Many Europeans denied this. Guys wrote that, although Europeans had in the past been favored over local people in regard to custom duties, in his time Europeans and local merchants paid the same. British consuls-general agreed. In truth, however, Europeans continued to be favored by the law, and that is why local merchants tried to transact business in the name of foreign companies and why they resented the foreigners' presence.[38]

What economic privileges the European merchants could not secure by legal means, they tried to extort through consular pressure. These consuls, often businessmen themselves, were the spokesmen of European imperialism in the Middle East. Whenever Ottoman authorities did not enforce commercial treaties — and sometimes even when they did — the consuls came to the defense of their conationalists. Consular reports abound with complaints of Ottoman misuse of power and abuse of European rights. Sometimes persuasion but, as Western power became greater, more often pressure and protest were used. The consular reports from Beirut alone show a tremendous change in tone from the beginning of the century, when consuls worried about whether they had been properly received by an Ottoman governor, to the late nineteenth century, when consuls-general openly called for a governor's removal because of lack of cooperation toward European interests. These complaints no doubt reflected growing Ottoman irritation at European interference.[39]

Consuls confronted not only local authorities but other consuls. Although the same merchants and consuls did not hesitate to join forces to complain against local authorities when it seemed useful, this did not prevent them from undermining the interests of other nations whenever they had a chance. In Beirut, rivalry was most common between the French and British consuls-general. On one or another occasion, the British consul-general accused his French counterpart or French merchants of abuses, of which the British themselves were naturally innocent. They accused the French of abusing their legal privileges and rights, of smuggling and other illegal acts, and — worse, surely — of acting not as merchants but as agents of the French government by interfering in local politics: importing and selling gunpowder, encouraging sectarian insurrections, and the like. The British and the French also bent every effort to beat each other in economic deals. Over and over again, British consuls-general expressed their displeasure at the influence the French exerted on the local scene.[40]

The ground had been prepared for the settlement of French merchants in Beirut through various government and private agencies cultivating a whole network of educational, military, and political links among France, Beirut, and Mount Lebanon. French religious and educational agencies were active. The Catholic Sisters of Charity had a convent, a school, an orphanage, a hospital, and churches in Beirut and in Mount Lebanon, which during the 1860 civil war provided relief for refugees. Their orphanage in Mount Lebanon trained young women for silk-reeling work. The Dames de Nazareth had a convent, a school, and a church in Beirut and Mount Lebanon. The Lazarists, the Capucins, and the Frères de la Doctrine Chrétienne were also active. Far and away the most prestigious and influential were the Jesuits. They opened a college in Ghazir in Mount Lebanon and then moved to Beirut in 1874. There they built a beautiful college, inaugurated in 1875 and enlarged with a medical school in 1883. It had a printing press, a faculty of Oriental studies, a newspaper (*al-Bashir*), and a journal (*al-Mashriq*). It soon became the most important French educational institution in Syria. The Jesuit College in Beirut was founded by Jesuits from Lyons, the same home base as the French silk trade and a city that thereby became the center of French involvement in Syria.[41]

The French military was also active. After the outbreak of 1860, France landed troops in Beirut to save the Christians. But whether as protector or not, this was still interference from an outside power. The French intervention was the most flagrant example of what had always been regarded as French favor toward the Christian minorities, particularly Maronites, and French influence in Christian circles generally. France could exercise that influence through pressure on local authorities in political and economic matters and, at the same time, enhance its own power and prestige to the benefit of French investors and merchants. French interests, backed by the government and its representatives in Beirut, controlled the largest share of major construction projects. French investments in the port of Beirut and in railways in Syria and Palestine amounted to about 168.3 million francs. Of these investments, the Beirut-Damascus road, the railway, and the new harbor were the most important, but French merchants were also paramount in the silk industry, particularly in export.

As demand for Syrian silk grew, so did French shares in its export; between 1904 and 1910, the share of French merchants in the export trade went up from 17.23 percent to 42.23 percent. In silk reeling the biggest factories all belonged to Frenchmen, the rest to local merchants. The number of Frenchmen owning factories might be small — and in fact became smaller with time — but the proportion of basins owned by Frenchmen was higher than the proportion of factories.[42]

French merchants were also involved in a range of other commercial, industrial, and financial transactions. The merchants who controlled silk processing and exports were necessarily involved in import trade, banking, insurance, and maritime transport. Four of the largest silk reelers — Casimir Eynard, Mourgue d'Algue, Portalis, and Veuve Guérin — also imported silk eggs, manufactured silk and soap, and exported raw silk and acted as agents for French insurance firms and banks.

Though French interests dominated the economic life of Beirut, other Europeans were not excluded. French travelers emphasized the French contribution to Beirut's commercial liveliness, but had to recognize that it would be — in the words of one author — "incorrect and unjust" not to acknowledge that of other Europeans.[43] Among them, the British were the most important.

As with the French, British economic interests in Beirut and the region were backed by England's power. Whereas a great deal of France's influence derived from its missionary and educational activities, English missionary and educational activities, though obvious enough, were secondary. The British investment in education at Beirut was greater than in the rest of Syria, to be sure: twelve British schools in Beirut as against twenty-nine everywhere else. The twelve included an orphanage for Muslim and Druze children run by a Miss Taylor; a Church of Scotland day school for Jewish boys and girls; and the British Syrian Mission schools, founded after the civil war of 1860 by Mrs. Bowen Thompson and run in the late nineteenth century by Mrs. Mentor Mott. They also included a boarding school for girls, a blind girls' school, a blind men's school, a Muslim girls' school, and a training institution for teachers.[44]

Nonetheless, British missionary and educational influence was limited, partly because native Protestants were very few, and no one Protestant denomination was large enough to wield influence in the same way as the French could work through the Maronites and Greek Catholics. The British government was also not as committed as the French to these avenues of influence and did not fund them so generously — to the regret of British consuls-general in Beirut. The only well-funded Protestant mission in Beirut was not British, but American. The American Syrian Protestant College (renamed the American University of Beirut in the twentieth century) was established in 1866 and soon dominated Protestant educational and missionary activities.

British influence was established in other ways. The greatest imperial power in the world in the nineteenth century, Britain held particular sway over the Ottoman empire. The British ambassador had considerable authority in Istanbul and, after the British occupation of Egypt in 1882, so did the British consul-general in Cairo. In Mount Lebanon, British influence was strongest among the Druzes, although never as strong as the authority the French exerted over the Maronites. The British were also popular with the Sunnis and some Greek

Orthodox, who also, however, had other supporters: the Ottoman government in the case of the Sunnis, the Russians and Greeks in the case of the Orthodox. But England's influence over the Sublime Porte meant that British consuls-general in Beirut carried a great deal of weight with Ottoman representatives, an influence that the British consuls-general used to the fullest to promote the interests of British merchants in the city.

At first British merchants were not much interested in Beirut. The Ottoman empire included no major centers of British trade. What had once been a flourishing trade in Aleppo between the British Levantine merchants and the Ottoman empire had declined sharply in consequence of a diminishing demand for goods from the empire and a consequent decline of imports from England (and Holland). But at the end of the eighteenth century, British merchants were attracted back to Syria by Bonaparte's expedition to Egypt and Palestine, which temporarily weakened French trade in Syria and opened the field to others; political concerns on England's part over Muhammad 'Ali's expansionist aims in Syria, which encouraged the British government to take an active interest in Syria; the growth of the British cotton industry, which needed an expanding market; and the realization from all this that Syria provided economic advantages.[45] In the 1830s British merchants busily fought problems of local competition, new dues on imports and exports, and lack of facilities. In 1840, bombing by the British during the war against Muhammad 'Ali may have created a temporary setback to British merchants in Beirut, but in the long run this show of power probably helped them. Beirut continued to draw more and more British interests to the city and the region. By 1861 the British colony in Beirut, though not numerous, included employees in the consulate-general, other diplomats on mission, army staff, doctors, engineers, clerks, scribes, teachers and governesses, as well as merchants. The merchants probably came second in importance only to the higher echelons of the consulate. Merchants were often selected to represent British interests. Whenever committees were set up in Beirut, whether to deal with the antiques market or relief to refugees, leading merchants were involved. British merchants were on the Tribunal of Commerce established in Beirut in 1850, and on educational boards, including the board of the Syrian Protestant College.[46]

British economic enterprises were diverse. They rebuilt Beirut's water supply system in the 1870s. For centuries, a Roman aqueduct had been the main water source for the city, and water shortages appeared to be a permanent handicap to Beirut's further growth.

Under the Egyptians, efforts to dig more artesian wells proved in vain. In mid-nineteenth century, municipal authorities looked into ways of increasing the water supply, but were again unsuccessful. The city continued to be supplied by the ancient aqueduct until the second half of the century, when the British-formed Beirut Waterworks Company went to work. The company built a waterworks system equipped with engine horses and filtering beds. The new system, completed in 1875, piped water from the Nahr al-Kalb (the Dog River) miles from Beirut, and provided a clean and abundant supply until the 1920s. The company itself, however, clashed with the French-backed Société Ottomane du Port, des Quais et des Entrepôts de Beyrouth over rights to supply water to ships, use of storage facilities near the port, and management of heavy goods deposited on the quays and not handled by the port's employees.[47]

Banking was another sphere in which the British were active. Banking channels between Syria and England were limited in the nineteenth century, but they were better in Beirut than in Damascus or elsewhere. At least one British bank, William and Robert Black and Company, was registered in Beirut, and another British company, Henry Heald and Company, acted as agents for London's Coutts and Company. In 1856, the Ottoman Bank established a branch in Beirut, backed by British capital and run by British managers, with British accountants. Duthesne Stussy and Company brought another British bank to the city in the late 1850s or early 1860s, but after 1866 Henry Heald replaced it in the Banker's Almanac; possibly Heald had absorbed it.[48]

A number of British merchants were in the import-export business trading cotton, silk, tobacco, coal, iron, machines, mules, horses, and probably more. Two British firms owned silk-reeling factories, the first taken over in the 1840s by London's Courtauld, Taylor, and Courtauld from two French noblemen, Le Ferté-Champlatreux and Lemont, who failed to meet their payments to the British firm. In the early 1840s, another Englishman, John Gordon Scott, built a silk-reeling factory with sixty wheels in Shamlan in Mount Lebanon and exported silk to a firm in England. Other British subjects active in Beirut in mid-century were James Black from Roxburghshire, partner of the firm of Robert and William Black; William Riddell, also from Roxburghshire, who dealt in coal; and C. P. Lascaridi, a naturalized Greek, who acted as agent in Beirut for Lascaridi and Company of Marseilles and London.[49]

As the years go by, the names of some of these merchants and commercial houses keep recurring, but new names crop up as well: C.

Peart and Company; William Thompson; W. G. Horden, the only British merchant in the iron trade; James Nixon, resident British merchant in Beirut exporting tobacco who was also Danish consul in the city; R. Williams, who ran a stream-powered flour mill in the 1880s; R. Somerville, who had been in Beirut for thirty-five years in 1896, when he imported a steam engine; E. Joly and Company, owner of boats and exclusive supplier of water ships to entering the harbor in the 1890s (later it merged with Henry Heald). The four most important British firms in the mid-nineteenth century remained William and Robert Black; Henry Heald; Riddell; and Whitehead, Peart. Riddell dealt in coal, Whitehead, Peart in cotton, and possibly both in other goods as well.[50]

Black and Heald were the two most diversified companies. Black was probably the leading commercial house in Beirut; it is certainly the one most often mentioned in consular reports. Established in Beirut in 1843, it acted as the representative for England's Lancaster, Watson, and Kinnear Company; it traded in cotton; exported tobacco; acted as agents for the enrollment of drivers in Beirut for the local Transport Corps; and was involved in other businesses, including banking.[51] Its members all sat on major committees that dealt with petitions and matters involving British subjects in Beirut. Lewis Farley, an accountant at the Ottoman Bank in 1857 and 1858, writes that the Black family head was "known all over Syria for his high principles of integrity and commercial probity."[52]

Heald merged with the Joly family company in the twentieth century, and their records still include information on the founders that illustrates how such a company functioned. Henry Heald, its founder, was born in Leeds in 1803, one of four sons and three daughters of Elizabeth and William Heald, a wool stapler. How Henry ended up in Beirut is not clear; it is recorded simply that he went there for the first time in 1837. The earliest reference to him in consular records is dated 1838 when the asked the British consul-general in Beirut to act as referee in a dispute with his landlord; a copy of the lease attached to the letter indicates that he rented the house on January 1, 1837. By 1842, he was prominent enough to help the consul-general welcome the visiting Anglican bishop of Jerusalem to Beirut. In the 1850s, Farley writes that Heald and Riddell, another merchant in Beirut, "while sustaining the honourable character of the British merchant, are equally distinguished by the urbanity and hospitality of the English gentleman."[53] The Jolys concluded from these records that the firm was established in 1837, and this seems to be corroborated by a letter dated in 1838 that refers to commercial treaties signed by William and Robert Black and Company, agents of Lancaster, Watson and Kinnear, and by Henry Heald, agents of Count Roquerbe and Company.

The Heald company dealt primarily in shipping insurance. In 1838, Henry Heald was also appointed Lloyd's agent in Beirut and, in 1844, a correspondent of the bank, Coutts and Company. In 1847 he opened an account with Coutts which remained open until 1914. He apparently also acted as correspondent for the London County Westminster and Parrs Bank. In 1863, the company adopted a different style when Henry Heald's nephew joined him as a partner. It acted as agents for Liverpool Steamers and may have been involved in other business as well. Heald also considered getting involved in silk reeling, but he gave it up because there was no family member available to run the project.[54]

Heald was a family business, as were many of the commercial houses of that free-wheeling era. Henry himself apparently had no children, at least none who joined the company, though he got married in 1849 in Beirut ("out there," as Henry Heald's niece put it). His wife was reportedly the consul's daughter in Beirut, a reflection perhaps of Henry's social position. The Healds disapproved of the marriage but, as the niece puts it, the family would have condemned anybody Henry married whether as "irreligious — or a Roman Catholic — or frivolous and a gadabout — or merely indolent. I am afraid they were easily censorious."[55] However, the family was not so incensed by the marriage as to discourage two sons of one of Henry's sisters from joining him in Beirut. They eventually became, with their uncle, the three members of the firm.

Frederick Heald Smith, the first nephew to go to Beirut, arrived in 1849 at the age of eighteen. A family financial crisis forced Frederick to leave school when he was twelve to work in an office in Leeds and put his brothers through school. It was probably financial need again that sent him to Beirut a few years later, to "an unknown uncle in an unknown country . . . armed with two golden sovereigns, a box of improving literature, and 10 pounds of gingerbread." Hard work and discipline from his early teens probably accounted for Frederick's righteous and stern temperament: he was scrupulous in his work, his family responsibilities, and his duties toward the church; he was also lacking in imagination and so self-righteous that he turned down the first offer of partnership his uncle made in 1853, essentially on the grounds that he could not bear to live ten more years among people whose tastes and manners did not agree with his. He was concerned over his health (and for his parents back in England) and Beirut, as he put it, was a dangerous place where people neglected the true principles of religion and lived idly and carelessly; a place where Europeans professed to be Protestants and went to church but then, on the way home, went to gaming houses and spent whole days at picnics. Despite all this moral laxity, Frederick was persuaded to stay, and in 1862 he signed a seven-year partnership agreement. In the end, he spent some twenty years in the business.

In the meantime, Frederick had been followed to Beirut by his brother Charles Alfred Smith, a man of very different character, younger by some fourteen years. Charles had intended to become a parson, but gave up the church to go to Beirut and in June 1874 took over the firm a few weeks before Henry died. Henry Heald trusted him enough to leave the firm in his hands, but nonetheless left him some words of wisdom:

> And now, Charlie, accept a few words of advice. Keep steady and temperate, be attentive to business, punctual in meeting all your engagements, honest and truthful in all your transactions, civil and polite as far as possible with all you have to deal with. Civility itself is a good capital in business. Be careful to maintain and keep up the reputation of the old firm. Keep your eyes and judgement wide awake not to be overreached if you can possibly avoid it. Be very careful to have your books well kept and written up to the day as nearly as you possibly can, and may God bless and prosper you in the sincere prayer.[56]

Despite the successes of merchants like Henry Heald, their numbers remained small. Although visitors often commented on the many foreigners in Beirut, it was mostly because they did not expect to find any at all or because there were so many fewer in other Syrian towns. In terms of Beirut's total population, Europeans were few, and their numbers never increased very much despite the city's population explosion. In Beirut's foreign colony, the French remained the most numerous. In 1848, there were sixty-five of them, and although that number probably increased in the course of the century, it was not by much.[57]

The number from Britian was even smaller. Figures are vague because sometimes they included British subjects living outside Beirut who also fell under the jurisdiction of the consul-general, and sometimes included colonials. The number—including Ionians (until 1864) and Maltese—in 1843 in Beirut was 84; in 1846, 163; in 1848, 227; and in 1851, 282.[58] In 1891, 132 British subjects were recorded by the consulate in Beirut, lower than for the mid-century, but this may just mean only people born in the United Kingdom were counted. In 1847, a subscription for Ireland (in relation probably to the Irish potato famine) did not draw more than 39 signatures and, among those, several represented local people who were not British. In 1848, a farewell letter from the "English residents at Beyrout and Mount Lebanon" to a consul-general who was leaving his post included no more than eighteen names. A list of the British colony in Beirut in 1850 contained fourteen households (the number of people they represented is not given), and in 1861 eighty British-born people (excluding Maltese, Ionians, and other British colonials) lived in Beirut.[59] Of other Europeans in Beirut we know only that in 1863 there seems to have been over a hundred adult Greeks. In 1857 a petition by American citizens resident in Syria and signed in Beriut included ten names.[60]

An even smaller number represented European merchants and European commercial houses. In 1848, there were fourteen French houses in Beirut, almost double the number of British commercial houses but still not very many. In 1834, fifteen British merchants were listed in the area (including Acre) served by the Beirut consul-general. Of these, seven had English names; the rest were Ionians, Maltese, or other British subjects. In Beirut proper, there were six British and two Maltese commercial houses in 1842. In 1858, a petition from the "British bankers and merchants" of Beirut carried seven signatures.[61] In 1861, eight British-born subjects listed their profession as merchant; one as manager of the Ottoman Bank, one as accountant in the same bank, one as "banker," seven as clerks. Some of the clerks were clearly involved in Beirut's commercial life: Frederick Heald Smith of the Heald company was among them. In 1884, thirteen British merchants signed a petition, among them one engineer, the manager of the Beirut Waterworks Company, and the director of the Ottoman Bank. The British consul-general commented in 1890 on the few British merchants in Beirut.[62]

American merchants were even rarer. Most American citizens in Beirut were connected with educational institutions or were actually Syrians who had emigrated to the United States and then returned bearing American passports.[63] Greek merchants were visible and active. But since the term "Greek" was applied to any local people belonging to the Greek Orthodox or Greek Catholic Church, who need not have been Greeks at all, they may not have been as numerous as it appeared. Still, Greek merchants were active in commerce and trade throughout the Ottoman empire, so there is good reason to believe that there were quite a few in Beirut as well.[64]

The number of Europeans merchants in Beirut actually decreased over the course of the century. Even in the 1830s, Boislecomte, could comment that Europeans were having diffculty penetrating the Syrian market, which was still largely conducted by the many local commercial houses. By the 1840s, the British consul-general in Beirut reported that the local merchants could account for only a quarter of British imports to Beirut. But at about the same time Guys could still comment that Arab merchants, "inspired by their natural greed," were taking over the trade with Europe, making it difficult for Europeans to sustain the competition of local merchants. The local merchants' successes became even more pronounced in the second half of the century. French houses, which owned 56 percent of the silk-reeling factories in Mount Lebanon in 1852, owned only 3.59 percent by 1913.[65] Nor did British merchants keep up with the city's expansion. Farley noted the "extraordinary improvement" in Syria's commercial prosperity after 1850 and warned British traders that they were not taking sufficient advantage of it; they apparently did not heed his advice. He commented: "A few years ago, our principal merchants were foreigners, now they are natives; they now do all the exporting and importing business, and to them foreign ships come consigned." In 1876 a British consular report included a reference to the transferral of trade from British to native hands, and by then that transferral had indeed taken place.[66]

7 The Local Entrepreneurs

That local entrepreneurs participated actively in the economic development of Beirut, in the age of Western imperialism, is worth emphasizing because most people tend to think of economic development at that time and in non-Western areas as largely a European undertaking. In fact, however, the degree to which foreign entrepreneurs acted as agents of change varied enormously from region to region.[1] In Beirut, foreign entrepreneurs played a smaller role than they did in Alexandria or in North Africa; instead, local entrepreneurs were often the "agents of change," though in an age of Western domination they often filled that role by first of all securing Western consular protection.

Originally, protection was an Ottoman concession made to foreign consulates that allowed them to protect their own nationals when they traveled or resided in the empire. As elsewhere, so in Beirut this concession was gradually enlarged to include local inhabitants who were in the service of consuls and foreign merchants. In the early nineteenth century, these European protégés came to number in the tens of thousands throughout the empire.

Both the Europeans and the Ottoman government tried to restrict this abuse of consular protection, but without much success. As early as 1781, the French stated that protection went with a position; it was no longer an individual privilege. In the mid-nineteenth century, various countries tried to limit their protection to consular employees, but even those could be multiplied as the consul wished. The Ottomans were constantly issuing circulars complaining that various consuls were abusing their privileges, but these protests were of no avail. Everyone agreed, and complained about local people abusing consular privilege, but they themselves helped to perpetuate the system. The French and Russians exploited it most, the English were close behind; but to one degree or another, all Europeans were guilty.[2]

Consular protection provided Europeans with services from local people indispensable to the conduct of business; in return it gave local people privileges and exemption from the personal and other taxes the Ottoman government levied upon its subjects. They were eligible for the same judicial, financial, economic, and other privileges granted to Europeans in the empire, which were of great advantage in business. Christians and Jews benefited particularly, since they predominated in the trade between the port of exchange and the West. Trade with the interior, which conveyed goods between the port and the hinterland, and where consuls would be less involved, was dominated by Muslims. The few Muslims who worked in consular service were largely in lower-echelon jobs.[3]

Not all Christians benefited equally, since benefits were tied to position and to those Christian denominations most closely linked to the Western powers. The Greek Orthodox predominated among the Christians in Beirut, and Greek Orthodox merchants, both oldtimers and newcomers, found easy access to Russian and Greek protection, as well as French and British. The Maronites in Beirut took advantage of their ties with France at a time of growing French influence in Beirut and Mount Lebanon, and greatly improved their lot. The Greek Catholics had easy access to both France and the Austrian empire, an advantage they made full use of. Within these broad lines of affiliation, local merchants did not hesitate to switch from one consul's protection to another's, according to the needs of the moment. In fact, so overriding was entrepreneurial concern that, when it suited their interests best, they abandoned consular protection altogether. At those times, they claimed to be first and foremost Ottoman subjects, at least until they won the matter at issue, usually a judicial case.[4]

Most of the time, however, merchants were eager to be considered protégés, and the best way to achieve that aim was to be indispensable. They offered their services — if need be, free of charge — to consulates, as *dragomans* (interpreters), scribes, or in any other capacity, and to European commercial houses as employees. And they often were indispensable. In the consulates, their services as interpreters, their easy understanding of how the local bureaucracy worked, and how to get things done at customs, at court, and with the local government were essential to inexperienced and impatient European officials and businessmen. Local merchants served as intermediaries between the European wholesaler and the local retailer, whose language they spoke and whose needs and tastes they knew. They acted as brokers between the European merchants and cultivators of various crops. They eased the way for European entrepreneurs eager to start a business. Before 1856, restrictions on ownership of land by foreigners could be gotten around by entering into partnerships with locals, whose names could then be used for the sale. They were indispensable as cashiers and storekeepers and, for that matter, almost all other transactions.[5]

From acting as intermediaries for Europeans to getting the upper hand over them was a short distance easily transversed. Local merchants became so important as middlemen between the cultivators of silk — peasants, clergymen, feudal lords of Mount Lebanon — and the European exporters of silk that they were soon able to impose their own conditions on the sellers and buyers and to earn substantial profits in the process. They lent money to silk cultivators at rates that secured them real interests of 20 to 50 percent, and then sold the crops at high prices imposed on the buyers. Commenting on these money-lending deals, Guys wrote that "credit was at the heart of all their speculations." What gave the local the advantage was that he could sell his merchandise at a loss if need be, so long as he got enough cash out of the deal to invest in more profitable speculations.[6]

Local merchants soon moved from middlemen to manufacturers. Since their services were indispensable for acquiring the land to build a factory and establish its management, and since in the process they learned the ins and outs of the business, they were soon establishing factories themselves. When they did, European factory owners found it difficult to compete, for the local owners knew the language and customs of the country better than the Europeans did and could operate more cheaply. The initial investment was lower. Often they built the factories on property they already owned; they did not need outside managers or interpreters. They quickly learned to exploit these advantages and, since most of them went into silk reeling, this explains why the number of European silk reelers declined. They also knew how to manipulate consular protection to avoid local taxes and regulations, overspeculate, enter into questionable business deals, and in general operate under total immunity from the law. No wonder, then, that merchants sought consular protection so assiduously.[7]

Even though it seemed to European and Ottoman authorities that there were too many of them, the protégés actually comprised only a small elite. Available figures show that in the 1840s there were forty-four British and ninety French protégés in Beirut. How many protégés other consulates had enrolled is unknown, but there probably were more Russian and Greek protégés, since the dominant merchants of Beirut were Greek Orthodox. The number seemed to increase with the number of unpaid consular authorities who sold protection to local people. Despite official efforts to end the practice, many continued to enjoy that status, and the protégés soon formed a whole new class of entrepreneurs. In 1863, acting consul-general William Wrench complained that every affluent Jew wanted protected status; the same could have been said of every affluent Christian.[8] Protested the governor-general of Beirut:

> They are all leading Merchants . . . In order to be protected some of them assume the denomination of Brokers, some that of Secretaries, others that of Servants altho' when their position is considered they themselves have in their service brokers, secretaries, and servants. Besides the Merchants and Shopkeepers there are the inhabitants, natives of the town, and who have properties and possessions greater than those who are not protected.[9]

An indication of what kind of person became consular employees can be had from a list of dragomans at the service of the British consulate-general in Beirut in 1876. (1) John Abcarius, paid by Her Majesty's Government, first dragoman, son of another British consular employee, Jacob Abcarius, who had been consular agent in Sidon. John Abcarius was about to retire, and his consular protection was granted for life as a reward for services by himself and his father to the consulate-general. To replace him, the consul-general proposed Esper Shoucair, who also belonged to a family with British ties.[10] (2) Francis Misk, second dragoman, very aged and infirm, member of a family with a tradition of service in the British consular service and hence a family granted British consular protection. (3) Alexander Misk, unpaid, Francis Misk's son. He assisted his father and "renders himself generally useful in the office, when his private affairs permit him to do so . . . I should have desired to appoint [him] first Dragoman had he possessed the necessary capacity which unfortunately he does not." (4) Saloom Bassoul [Sallum Bassul], unpaid, whose services are occasionally required "upon a pressure of work and when he can spare time from his own business.[11]

The names are all of Christian merchant families, some of whom were more newly rich than others, but all of whom had accumulated wealth or connections through association with European representatives in Beirut, gained consular protection, and then used it to get ahead. The Misks were a family of "some standing," acquired through hard work, successful investments, and good connections. They were landowners, employees in banks, honorary dragomans in Damascus and dragomans in Beirut, and probably involved in other things as well. The Bassouls belonged to an old Beiruti family — a local tradition had it that the family earned its name, which means "courageous," in the early nineteenth century when it lived outside the walls, a location regarded as dangerous. In the mid-nineteenth century, they owned a hotel sometimes called Bassoul, sometimes Belle Vue (also the name of another hotel of the time), and finally Grand Hotel d'Orient. Although not luxurious, the hotel was one of the oldest of the few hotels in Beirut. It enjoyed a beautiful view of the bay of Saint George and was frequented by European and Ottoman officials.[12] Its owner in the 1850s was Nicholas Bassoul, no doubt a relative of Sallum and a "highly respectable Arab" who "prides himself not a little on the support he receives from the Americans and the English." He, like Sallum two decades later, was a dragoman. In addition to owning land, the family was involved in trade. Bassoul and Sons were in the silk business and were one of the three biggest exporters of silk in Beirut in the early twentieth century.[13]

Kinship ties were extremely strong in Beiruti society, and the business of local merchants was often a family business. Several members of the same family were also in consular service. Urban growth was not accompanied by the weakening of family ties otherwise so typical of modern industrial towns. To the contrary, one consequence of the growth of Beirut's population through immigration was the preservation, and in some respects the accentuation, of family and other traditional ties. Consular protection was used to help whole families. Consular records are full of requests by protégés to gain some advantage for the rest of the family as well.

The Abela (Abila) family provides an example of how the system worked. The Abelas were descendants of a Maltese doctor who accompanied Napoleon to Acre and remained behind when the French troops left. One of his sons also practiced medicine and served as a British consular employee in Sidon. Later he settled in Beirut, where another branch of the family had already become established, and eventually there were Abela family members all over the Syrian region.[14] One of them — Habib — acted as confidential interpreter for the British consul-general when he traveled around Syria. Habib Abela became an unpaid British vice-consul in Sidon — not an unusual practice — performing what the consul-general described as indispensable services. At the same time—not unusual either—he was engaged in trade in partnership with his younger brothers. The Abela brothers conducted their business in "an honourable manner" and succeeded in "acquiring by their exertions and industry considerable property both real and personal. Their operations consist in cultivating their lands, buying, selling, and exporting produce of various kinds, as well as making advances on the security of crops and lands, as it is usual for merchants, Foreign and native to do in this country."[15] Wealth brought other consular appointments, as well as marriage into some of the best families. The result was more power, which was preserved and increased by the family:

> They [the Abela brothers] all hold Consular appointments under various Foreign Governments, and are connected by marriage with all, or almost all, their colleagues as well as with many wealthy and important families of the native Christians of Sidon, and likewise of Beyrout, Damascus and other places in Syria. They thus form a compact family body which certainly gives them a great advantage in addition to the privileges which they enjoy in virtue of their consular functions.
>
> This union of families gives these consular Agents and their friends an advantage over their neighbours and rivals in trade, who cannot be otherwise than jealous of their success.[16]

The same spirit of solidarity was extended to the families with whom the Abelas intermarried. Since they were also merchants and families who enjoyed consular protection, they represented not only an extended family but an elite with the same privileges, class, and family interests: "In any matters in which the interests of one of the family are concerned the Authorities find these interests are supported by the whole of his colleagues, a position which cannot be otherwise than galling to the Authorities." This privileged extended family was then used to further their interests against others of the same standing in business competition with them.[17]

The Medawar (Mudawwar) family were Greek Catholics from Mount Lebanon who in the nineteenth century had landholdings, trading enterprises, and financial interests. Their success was in part a result of their skill in their aggressive pursuit of new ways of making money. In the 1850s, they experimented in the cultivation of red-dye cochineal in the Beirut countryside. When their experiments succeeded, they applied to the government for exclusive rights to the cultivation of cochineal in all of Syria for ten years, pleading that privileges of that sort were granted in other countries to the developers of new and beneficial inventions.[18]

The Medawars brought the same spirit to their other businesses, cultivating ties with the French consulate-general, which soon resulted in consular protection. They served as dragomans and writers at the consulate, and enjoyed a close relationship with the consul himself, a sign of their high status in society and of their usefulness to him. So strongly did they identify their own interests with those of the French that on one occasion they even sided with French interests against the Ottoman government. But they were shrewd enough businessmen to know they also needed the ruling power on their side, and at least one Medawar held a responsible position in the government as head of chancellery.

The Medawar brothers had inherited a fortune, but they multiplied it several times over by exercising their skills and manipulating their protected status. The family functioned like a "wisely administered government," with each of the six brothers having a distinct role. One managed their considerable rural holdings; two others managed the extended affairs of their trade and correspondence; a fourth was busy at finance; and the last two were responsible for public relations (*relations de ville*) and legal problems.[19]

The most spectacular social climb in the nineteenth century, however, was probably the rise of the Sursock family.[20] The name originally (probably Sarsak) is Ottoman Turkish; and the family can be traced to Mersine, a town near Adana in southern Turkey, much of which was built on Sursock land. In the seventeenth century, or perhaps earlier, the Sursocks became tax farmers for the Ottoman government and in that capacity came to Barbara, a village in the district of Jubayl near Beirut. There they acquired land, probably *miri* or state property, which was a reward for their services to the Ottoman government. It is not certain when they moved from Barbara to Beirut, probably sometime in the late eighteenth or early nineteenth century.

By 1832, the time of the Egyptian occupation, the Sursocks had acquired sufficient prestige in Beirut for a member of the family — Dimitri (Mitri), described in a report to the Egyptian government as a "private merchant" — to be made dragoman to the newly appointed American consular representative. Another Sursock, Nicolas, who headed the business firm of N. Sursock and Brothers, traveled on a Greek passport in 1839 and remained under Greek protection at least until 1862. A Sursock of the same business firm (his name is not given) was in the service of the French consulate in 1856. In 1865, Nicolas was third dragoman at the Russian consulate in Beirut, and the firm was under Russian protection. Nicolas and perhaps other Sursocks were Russian protégés in the 1870s as well. In 1875, 1881, and perhaps sometime in between, Musa Sursock, a brother of Nicolas, was under German protection.[21]

Sursock and Brothers was in the nineteenth century managed by the sons of Mitri (probably the same Mitri who was dragoman of the American consular representative in Beirut in 1832), in all seven brothers and half-brothers including Nicolas, Khalil, Musa, Ibrahim, Joseph, and George. Two sisters — Clémence and Mariana — completed the immediate family. The firm acted as agents in Beirut for Lascaridi and Company, in the 1850s and 1860s, and shipped grain to London, Cyprus, and elsewhere. They were also bankers and speculators in the stock exchange. They invested in the Suez Canal Company (the canal was opened in 1869), in the Beirut-Damascus road company, the port company in Beirut, and other enterprises.[22]

The firm's financial investments in Egypt illustrate how successful entrepreneurs secured the support of local rulers as well as European protection. The Sursock brothers went to Egypt at a most opportune time for bankers: during the extravagant regime of Muhammad 'Ali's fourth son, Viceroy Sa'id (1854–1863), and the even more extravagant rule of his nephew, Khedive Isma'il (1863–1879). Both Sa'id but especially Isma'il spent generously on public works, embellishing Egypt's main cities, founding institutions and societies, including a national museum and library, and expanding into the heart of Africa — all to propel Egypt into the modern world. It certainly propelled Egypt into bankruptcy: by 1876, the Egyptian treasury was in debt to the sum of £ 100,000,000 of which £ 68,000,000 were in foreign loans. International creditors and the Khedive tried, the first to pressure and the second to resist, until finally the British and French governments pushed the Ottomans to depose Isma'il, as he found out when he received a telegram addressed to the "ex-Khedive Isma'il Pasha" in 1879.[23] Isma'il was out of power, but not before the Sursocks had acquired shares in the Suez Canal Company. If local rumor is true, the Sursocks, who were close friends of both viceroy Sa'id and Khedive Isma'il as well as their bankers, refused to support British and French creditors when they tried to pressure Isma'il into paying his debts. In gratitude the Khedive paid back what he owed them in shares of Suez stock. Whether the Sursocks acquired those shares because of their loyalty to Khedive Isma'il or because of their loans to him, their connections with him were certainly important to their successes in Egypt.

Beirut remained their base of operations, however, and they returned from Egypt in the 1860s to build elaborate homes in the Ashrafiyya suburb east of Beirut. The family of Musa Sursock returned at the urging of Musa's wife, who did not want her daughters to marry and settle in Egypt. Other considerations no doubt also played a part, but in any case success breeds success, and in Beirut the Sursocks' fortunes continued to grow through investments in trade, banking, real estate, and silk manufacture. In 1872, when the Russian Grand Duke Nicolas visited Beirut, he was taken to visit Nicolas Sursock. D. A. Skalon, who accompanied the grand duke, refers to Nicolas Sursock in his account of the trip as a "rich Syrian" and adds: "We were told his annual income amounted to £ 60,000."[24] Between 1887, when Musa Sursock died, and 1890, when his will went into effect, his share of the Sursock fortune was divided among his partners (brothers still living and nephews replacing deceased ones), his wife, his sons George, Michel, and Alfred, and his daughters Malvina, Labiba, Rosa, Mariam, and Isabelle. Musa's inheritance included extensive real estate — residences, warehouses, shops, and vacant land in and around Beirut, in Mersine, Tarsus, and elsewhere in southern Turkey, and in Alexandria. It also included extensive rural holdings, including whole villages, in Egypt and Palestine. In addition, the family owned property in Mount Lebanon, including the house they had built in 1880–81 in Suq al-Gharb, and land in Sofar that became, in the first decades of the twentieth century, a fashionable resort for the cream of Beiruti society and for tourists.

The Sursocks' success was measured by their admission to the highest circles of both Ottoman and European high society. They were intimate with officials in Istanbul; people often approached them to intercede on their behalf with the Ottoman government. One sign of their closeness to the sources of Ottoman power was the appointment of Alfred (Musa's son) to the post of secretary at the Ottoman embassy in Paris in 1905. Alfred moved in the titled circles of Europe and married Maria Serra di Cassano, from an old Italian princely family. Their daughter Yvonne eventually became Lady Cochrane. Alfred's first cousin Nicolas married Alfred's sister-in-law; Nicolas' eldest sister married Marchese Alberto Theodoli, and his youngest married the head of the Colonna family. The Sursocks were part of an international set that circulated amid Alexandria, Istanbul, Beirut, and Paris, Rome, and other European capitals. Their wealth and sophistication were also reflected in their residences, equal in elegance to any Italian palazzo.

To be truly successful as a socialite, however, one must also be recognized at home. The Sursocks were, moving into the highest circles, close to Ottoman and European representatives in Beirut, and intimates of the Greek Orthodox archbishop. Michel (Alfred's brother) became a delegate from Beirut to the Ottoman parliament in 1914.[25] The family was active in charities. Emilie Sursock founded the girls' school known as Zahrat al-Ihsan. In short, the Sursock family had become one of the "Seven Families," the cream of Beirut's merchant nobility.

The Greek Orthodox Bustros are another example of rapid rise to prominence. The family had come from Cyprus in 1600 and settled near Beirut. During the troubled rule of al-Jazzar and part of 'Abdallah's rule, they kept away from Beirut, as did Christians generally, but they remained firmly established among its notables. In the 1820s 'Abdallah Pasha went out of his way to invite the Bustros back to Beirut along with a number of other Christians, offering as inducements trade partnerships and authority to levy customs.[26] In the 1830s, George Bustros still possessed the authority to levy customs, and another Bustros was among six Christians chosen for an advisory committee set up by the Egyptians. In consular reports they were referred to as the leading Greek Orthodox family of Beirut, and they were visited by Ottoman officials and European dignitaries. They lived in a mansion in Ashrafiyya not far from the Sursocks, and they too were regarded as one of the Seven Families.[27]

The Bustros achieved all this partly by sticking to what they did best, making solid investments in traditional ways. The four sons of Antoun Bustros — George, Bustros, Joseph, and Musa — were already rich enough to build a mansion for the family early in the nineteenth century. It became the family headquarters. Joseph died at the age of twenty, but George, Bustros, and Musa carried on the business together. George and Bustros also married into two of the oldest and richest Christian families of Beirut, the Jubaylis and the Fayyads, which helped to spread their influence and connections. Then, sometime before 1850, George and Bustros both died, leaving Musa to associate with his nephews and form what became M. Bustros and Nephews, a commercial and investment house. They became still richer by investing well in land, trade, and finance. They acquired real estate in Beirut and landholdings all over Syria and Egypt. They traded in agricultural products, since they owned large olive and mulberry plantations. The money used to finance these ventures came from the new economy.

The Bustros had the ear of Ottoman officials and of several European consuls-general; they were the protégés of the Russians and perhaps of others. Musa Bustros and Nephews was the agent for a London firm, Spartali and Company, in Syria, and they traded in grain between Europe and the Syrian region. They were also agents of the British Liverpool Steamers, owned shares in the Beirut-Damascus road company and the port company; they played the stock market and carried on a considerable business in Egypt.[28]

The Abelas, the Medawars, the Sursocks, the Bustros, and other wealthy Christian families were successful because they exploited the new avenues to riches at their disposal as well as the traditional social ties they had always lived by. They put Beirut's growing trade and the increasing Western influence at their service by furthering the interests of both, and in so doing increased their family fortunes. This ability allowed the old established merchant families to join in the scramble for new wealth while keeping to their traditional ways of conducting business. All they had to do to stay at the top was to penetrate the new market. Personal contacts, family connections, and investment in land, jewelry, and other traditional securities gave them a headstart over newcomers, so long as they remained flexible enough to move with the times. The most spectacular succcesses were Christians because their European ties made the transition easier for them, but some of the old, established Muslim merchants were almost as successful, maintaining and adding to their prominence and wealth in the face of a changing economy.

But the conditions under which they did so were somewhat different. Unlike the Christians, they could not count on consular protection, nor would they have wanted to, since they had little sympathy for Western interests in the region. They relied on other means, particularly government influence, to preserve their economic position. Even more useful than government support was their control over internal trade. Historians have too often relied on European archives for their material. These, naturally enough, deal largely with export trade involving Europe, which was very much in the hands of Europeans — or at least non-Muslims — and overemphasizes the role of both foreigners and local Christians in the economy of the Middle East. To be complete, however, the story of the region's economic development must also include ties between the hinterland and the port cities, and it was there that the Muslims secured their place.

Beirut's merchant Muslims included some old established Beiruti families — 'Itani, Agharr, Barbir, Bayhum — and several newer ones — 'Anuti, Sarduq, Ghandur, Idris, Salam, 'Iraysi, Da'uq, Ayyas, Yasin, Husami, Baydun, Tabbara, Biqdash, al-Wazzan, al-Qarut, Khattab, Quraytim, al-Yafi, and Kronfol. They traded with Damascus, Baghdad, and other centers in the interior, and much of their trade was nonspecialized. In contrast to the Beiruti Christian merchants who concentrated on a few major enterprises, the Muslims simply traded in whatever product, manufactured or not, that exchanges between the hinterland and Beirut might at any point involve. They also traded with Egypt and other parts of the Ottoman empire, and invested in land around Beirut.[29]

Although this internal trade was more common, it remained true that only those Muslim merchants who managed to involve themselves with Western trade were in a position to become really rich; they alone could cheaply acquire the Western manufactured goods that the hinterland craved. The others could only resent the presence of foreign merchants and investors and, at times, local protégés. Since Ottoman officials shared that resentment, it occasionally flared in the open. One reason the two French noblemen who tried to found a silk-reeling factory in Beirut had to give it up in the 1840s was that the Muslims opposed it. When the new port of Beirut was built, about seventy Muslim merchants signed a petition against the exactions of the French port company (exactions that European merchants also criticized vehemently and repeatedly in consular correspondence), which claimed that French ownership of the port represented a danger to the Ottoman empire. Although open expressions of displeasure, in writing at least, at the European presence in Beirut are relatively rare, the few there are were clearly inspired by the resentment of Muslim merchants who felt deprived of their share.[30]

The Beiruti Muslims who managed to break into the trade with Europe were for the most part established houses, which had early made contact with the Western-dominated trade of Beirut and were able to maintain and exploit those connections through their experience, wealth, and entrepreneurial skills, and the ties they cultivated with local Christian merchants. Because Beirut's merchant class was small and because Muslim and Christian merchants needed one another, this was not difficult to do. By and large, however, the Christians dealt in exports and the Muslims with internal trade, and they worked together to move goods between city and hinterland. The correspondence of merchants in Beirut often has a Christian merchant at one end and a Muslim at the other. Sometimes even formal partnerships grew out of these interactions.[31]

The Bayhums were typical of the established Muslim families who exploited the new trade between Europe and Beirut. Descended from the 'Itani family, of Spanish origin, who settled in the Syrian region in the "Middle Ages" (it is not specified when), they split off from the 'Itanis in the late eighteenth century. Mustafa Husayn, son of Nasir 'Itani, was said to have received the name *bayhum*, colloquial Arabic for "their father," because of his generosity and benevolence toward the poor. His sons and their descendants assumed it as a surname. He had six sons: Nasir, Muhammad, Yusif, 'Umar, 'Abdallah, and Mustafa. They were all merchants of high standing and great wealth. Yusif became a prominent political figure as well.³²

The Bayhums remained a family of merchant notables, well connected to the local sources of power, particularly to the princes of Mount Lebanon, the Shihab emirs. So close was Yusif Bayhum to Emir Bashir II that the emir supplied his family with provisions when the Bayhums sought refuge in 'Ayn 'Aynub, a village in Mount Lebanon, during a cholera epidemic. Throughout the century, consular reports refer to them as the richest, most influential, most respected Muslim family in Beirut. They sat on municipal committees and were elected to represent Beirut at the national assemblies called in Istanbul.³³

They managed to stay on the top because they were able to grow still richer by exploiting the new trade. Like Christian merchants, the Bayhums' business was run in the traditional family way, though some of the brothers maintained their own businesses independently. Mustafa, for example, transacted business on his own and lost money when the government withdrew from him (and others) the *iltizam* of salt. It is also clear from the correspondence that the business involved a great variety of goods, including agricultural products, spices, silk, and cotton, and that they had immense urban and rural landholdings as their traditional form of wealth.³⁴

One of their moneymaking schemes involved economic deals with the feudal lords of Mount Lebanon who became indebted to them, a practice that marked a decline in the power of the mountain lords. The Bayhums were also involved in the silk trade and maintained their own agents in their active and lucrative trade with Europe, for they were among that minority of Muslim merchants who managed to penetrate the export business. In the late 1840s, only three out of twenty-nine local merchant houses trading directly with England were Muslim; the rest were all Christian, and similar proportions remained throughout the century. The export of silk was almost entirely in local Christian and European hands. Between 1904–05 and 1910–11, Muslim-owned silk exports equaled less than 1 percent of the total (167 bales of silk out of 20,962), and five Muslim commercial houses, 'Abed and 'Abdul Mukhtar Bayhum, Muhammad Rashif Siba'i, M. Bissar, H. Kronfol, Ghul and Hajj, accounted for most of that. Silk manufacture was predominantly Christian both in ownership and employment. The Druzes ranked far behind the Christians, and the Muslims far behind the Druzes. Only 100 of the 1,400 workers in the silk industry were Muslim in 1911.[35]

The imbalance in economic opportunities between wealthy Christian and Muslim merchants was even more pronounced in the rest of the population. Before the nineteenth century there were no avenues for success for them except making and trading in the necessities of life or service in government or the army.[36] On the whole, people were born rich or poor and stayed as they were born. But the expansion of Beirut provided new opportunities, especially those of the Western-oriented economy.

Immigrants who arrived in Beirut with little or no money could find opportunities in the city. We have seen how in 1860 Dimitri Debbas arrived in Beirut as a refugee who lived first around a school and then in Khalil Sursock's house, dependent on charity for his livelihood until an opportunity for making money presented itself, and he began his progress from refugee to budding entrepreneur. Dimitri and a relative took tobacco and local piastres to French soldiers camped in a forest nearby, sold the tobacco and changed money for them, a fairly common way of launching a career at the time. Money changing was not a very exciting occupation, but it probably made it possible for him — and no doubt a number of his friends and relatives as well — to make a living. Eventually he moved on to Sidon, where his experience with silk reeling proved more useful. He worked in an acquaintance's silk mill, which "put an end for us to beggary and food rations and the carrying of bread daily from the barracks."[37]

Sometime in 1861 the French army departed. This left Dimitri and his companions without protection in Sidon, so he returned to Beirut. Then, again with the help of friends and relatives, he went to Athens where a hundred or so other Beiruti families had already fled after the French departure. The archbishop of Athens provided the refugees with food, but bread alone was not enough, and they decided to take their chances and return to Beirut. From there they went to Damascus, where they managed to reclaim some of their lost riches, and returned once more to Beirut. This time they settled down to what they knew how to do best: manufacture silk, as they had done before the civil war. They acquired partners in both Alexandria and Beirut. Various members of Dimitri's family worked various areas — one brother, for example, in Alexandria; another in Damascus.

By 1870, Dimitri was well enough off to marry Mariam Ilyas al-Khuri, and from then on, as Dimitri phrased it, good fortune started to "pour down on us." The couple had many children. Hard times were over, and Dimitri could now shift the focus of his memoirs away from his business activities and toward his activities as local notable. Clearly by now the family was prosperous, though that first generation of Debbases never became rich—the rich are referred to in the memoirs as a class apart with whom Dimitri clearly did not consort.

But his willingness to take on any job as long as it was "honorable" had made him well off. The words that recur most often in his memoirs are "God" and "honor." The emphasis on nonbusinesslike values like honor should not, however, lead one to conclude that Dimitri was impractical; he was very shrewd and pragmatic—hard work, honesty, and perseverance might be emphasized, but they were placed at the service of shrewd business acumen.

The reward for hard work was a place in Beiruti society. He went to work on behalf of the Orthodox hospital of Saint George and later for the Orthodox church of Saint Dimitri (Mar Mitr), which was in financial trouble, bringing to his charitable enterprises the same sharp mind he had brought to business. The church's cemetery was refurbished, and its plots sold at substantial profit. The church edifice was torn down and rebuilt on a grander scale. It became so prosperous that it was counted one of the "nicest" in Beirut supported by a community that was the city's "biggest and richest," as he put it. By 1908, the church was doing so well that its parishioners could provide its archbishop with a marble throne. The pride of a community was expressed in its church; the prestige of the notable of a community was reflected in his public service. Dimitri had indeed become a local notable.

Beirut also offered opportunities for advancement to Beirutis of modest background, such as Assaad Kayat, another self-made man. He was born in Beirut in 1811 into a Greek Orthodox family that already had a little money and some contact with foreigners. Kayat's father was a trader who spoke, but did not write, Greek, Turkish, and Albanian. One uncle acted as interpreter for a British naval officer in Beirut in 1799, and another had been in touch with some early American missionaries. From childhood, Kayat was ambitious. When he was eight, he saved his pocket money to buy old currency, which he then sold at a profit. His father made him learn Greek, and very early on Kayat put that knowledge to use. By the time he was ten, he was already hanging around the harbor, offering his services as interpreter and guide to visiting Greek captains. As he grew older, Kayat began to speculate in currency. He went on a pilgrimage to Jerusalem with the most unholy aim of furthering his career. In Jerusalem, he made his first contact with American Protestant missionaries, learned Italian from a Capucin priest, English from an American missionary, and settled down for a while as a teacher in an American mission. Soon, he returned to moneymaking, however. He came back to Beirut and joined with two Swiss merchants. When political tensions in the Ottoman empire in the 1820s drove them out of Beirut, Kayat went into business on his own. He was still only nineteen.[38]

Having developed his European connections, Kayat saw that it was now time to establish Muslim contacts, and he entered into partnership with a Beiruti Muslim merchant. He worked with him in Damascus, Homs, Hama, and Tripoli. On these trips, he formed other contacts with Christian and Muslim merchants as he collected his profits. Back in Beirut he turned to more complex and profitable trading operations involving currency and commodity speculation.

In the meantime, Kayat was careful not to neglect his European connections. First in Beirut and later in Damascus he was second and then first dragoman to the British consulate. He began to dress in Western fashion. He also went to England where he, as Kamal Salibi put it, "lost his soul" and cultivated ties with both British missionaries and British merchants.

Kayat then underwent what appears at first to have been a change of heart, but what was in fact another consistent step toward self-advancement. Back in Beirut, he resigned from his post in the consulate to devote himself to what he called "the welfare of Syria." In fact, however, this turned out to be more trade and more profits. He brought precious jewels from Baghdad and Iran and sold them at considerable profit in England. As he grew more and more successful, he neglected his ties with British missionaries, but reinforced those with the British foreign service. The ultimate reward for his efforts came in 1847 when he became first British commercial consul in Jaffa. The successful merchant was now a diplomat of sorts.

A very different success story is that of the novelist Jirji Zaydan, born in 1860. Zaydan's background was much more modest than Kayat's. He was born into a poor Greek Orthodox family whose only capital was the "desire to work." Zaydan's grandmother baked bread that she gave to his father to sell in the suqs of Beirut. From there he found employment in a bakery where he made bread and other foods. Then he opened a restaurant. When it began to bring in money, he could afford to get married, which he did in 1860, at the age of twenty-seven. The values of hard work and seriousness were thus instilled in

Zaydan from a childhood spent in a household of uninterrupted labor. Zaydan's father left for his restaurant at dawn and returned in the middle of the night. His mother worked all day long as well. This industriousness convinced Zaydan that "the human being is born to work and that to sit without working was a great shame."[39]

When Zaydan was eleven, his father took him out of school to work in the family restaurant, which had continued to prosper. Zaydan hated the work and wanted to go back to school, but his father argued that too much education would westernize Zaydan: he would begin to eat with a fork and a knife, and everything evil would follow from that. Zaydan capitulated but was so miserable that his mother suggested that he try some other livelihood, so he entered a promising new trade in Beirut, the making of Western-style shoes. Two years as a shoemaker, however, affected his health and drove him back into the family restaurant, which only exposed him further to the wastrels who loitered in the city's center and increased his distaste for laziness and failure.

An opportunity to move out was given at last when, at a neighbor's, Jirji met a young man, a watchmaker of some education. The two of them went on walks as they talked and recited poetry, and were joined by students at the American Syrian Protestant College. All this revived Jirji's yearnings for an education. When he heard from a customer at the restaurant about an English teacher who had opened a school, he finally convinced his father to let him study and set about it eagerly. He learned English, studied at the Syrian Protestant College, and eventually became a successful writer of popular histories and historical novels.

The social ladder that Dimitri Debbas, Assaad Kayat, and Jirji Zaydan climbed in their different ways was used by others as well. A good deal depended on talent and drive, but at least if the will was there, so were the opportunities. The will was everywhere, judging by the amazement expressed by travelers at the dynamism of Beirut's moneymakers, whether they were dragomans fighting over a client or rich merchants striving to get richer. The love of gain was said to drive Beirutis to cheat clients of even petty sums, and their Levantine cleverness was contrasted to the nobility of the Arabs in the Syrian interior.[40]

Money also brought self-assurance to Beirut's population, particularly its Christians. They exulted in money. Since their livelihood was tied to the expansion of trade with the West, people began to affect a Western style of living as well. Foreign observers were struck by the number of people who dressed in European garb, knew French or English, and had adopted Western manners. As the city expanded, the new quarters took on a European look, with Italianate villas, red-tile roofs, and Western furnishings. In the Ashrafiyya quarter on the edge of the city, merchants lived like aristocrats in European palaces. The splendor of the city's new quarters contrasted starkly with the simplicity and drabness of the old.[41] The new clothes and houses were accompanied by a new European cultural orientation, as a passion for all things European developed among the city's Christians.[42] Western ways were emulated, and Eastern ways were looked down upon. This new juxtaposition in Beirut of two ways of life was but one of the many challenges to sectarian harmony.

8 Sectarian Relations

Beirut was noted for its religious tolerance long before its growth as a port and manufacturing city. In the seventeenth century, d'Arvieux remarked that, aside from the Jews — and that exception may well have reflected d'Arvieux's own prejudices — Beirutis of whatever religion lived together in harmony. In the eighteenth century, another traveler noted that the Christians enjoyed landholding rights more favorable than their brethren held in Acre. Local histories rarely mention sectarian incidents. On one occasion, two Muslims were reported to have plundered a monastery of Beirut, but they were executed for the crime by the Ma'nid rulers. Coexistence was certainly strained by political insecurity in the early part of the century, but this had ended by the 1820s. Official Egyptian policy in Syria and Lebanon in the 1830s was one of tolerance toward Christians and other non-Muslim groups.[1]

Beirut also allowed more religious services and privileges than were provided to the Christian citizens in other towns. Blondel, at a loss to explain a Muslim tolerance that no doubt ran counter to his generally antipathetic attitude toward Muslims, claimed that it was only because Muslims were in a minority. The great variety of religions in the city, he reported, was best observed in the bazaar, where it was rare to see all the shops open at the same time, because one segment of the population or another was always celebrating a saint's day or some other religious feast. Three days of the week were always holidays: Friday for Muslims, Saturday for Jews, and Sunday for Christians. The French consul, Henri Guys, wrote a novel in the 1830s in which the hero, an Algerian Sufi, remarked on Beirut's tolerance and the liberty enjoyed by Christians and others, but this did not prevent Guys from commenting at length in his memoirs on the fanaticism of the city's Muslims. Even there, however, he at least qualified his comments by adding that nonetheless many Muslims maintained cordial relations with Christians.[2]

Social intercourse between any two communities is an indication of mutual acceptance, and Guys's reference to social interaction is one of the few available. Although he could not resist adding that the many Muslims who had friendly relations with Christians were most apt to be those who liked to drink, it is unlikely that conviviality was the real explanation, since even today alcoholic consumption is relatively rare in the Middle East.[3] What Guys's comment probably tells us is that sociability among them was so common that even someone with his prejudices could not fail to mention it, but he had to give it an explanation in harmony with his way of thinking. It is not clear how representative it was, however, if only because life in Beirut in the early part of the century was simple, with few luxuries or social gatherings. Guys claims that Christians did not venture out at night from caution, but he also says that Muslims rarely entertained people even of their own community.[4]

However common their actual social contacts may have been, the two groups undeniably shared a way of life. There were superficial differences between the communities, to be sure — Guys describes at length what constituted "Muslim" and "Christian" habits.[5] Differences in clothing also existed — by law non-Muslims had to wear distinctive dress — as did differences in customs, resistance to diseases, and the like.[6] But even some of these differences, clothing for example, were slowly eliminated, and others — such as incidence of disease — are better explained by differences in the socioeconomic levels of the two groups as a whole. Behavior at home, at work, at leisure — sitting in coffeehouses and listening to storytellers; riding or walking to the pine groves on the outskirts of the city — were the same. When Kayat contrasted Eastern life with English habits by comparing the life of an inhabitant of Beirut or Damascus with that of an inhabitant of Liverpool or London, he said that the Muslims might go to a mosque and the Christians to a church, that they might pray a different number of times a day and in different ways, but that they otherwise shared a common way of life. Guys himself, after trying to distinguish between Muslim and Christian habits, ended up by noting that he could distinguish little difference and lumped them all together as "Syrian" or "Eastern."[7]

This shared way of life was based on a common set of values regarding what mattered and how one was to behave toward family, friends, and associates. At least until the mid-nineteenth century, Christian and Muslim shared social values, character traits, and a local culture.[8]

In principle, economic interaction among members of different communities need not imply social mingling, since economic interest can drive even opponents into collaboration. Christians participated in enterprises where they had to transact business with a predominantly Muslim government and most likely, in the process, with merchants of other communities. After Abdallah Pasha drove the Christian merchants away from Beirut at the time of the Greek raids on the city, he then had to pressure some of these same merchants into doing business with him because he could not function without them. He provided capital for joint business ventures with himself as partner and farmed out customs collection to them. Under the Egyptians, Christians were also customhouse collectors. State monopolies were another form of joint enterprise in which not only Christians but merchants of all communities interacted with the government and with one another.[9]

Merchants of the various communities could also be partners in private business ventures. Christian merchants may have entered into these partnerships partly to protect themselves from the government, but the more likely reason was that with Muslim partners they could frequently make more money. Guys spoke of economic collaboration between Christians and Muslims as if it were a usual occurrence, and even admitted that Christians were very eager to do business with Muslims.[10] On the Muslim side, there was not quite the same need to do business with Christians, but they did so quite regularly. Wealthy Christian and Muslim merchants cooperated in trading transactions and landowning deals. The Bayhums traded with other Muslims in the Syrian interior, but with Christians and sometimes Europeans in Beirut. The Bustros' landholding records show that they sometimes bought land in partnership with such wealthy Muslim families as the Bayhums, and there is ample documentation for other sorts of joint commercial and financial transactions.[11]

Among middle-class merchants, we have the example of Kayat, who at the age of nineteen entered into partnership with a Muslim merchant of Beirut by the name of Hajj 'Abdallah. The Hajj gave Kayat a hundred gold pieces and a letter of credit to his correspondent in Damascus. Kayat was to make as much money as he could and divide the profits with his partner. His business with the Hajj took him to Damascus, Homs, Hama, and Tripoli and was indeed profitable.

Not surprisingly, relations were most harmonious between Muslim and Christian when their partnerships were successful. Kayat was full of praise for his partner Hajj 'Abdallah, "a most respectable" Muslim merchant of Beirut. "There cannot be more honorable men of business than these Muslim merchants." His eagerness to impress his readers with his Christian piety in no way inhibited his praise of Muslim merchants, perhaps because the Greek Orthodox and the Muslims had so long lived side by side.[12]

Economic collaboration among members of different sects and communities is particularly easy when the interests of a city are based on trade. Merchant communities in port cities are accustomed to dealing with all sorts of people, and merchants ranked so high in the social hierarchy that their occupation took precedence over their communal affiliation. The inhabitants of Beirut were more apt to be at odds with outsiders, whether or not they shared their religious affiliation. During the Egyptian occupation, when armed men from Mount Lebanon came down to the coastal cities and established garrisons there, the Christian inhabitants of the coastal cities were as indignant as the Muslims were. A British report of 1840 even mentions that the population of the towns, including Christians, were opposing the inroads of the rebellious Druzes and Christians of Mount Lebanon. The Christians of the coast — including Beirut — were, of course, predominantly Greek Orthodox, and the Christians of the Mountain predominantly Maronite, and this no doubt contributed to Christian hostility against the intrusions of the mountaineers, but in the end the inhabitants of Beirut simply saw themselves as members of an urban merchant community resisting a hostile element that interfered with business.[13]

Little is known about Beirut's physical layout in the early part of the nineteenth century, but available evidence suggests that it conformed to the traditional Middle Eastern pattern of neighborhood distribution where rich and poor were grouped together according to religious affiliation, ethnic background, and place of origin. These quarters were distinct, relatively homogeneous and self-sufficient units.[14] But references in the 1830s show Muslims and Christians buying land side by side in the newly developing area of town or the outskirts of the city. The records of the Mahkama Shar'iyya for the 1840s abound in detailed descriptions of houses bought and sold. They make clear that intercommunal mixing even in the center of town was greater than is usually assumed. In one of its oldest areas, the bazaar, groups worked side by side. Travelers all remark that the streets of the bazaar were organized by profession and not by religious affiliation. While there was probably some correlation between the two, it was still profession and not religion that determined location. Blondel spoke of individual shops — and not of whole sections of the bazaar — closing down for all the various religious feasts.[15]

The remarkable similarity of the city's architecture in itself provided homogeneity. The bazaar was architecturally strikingly uniform, and even when the quarters were defined in terms of religious or ethnic identity, no obvious physical differences could be discerned between them. Poujoulat found what he called the "Muslim quarter" to be dark, but this was probably true of all the old quarters, since the houses were so close together. Contemporary descriptions suggest that houses were similar both inside and outside, whatever the religion of the occupant.[16]

The good will that often existed between Muslim and Christian was put to the test by the troubled middle decades of the century. The weakening of Ottoman power, the growth of European influence and of European protection of groups of Ottoman subjects, the changed status of the subject peoples and communities of the empire after the *hatt-i şerif* (imperial rescript), threatened to undermine communal relations. That edict, issued in the park of Gulhane in Istanbul in November 1839 and therefore known in history as the *hatt-i şerif* of Gulhane was the first edict of what came to be known collectively as the *Tanzimat*, or orderings, a series of laws promulgated between 1839 and 1876 which were intended to strengthen the Ottoman imperial administration. Although the rivalries that resulted had their purely local manifestations, they reflected a more general phenomenon. As the Ottoman government became weaker and European influence in the empire became stronger, the relative status of the various communities within its borders began to shift as well. The Muslims began to lose ground to the outsiders. In the Arab world this meant that Arab Muslims, the great majority of the population, no longer enjoyed the advantages either of being in the majority or of adhering to the official religion. Christians, who, along with Jews and other *dhimmis*, or protected people, had been second-class citizens (they paid special taxes and did not serve in the army), began to gain the upper hand. Step by step between 1839 and 1876 the Tanzimat provided a legal basis for this increasing power by making all Ottoman subjects, regardless of religion, equal before the law.

The frustration of Muslims at their loss of status, the growing power of non-Muslims and foreigners, and the rebellion of non-Muslims, particularly the Christians no longer content with their second-class status, soon resulted in tensions and conflicts. The growth of the new European-based economy, from which the Christians benefited more than Muslims did, abetted the process. Non-Muslims were also in closer contact with Europeans and were generally quicker than Muslims to abandon their traditional ways of life and to adopt Western ones, particularly in the great cosmopolitan trading towns and in the Lebanon where Christians predominated. Many Muslims also became Westernized, but not until considerably later.[17]

It is difficult to assess the amount of hostility based on sectarianism in Beirut at the time, partly because recent events encourage the tendency to interpret the past exclusively in sectarian terms.[18] Religious identification was strong and gained still more strength in the nineteenth and twentieth centuries as regional and international changes in the balance of power between the Ottoman government and Europe encouraged the confusion of political with social identification. Written and oral history both suggest that people continued to think of themselves in terms of a particular religious community, and very often chroniclers continued to identify contemporaries in terms of their religious affiliation and evaluate events in terms of their impact on that.

But this is not to say that tensions between Muslims and Christians or Christians and Druzes were particularly noticeable. Communal identification should not be confused with a too narrowly drawn sectarianism; nor did sectarian and communal identification always exactly coincide, if one defines the community in terms of the larger groups — Christian, Muslim, Jew, Druze. Denominational antagonisms were often stronger than sectarian ones. Differences among Christians sects, for example, could be taken just as seriously as the differences between Christian and Muslim, and converts from Islam to Christianity were no more ostracized or persecuted by Muslims than converts from one Christian denomination to another by members of the denomination they had left behind. Since shifts between one Christian denomination and another were more common than conversion from Islam to Christianity, stories of persecution of Christians by other Christians are far more common than stories of persecution of Christian converts by Muslims. Emphasizing hostilities between Christians and Muslims, or Christians and Druzes, or Druzes and Muslims, misses the point that, until the end of the nineteenth century, sectarian hostility in the city was as much within as among the major communities. In particular, hostility among Christians, Muslims, and Druzes was typical only in time of political crisis.[19]

As this suggests, sectarianism is essentially a political phenomenon. Not only can conversion itself be politically motivated, but often hostility toward a convert by the coreligionists he has deserted is rooted in political pressures.[20] Conversion may constitute a threat to one's beliefs, but it also undermines the strength of the sect as a whole. On the other hand, religious loyalty need not necessarily gain intensity at the expense of confessional harmony. Recent migrations to Beirut's suburbs by groups of Shi'i villagers, for example, intensified sectarian loyalty at the expense of family allegiance, because Shi'a replaced family as the channel for participating in local politics.[21]

One reason that people have assumed that sectarianism was common in the nineteenth century is that they fail to make a distinction between official policy and the way people actually behaved. Governments might or might not discriminate against non-Muslims from time to time, but that had little to do with the attitudes and relationships of oridinary Muslims and Christians to one another. Christians and Druzes in Beirut worried considerably more about what the government would do next than they did about the attitude their associates or neighbors might have. When Christians left Beirut, it was mainly because of oppression by an intolerant pasha, as was the case during the rule of al-Jazzar and 'Abdallah Pasha. When the pasha disappeared, they came back. The Druzes were also made to feel uncomfortable in Beirut after the city was separated from the jurisdiction of Mount Lebanon in the late eighteenth century, and under al-Jazzar (1775–1804) the Muslims had their turn along with the local Christians.[22]

When real tensions did begin to develop in Beirut, they assumed special forms, most of them confined to the poor and working class. The most common expression lay in making a public show of the newly acquired Christian privilege of ringing church bells, or tearing down posted reports of Muslim attacks on Christians, as happened in Aleppo in 1850, or refusing to support members of other communities. In the 1850s rumor spread among Christians that the Muslims of the city were hiding firearms in their houses and shops to use against them. Occasionally, too, there was a public demonstration: in 1842 boys in the streets of Beirut followed the Greek Orthodox archbishop singing what was described as "Druze songs," and one of the boys spat at him.[23]

Hostility did, however, crop up occasionally even among the rich. In 1853 a Muslim assaulted a "respectable" Christian merchant who was the agent of a French mercantile house in Beirut. Perhaps the incident had more to do with commercial jealousies than with sectarianism; we cannot say. In 1855 the British consul-general Noel Moore also mentions a "fanatical" Muslim party that was small but carried some weight because of the social standing of its leaders. Its fanatical leanings amounted to opposing the current pasha of Beirut because he had shown signs of being well-disposed toward Christians.[24]

Tensions could also be expressed through opposing or supporting a foreign power or an outside faction. The latter course was made easier by the growing involvement of Beirut in the affairs of Mount Lebanon and reflects the divergence of interests any outside involvement caused among Beirut's expanding and changing population. The Muslims and Christians of Beirut are reported to have reacted very differently to the presence of European warships in the harbor. Muslims were alarmed at their presence and happy to see them depart; Christians were pleased to see them arrive and sorry to see them go.[25] As more and more Christians settled in Beirut in the middle decades of the century and after Beirut's Christians became involved with Mount Lebanon's Maronite interests, petitions dealing with problems in the Mountain were signed by Beirutis appealing for help to consuls and other influential people on behalf of coreligionists in the interior. Much of the agitation in Mount Lebanon was also attributed to coreligionists in Beirut. One famous agitator was the Maronite Bishop Tubiyya 'Awn, who was active in stirring up Maronites against Druzes and in 1860 organized a Maronite Young Men's League that openly provoked them.[26]

One difficulty in assessing the amount of sectarian hostility in Beirut in the mid-century stems from the sources themselves, since most of them are Christian, and usually European. This explains, for example, why all references to hostility among the well-to-do make Muslims the aggressors.

Another difficulty is that these observations are colored by their authors' relationships both with local groups and with rival nations. It is difficult to decide, say, how to assess the information provided by consular reports. They can be useful for their detailed accounts, and their overall reliability makes it hard to disregard their comments on sectarian feeling entirely, but their fondness for the word "fanatical" as applied to Muslims is certainly suspect. One report says that even "the most fanatical" and wealthiest Muslim merchants of Beirut insist on having their legal suits brought before the mixed tribunals of commerce lately established in Beirut, instead of the Muslim courts of law, because the Muslim merchants acknowledged the "superiority of Christian justice." Those tribunals were composed of equal numbers of foreign and local representatives and based on rules of evidence and procedure inspired by European practice. That insistence may well have been more indicative of good business sense than of admiration for Christian justice, but in any case the only fanaticism apparent in this particular report is that of its author against Muslims.[27]

Despite complaints, it is undeniable that Beirut continued to be at least more tolerant toward non-Muslims than most other towns, even on the governmental level. After the restoration of Ottoman power in Syria and Lebanon in 1840, many non-Muslims claimed that the Ottomans had taken away privileges the Egyptians had granted them. Even when the Ottomans decreed reforms in their favor, they claimed that the reforms were not properly enforced. Christian evidence in court was not given the same weight as evidence provided by Muslims. Incidents between Ottoman officials and local Christians in Beirut in the 1840s and 1850s reveal considerable mutual distrust, but non-Muslim rights remained at least better protected in Beirut than in other places, where consular presence was weaker and Ottoman representatives were lower in rank or less conscientious in enforcing new regulations.[28] Most of the reports concerning the violation of Christian rights after the Egyptian withdrawal involve merchants outside Beirut. In Damascus Christians were not as well treated as their coreligionists in Beirut, and sometimes the sources even admit this: after at first criticizing the criminal court established in Beirut in 1850 for its injustice to Christians, consular reports subsequently admit that it treated Christians fairly, in marked contrast to the justice meted out in other cities.[29] The fact that Christian rights were better protected in Beirut probably accounted for much of the continued Christian immigration.

The mutual tolerance that prevailed between Muslims and Christians was a remarkable achievement given the considerable tensions that always surrounded the city. Even people who belonged to the small but influential "fanatical" party of Muslims to which consular reports repeatedly refer seem to have been friendly enough toward individual Christians. In 1851 a number of highly placed officials who had hitherto been thought ill-disposed toward Christians were dismissed from their offices by the Ottoman authorities. Among them was the Mufti of Beirut, the most important Muslim figure in the city. The reasons given for the dismissal was collaboration with Christians, in particular sanctioning the intervention of the Greek Patriarch in a controversial affair involving inheritance and land property.[30]

Personal ties between members of the various communities helped to diminish tensions. In Beirut everyone knew everyone else, and Muslims and Christians continued to meet at official functions; they sat on courts and committees together. In 1851, three Muslims and three Christians were members of a majlis (council) for the trial of criminal cases. Four Muslims and four local Christians as well as some Europeans were appointed to a mixed commission established in 1855 to judge a case involving French and British agents. Whatever their private feelings, merchants continued to put business first and to cooperate in matters involving their trading interests. In 1852, a few Christian merchants joined the Muslims in supporting the local *majlis* against an attempt to install a steam press in one of the khans of Beirut. In 1854 European, Christian, and a few Muslim merchants raised a loan demanded by the local government: the specific purpose of that collective effort is not known, but the collaboration it involved is clear.[31]

Much of the hostility evident in Beirut in the middle decades of the nineteenth century erupted between, not Muslim and Christian, but the various Christian sects and factions. As the numbers of Greek Orthodox, Maronites, and Greek Catholics increased, so did factionalism.[32] Christian rivalries even extended to the few resident Protestants, the latest to arrive on the local scene. Jessup, who lived so long in Syria and whose opinions were probably shared by other Protestants, was at times harsher on "nominal Christians" of other sects — especially the Greek Orthodox — than he was on Muslims, and he made it a point to mention that Muslims differentiated between Protestants and other "creature worshippers."[33] Even when warfare broke out in the Syrian interior and in Mount Lebanon in the 1840s and 1850s, Christian sects continued to argue as energetically as ever, and perhaps even with greater zeal.

The civil war of 1860 certainly brought animosity between Christians and Muslims, but this is only part of the picture. When the Christians of Beirut supported their coreligionists outside, the Muslims responded with demonstrations — one Muslim riot that occurred on July 23, 1860, was the closest Beirut came to civil war.[34] But cooperation also continued: Muslims "both of lower and superior classes" came to the rescue of Christian refugees and collected money, to feed, clothe, and shelter them.[35] Many claim that strong European influence — and the presence of European ships in Beirut's harbor — prevented bloodshed in the city in 1860, but the real reason behind Beirut's avoidance of bloodshed must lie with the population itself and with the restraining influence that individuals were able to exercise. European influence remained but could not prevent bloodshed later on, for if some spirit of mutual tolerance survived in 1860, little remained afterwards, as the thousands of Christian refugees in the city mourning the loss of relatives and friends wept and wailed in the streets of Beirut, and cheered the arrival of French troops. Conscripts from Damascus were taken to Istanbul by way of Beirut, and as they passed through the streets a Damascene Christian pointed to one of the conscripts and cried out in rage: "This is the murderer of my brother!" A Turkish soldier struck him down; the French protested, and the Turk was punished. The house of General Beaufort, the French commander, was "frequently surrounded by crowds of Christians, mostly women, who wail and sing their funeral songs under his windows." At a public ceremony in Beirut honoring the newly appointed governor of Mount Lebanon, Daoud Pasha, "the proceedings were more than once interrupted by the painful incident of a number of widows of Deir El-Kamar and other places where massacres were perpetrated making their appearance on the ground wailing and shrieking for their lost kindred and clamoring for vengeance on their murderers." Even after the refugees had been more or less integrated into the population, they kept their memories. At the turn of the century, they were still dating events in terms of the civil war.[36]

Muslims were not immune either. They resented it when the Muslims in the war were punished, and humiliated when foreign troops were brought in to protect the Christians. Week after week, Muslims watched the arrival of thousands of Damascene Muslims, sometimes members of the noblest families, conscripted into the army, "all with their wrists fastened in wooden stocks, nailed fast."[37] It is hardly surprising that they, too, occasionally responded with violence to the open joy of Christians welcoming French troops, and they picked quarrels with the Christians who almost a year later surrounded General Beaufort's house. Nor is it surprising that although Europeans stayed out of the war, a Muslim struck a blow at a French shopkeeper in Beirut; or that as the French army left, a procession of Muslims on a feast day sang war songs and jeered the departing troops.[38]

The humiliations to which they were subjected in reprisal for their rebellion and the landing of foreign troops in their land told the Muslims of Beirut that the alteration of the status of non-Muslims in the empire would leave the Muslims powerless, and it soon became more and more evident what that change would mean in Beirut. As peace returned and Beirut consolidated its economic and political position, Christians began more and more rapidly to supersede Muslims in numbers, wealth, and influence. The presence of Western representatives constituted a growing source of power, and the increasing number of Christians in Beirut allowed them to use these new privileges to the fullest. Nowhere else did the benefits the Christians thus acquired become so visible as in Beirut; nowhere else did these benefits result in so visible an imbalance of advantage to Christians and Muslims living side by side.

The result was sectarianism of a new kind. Although it continued to be affected by regional and international developments, it was now tied primarily to developments within the city, particularly the increasingly evident socioeconomic and cultural gap between two communities benefiting unequally from urban growth. The Muslims found it hard to accept the advantages accruing to their Christian neighbors and not to themselves. They had always been on top and saw their superiority as natural. Now the tables were turned, the times were out of joint, and Christian appetites grew with the eating, the more so as the new emigrants from the Mountain came devoid of the urban instinct for coexistence and compromise.

As a result, the city that had once been a refuge became the focus of Christian-Muslim tensions. In 1882, the year of the British occupation of Egypt, Beirut Christians were reported to have fled the city because of incidents connected with Muslim religious festivities.[39] By the first decades of the twentieth century, Beirut's name was so closely associated with sectarian warfare that Edward Atiyah started a chapter on "Beyrouth" with the following words: "Christians *versus* Moslems: this was my first notion of collective human relationships. To my mind at the age of five or six the world consisted of Moslems and Christians in antagonism to one another — two natural inevitable groups, as natural and inevitable as the world itself . . . From my earliest days I was hearing talk about 'Christians and Moslems.'"[40]

Sectarianism remained most evident among the poor. At the margin of every society, the poor suffer most from any shift in status that adds to the precariousness of their livelihood. Interdenominational rivalries receded in the favor of rising hostilities between Muslims and Christians. By the turn of the century, people were talking less about intracommunal differences and more about intercommunal ones.

No opportunity was lost to further the contest. Zaydan, who has left an account of the pastimes of the common people of Beirut, relates how a sword game between a Christian and a Muslim turned into a battle that required police intervention and led to prohibition of the game. Popular gatherings on religious feasts or official occasions could cause an incident. A procession in the streets of Beirut honoring a gift to Beirut's Muslims by the Ottoman sultan, three hairs of the Prophet Muhammad, gave rise to demonstrations against unbelievers. More and more often, however, it was a quarrel between individuals of different communities or a settling of accounts that started the trouble. As these incidents became more and more frequent, pretexts became flimsier until people from different communities were attacking one another for no obvious reason at all. By the beginning of this century, Christian-Muslim clashes were so common that rarely did a week go by without an assassination, or a year without a riot. According to Lewis Gaston Leary, who spent some years in Beirut as an instructor in the American Protestant College and published a book on Syria in 1913, in one winter there was a murder every night for six weeks. Christians and Muslims were killed alternately with such regularity that one man postponed an evening visit on the grounds that "this is the night for a Christian to be killed."[41]

Hostilities also became more violent. A boy spitting at an archbishop was a hostile act in the mid-nineteenth century; twenty-five years later people were attacking with weapons. In 1871, the Christians were set upon in several quarters by bands of Muslims with sticks and retaliated by attacking the Muslim guards near the governor's house. Soon wooden bats were not enough. In 1881 a quarrel broke out between Muslim and Christian boys playing in the developing Christian Mazra'a quarter of town. When another Christian tried to separate them, he was beaten with clubs by three or four young Muslims and then stabbed to death. As the news spread, more Muslims and Christians collected on the spot where he died and fought each other with swords and guns. A number were killed or wounded.[42] In 1882 swords were brandished, if not used, by Muslims assembled at the funeral of a Muslim boy found murdered in a Christian quarter on the outskirts of town. In 1888 two Christian boys found their lost goat decapitated near a Bedouin house in the Mazra'a quarter. One of the boys shot at the Bedouin women inside the house, and thereby started a riot that ended in the death of several people and the wounding of several others. In 1896, Christians strolling in the streets of Beirut were fired upon in broad daylight; Muslims sitting in the shop of a tobacconist were then shot at by men in disguise, no doubt Christians. In 1897 and 1899 firearms were used repeatedly, escalating both the violence and the number of victims.[43]

Ringleaders emerged. The most famous of them was a Greek Orthodox man called Osta Bawli — "Osta" either is a corruption of the word "professor" (ustadh) commonly given to people with some education or position, as a sign of respect, or of the common word for a master craftsman.[44] Osta Bawli was stalked by the Muslims and became a folk hero to the Christians after he was finally stabbed in the back one night. He was

> a redoubtable champion, loved and admired by the Christians, dreaded by the Moslems. Every Christian in difficulties with the Moslems or with the Turkish Government was his protégé; every Christian murdered was sure to be avenged by him or his lieutenants; Christians in danger of being arrested sought refuge with him. He concealed them, gave them money, helped them flee to America. When he walked out he was surrounded by a veritable bodyguard of lieutenants, wearing caftans, and belts holding daggers and revolvers.[45]

All the violence was encouraged by the lack of an efficient police force. Although Beirut's police succeeded occasionally in checking riots, more often than not they failed. On more than one occasion they were accused by Christian sources of favoring the Muslims. The majority of the police were Muslim, and the few Christian policemen there were confined to the lower ranks. The police may also have been hampered by the city's unchecked growth; there may simply not have been enough of them — or at least enough able ones — to keep the situation under control.[46] Crime certainly grew with the city, and especially with the numbers of poor people who lived there. Sometimes riots involved people who were not necessarily criminals. When porters, carriage drivers, or donkey drivers fought in the streets it was clear that only working people were involved. At other times, however, it was less clear. Zaydan mentions incidents that clearly involved troublemakers. The Muslims who started the riot by threatening unbelievers during the procession honoring the hair of the Prophet, for example, were said to have been of "the baser sort," as were the Muslims who brandished swords and sang war songs at the funeral of the Muslim boy found dead in a Christian quarter. One incident involved a Christian of the "criminal class" who had escaped from prison and murdered a Muslim officer (zaptie). Several involved smugglers, whose arrest often triggered rioting. Of the Muslim smugglers, the most famous was 'Abduh Inkidar, who had once been on trial for the murder of a Christian.[47]

Sectarian hostility also increased among the rich, but there it assumed quite a different form. While the common people openly fought, the merchants and notables channeled their energies into political maneuvering, struggles for influence, and outdoing one another in charitable largesse. They founded benevolent societies, schools, and hospitals for their own communities. The Christians established the Greek Catholic Patriarchal College in 1865, the Maronite Ecole de la Sagesse in 1874, the Greek Orthodox school of Thalathat Aqmar, and in 1880 the girls' school Zahrat al-Ihsan supported by Emilie Sursock. Among Muslim schools were Dar al-Funun, a primary school founded in 1880, and the Maqasid Benevolent Society, founded in 1878 and destined to become the leading Sunni educational and medical center in Beirut. Schools and hospitals were often affiliated with various Christian denominations and supported by Italian, German, English, French, and American money. Of the learned societies, the two earliest (the Society of Arts and Sciences founded in 1847 and the Oriental Society founded by Jesuits in 1850) had both been Christian, but now a number of new ones were established. The Protestants founded an evangelical missionary society; all the officers were drawn from the ranks of local Protestants, a group formed mainly by converts from the Greek Orthodox church. Alumni associations became popular, such as the cultural society called Jam'iyya Shams al-Barr, founded by graduates of the Syrian Protestant College as a branch of England's Union of Christian Youth. Political and social clubs drew their members from the same class and group.[48]

Immigration contributed to the springing up of benevolent societies, which provided both social identity and security in a rapidly growing society. Dimitri Debbas established himself in society not only by working for the Orthodox church of Saint Dimitri but by being a founding member (in 1900) of the Society of Damascene Families in Beirut, its vice-president until 1909 and its president in 1911. One reason for creating such a society was the feeling among Damascenes that the Beiruti Greek Orthodox did not accept them. A dispute between rival patriarchs that involved church politics far beyond the interests of Beirut had resulted in estrangement between the Greek Orthodox of Beirut and the Damascene emigrés. As a result of their real or imagined humiliations, the Damascene Greek Orthodox decided to found a benevolent association of their own. It did not take them long, however, to realize that the surest way to be accepted by local society was to extend help not only to their own families but to other Greek Orthodox as well. After the first three or four years, the society opened its activities to all the Greek Orthodox of Beirut, with notable success.[49] The Greek Orthodox Damascenes to this day maintain their distinctiveness as a source of pride. The memory of 1860 was kept alive, but as an asset that could be at the same time a source of identity and of integration with their Beiruti coreligionists.

That merchants and other notables of all denominations established their own societies, schools, and hospitals may reveal a new tendency toward sectarian exclusiveness, but it certainly in no way resembled the hostilities in the streets outside. Still, social and economic fissures between elite Muslims and Christians and, even more visible, cultural gaps were forming as well, and they were encouraged by educational trends, especially the establishment of foreign — particularly French — schools among the Christians. Warring or not, one culture and one way of life survived among the common people; peaceful or not, the cultural cleavage among the merchants and notables of Beirut grew wider. What had begun only as a different way of dressing and living progressed to different goals and different outlooks on life. The full effects of this cultural schism were already apparent before World War I. Visiting Beirut in 1913, Maurice Barrès described the class of "uprooted" people that the study of French literature and civilization was creating among the indigenous population. In the long run, those separate cultural orientations would be harder to bridge than any gap in religion or income.[50]

Yet even this cultural division did not obliterate all similarities. Behind the westernized Christian merchant remained a basic attachment to traditional ways. Social and financial success was defined by Christian and Muslim merchants in identical terms. The successful man was active in politics both inside and outside the group. Traditional habits did not stop the Muslim merchant from adapting them to Western-inspired ideas. In 1865 a traditional Muslim family wedding featured a play in which new liberal ideas allegorically triumphed over Orthodox Muslim teachings.[51] On the other hand, this clinging to the past on both sides also ensured acceptance of both as members of a common merchant community. One of their common interests was to restrain the growth of sectarianism so visible among the poor. Notables of both communities joined against whatever elements, regardless of community, might threaten peace and prosperity.

The 1870s were crisis years for the Ottoman empire, and of them 1876 was the most difficult. The atrocities perpetrated by the Ottoman government against Bulgarian subjects had intensified tensions throughout the empire, and a crisis was unfolding at the highest echelons of the Ottoman hierarchy. In one year, three sultans followed one another to the throne: Abdulaziz was deposed on May 30, 1876, and committed suicide on June 4; Murad V was deposed on August 31, and Abdulhamid II succeeded him. Edicts in late 1875 and February 1876 promoted reforms to counteract the unrest. Upon his accession on June 1 Murad proclaimed that all subjects without distinction were to enjoy complete liberty, and plans for a constitution continued throughout the year. It was adopted on December 23, 1876.

The effects of these developments were felt throughout the empire. In Beirut, Muslims claimed that, if they were to be treated on an equal footing with Christians, conscription should be extended to Christians as well. Muslim notables tried to prevent popular outbursts. A consular report mentioned that, although changes in the Ottoman capital excited and alarmed Syrian Muslims, "the most respectable amongst them are doing their utmost to restrain the lower orders from committing any excesses," despite the fact that some Christians were provoking them. After the reading of the proclamation of Sultan Murad, certain Christians of Beirut "appeared desirous to bring about a collision with the Mahometans during the rejoicings," but authorities prevented that. Most likely, these Christians were from among the populace, just as the Muslim agitators were. Partly because of feeling in England against the Bulgarian atrocities, reports of sectarian agitation were included in consular reports, but this agitation was confined to a few isolated incidents among "the lower classes of the population." Among Muslim and Christian notables, all efforts were concentrated on restraining excesses.[52]

The collaboration of Muslim and Christian merchants was preserved, as it had been earlier, by personal relationships. Notables of the two communities continued to meet regularly at official functions. Although Christians had by then become more numerous than Muslims in Beirut, they continued to share equal representation with Muslims on committees, in itself a sign of their willingness to work together.[53] As the century drew to a close, more and more public committees were formed in Beirut in answer to the ever-growing urban needs of the city, and Muslim and Christian notables frequently sat together at public functions. The formation of the Ottoman parliament, to which Muslim and Christian representatives from Beirut were chosen, added a new dimension to that interaction.[54]

For the first time in the late nineteenth century, private societies and committees were also formed by Muslim and Christian merchants and notables who voluntarily joined together. These private societies and committees were intellectual, social, and political in character. Although their actual composition is unclear, it is at least known that some of the literary societies in Beirut had a multiconfessional following and tried to bridge those religious gaps. For example, the Syrian Scientific Society, or al-Jam'iyya al-'Ilmiyya al-Suriyya, had about 150 members of whom a number were notable Muslims, and a Masonic lodge established in Beirut had both Christian and Muslim members.[55]

There is also some evidence that Muslims and Christians joined a political underground society in 1880. Little is known about its activities, except that it posted revolutionary placards in Beirut and elsewhere, denounced Turkish injustices, and demanded that Arabs be treated equally with Turks. But the presence in it of both Muslims and Christians is the first hint that we have of the development of some form of national identification transcending communal loyalties.[56]

That trend became apparent after 1908 when the Young Turks came to power and launched the Ottoman empire into a policy of centralization and Turkification that alienated the Arab Muslims. In 1913 a Beirut Reform Committee was founded to demand recognition of Arab rights in the Ottoman empire, the appointment of an Arabic-speaking governor for Beirut, and the use of Arabic in court. It included Christians, Muslims, and Jews.[57] To the economic interests that had always bound Muslim and Christian merchants of Beirut were now added the intellectual and political interests arising out of the policies of the Young Turks.

How long Muslim and Christian merchants and notables would continue to restrain sectarianism depended on the continuing survival of their common interests, and those would last only so long as the merchant class remained open to members of both communities. By the time of World War I this merchant class was still predominantly Christian, and future sectarian harmony seemed to depend solely on how large a place in the sun would be guaranteed to the merchants and notables of both communities in the years to follow. But after the war, although a growing number of Muslims continued to join the Christian merchant elite, sectarian harmony had two new factors to contend with. One was the French Mandate, which transformed the nature of sectarian relations. The other was a new international situation. The fragile balance in modern Lebanon was destroyed by the presence of new groups who had no place in the traditional political power structure and who have been able to tip the balance by reviving old animosities, especially among the masses. But for merchants and notables, the acid test of the nineteenth century that their relations survived has helped them to withstand these new challenges to sectarian harmony.

9 Conclusion

The impact on its population of Beirut's prosperity deserves to be studied for several reasons. In the course of a century, Beirut grew from an insignificant port to the leading trade center on the eastern Mediterranean, and in the process it was the recipient and propagator of all sorts of influences and ideas. This radical improvement in its fortunes can be linked to changes in international trade routes and in the European balance of power. Technological revolution in Europe, the growth of Mediterranean trade, the advent of steamships, and improved regular communications with the West, all promoted the growth of the seaports to the detriment of the inland cities. Beirut may have become the center of the new trading network, but its growth was otherwise only the most dramatic example of what was in fact a general trend.

The answer to why Beirut prospered so much more than any of the other once famous Levantine ports — Acre, Tyre, Sidon, and Tripoli — lay partly in the power structure of the Middle East, for Beirut's growth is a striking example of the relationship between politics and urbanization. When Egypt ruled in Syria and Lebanon in the 1830s, Muhammad Ali decided to move the political center of his holdings northward to Beirut, and for the first time it acquired the trappings of government, including the establishment of European consulates. After the Egyptians departed in 1840 and the Ottoman Turks returned, they decided to maintain Beirut as the center of the vilayet of Sidon, and thus its political and administrative importance increased. In 1888 the vilayet of Beirut was established, ensuring its place in international and local political and economic affairs. As a commercial city it easily became an educational and cultural center as well, and this political and social function explains why the city was able to continue to grow, even in the twentieth century, when shipping had lost so much of its commercial importance.

The changes in the political and administrative roles of Beirut introduced by the Egyptians and continued by the Ottomans also enhanced the relationship of the city to the hinterland. The alliance between Ibrahim Pasha of Egypt and Emir Bashir II of Mount Lebanon made Beirut strategically invaluable and a political power base for Mount Lebanon, and the city's growing economic importance both strengthened and diversified that role and turned the close relationship between Beirut and Mount Lebanon into dependence of hinterland upon city. Beirut was the political collaborator and counterpart of Damascus, as well as its port. The Beirut-Damascus road, built in 1858–1863, was a physical manifestation of the link that had been forged.

Once established as an administrative center, Beirut reaped the advantages of security from upheaval. It was politically safer as well as economically more attractive than the surrounding countryside. Earlier, the inhabitants of Beirut had sought refuge from their enemies in Mount Lebanon; in the 1830s the tables were beginning to turn. In moments of crisis—after 1840 when the Mountain rose in revolt against Egyptian domination, and again in a more dramatic way after the civil war of 1860—more and more often people fled to Beirut. It received refugees not just from Mount Lebanon, but from other troubled areas in the Syrian interior. Increasing political power and stability in the city allowed it to sustain its role as an asylum when clashes occurred in Aleppo in 1850 and 1860. By the time calm returned to the interior, Beirut had grown to the point where it provided enough economic, social, and cultural opportunities to ensure its continued expansion even in the absence of crisis.

Because Beirut's population grew as a result of specific events, the composition of the incoming population is comparatively easy to establish. One has only to identify those groups in need of security because, since jobs were plentiful, most of those who fled there simply stayed. It was in this way that socioeconomic and political developments combined to alter both Beirut's population and its relationship with surrounding areas.

Immigration first of all altered the city's religious composition. As sectarianism intensified in the interior and Mount Lebanon in the middle decades of the nineteenth century, a great number of Christians from the disturbed areas came to Beirut. Since Christians of all sects tended to migrate to the city in proportion to their numbers in the areas from which they came, a Syrian city for the first time acquired a marked preponderance of Christians over Muslims. The fact that more Christians than Muslims migrated to Beirut also meant that Christians benefited more from the city's expanding economic opportunities, and this shifted the distribution of wealth among Beirut's religious communities.

Beirut's expanding opportunities also altered the ways its people made their living. In the early nineteenth century, the people had been limited to crafts, trade, or government service. Artisans, shopkeepers, and workers comprised the majority, ruled over by an upper class of government officials and wealthy people — Muslim notables and a combined Muslim and Christian merchant bourgeoisie. The expansion of Beirut's commerce, the establishment of foreign consulates and trading firms, and of new local merchant and moneylending houses broadened and diversified those avenues to wealth. A new, and now predominantly Christian, merchant class emerged. Unlike many of the renascent port cities of the Middle East where entrepreneurship and profit remained largely in foreign hands, the merchants of Beirut were quick to take advantage of the economic development of the city and to keep at least some of the profit for themselves. Even people of simple background through assiduity, ingenuity, and education could become self-made men by amassing capital as money changers and lenders, interpreters, small-scale venture capitalists, agents of foreign commercial houses, and middlemen in domestic trade.

As a result, Beirutis enjoyed a degree of social mobility that would have been unheard of earlier, either in the limited trading milieu of the small town of Beirut or in the hierarchical society of Mount Lebanon. The rich refugees who had taken their money and expertise with them to Beirut became its new merchant class, and in the course of the nineteenth century that class accumulated more money and, what was unprecedented, political power. From discretion and simplicity in clothing, housing, and custom, this new class began to display its wealth, and since the sources of that wealth owed much to the expansion of trade with the West, this display often came in the form of Western clothing, furnishings, and education. In the long run, the educational systems established in Beirut catered to this new style — and the proliferation of Western Christian schools and the reaction to it provoked in the form of a reaffirmation and expansion of Muslim education dug a potentially dangerous cultural gulf.

Beirut had been known for its tolerance throughout most of the nineteenth century, but by World War I it had become more sharply divided along sectarian lines than the nearby cities. The rapidity of Beirut's growth was in part responsible because people had not developed urban ways of living as they moved into the urban environment. The move to the city had simply reinforced their hold on the old ways, not an unusual phenomenon in periods of rapid urbanization and a common symptom among first-generation immigrants in all societies. Refugees of civil war and political turmoil also bring their memories with them, and finally animosities were exacerbated by an economic expansion that the Christians had been able to take advantage of more easily than the Muslims.

Sectarian tensions were most visible among the poorer classes. Among the wealthy the gulf was narrower, since they were less apt to let communal affiliation stand in the way of economic cooperation and social and political action. Merchants still had more in common with one another than they had with their European counterparts. The economic changes of the period created a socioeconomic group that cut across communal lines. Among the rest of the population, however, the uneven distribution of wealth between the communities, and the continuing immigration to Beirut that brought a steady stream of unassimilated newcomers, impeded the formation of a fully integrated urban community.

Tables

Selected Bibliography

Notes

Index

Abbreviations

A.D.A. Archives de la Direction Générale des Antiquités du Liban, Beirut
A.E.   Archives du Ministère des Affaires Etrangères, Paris
A.P.   Archives de la Compagnie de Gestion et d'Exploitation du Port de Beyrouth, Beirut
F.O.   Records of the Foreign Office, Public Record Office, London
N.A.E. National Archives of Egypt, Dar al-Watha'iq, Cairo
U.S.   U.S. consuls in Beirut, 1836–1906. American Consular Reports, Washington

Note: All dates are given in the order of day-month-year: 6–2–1847 stands for February 6, 1847. For F.O. and A.E., the first number given will be the series, the second the volume. For N.A.E., the first number given will be the folder's, the second the manuscript.

Table 1.   Population of Beirut

Year	Total	Source
1784	6,000	Volney, *Voyage en Egypte et en Syrie*, p. 290.
1823	6,000	Jessup, *Fifty-Three Years in Syria*, I, 25, 265.
1825	8,000	
1827	6,000	Laborde, quoted by Chevallier, "Signes de Beyrouth en 1834," p. 211, n. 5
1831	over 9,000 (including suburbs)[a]	Michaud et Poujoulat, *Correspondance d'Orient*, VII, 69.
1833	12,000	Moore, quoted by John MacGregor, *Commercial Statistics* (London, 1947), II, 125.
1833	ca. 12,000	Boislecomte, quoted by Douin, *La mission du Baron de Boislecomte*, p. 260.
1835	9,000 or 10,000	Hoche, *Le pays des croisades*, p. 583.
1836	5,000–6,000	Delaroière, *Voyage en Orient*, p. 45.
1836	15,000	Velde, *Narrative of a Journey*, p. 61.
1837	9,000 (without suburbs)	Schubert, quoted by Carl Ritter, "Beirut," *Die Erkunde von Asien*, IV: *Phönicien, Libanon und gebirgigen Nordsyrien* (Berlin, 1854), p. 449.
1837	10,000	Houry, *De la Syrie*, p. 49.
1838	15,000 (with suburbs)	Robinson, quoted by Ritter, IV, 449.
	15,000 (with suburbs)	Elliot, quoted by Ritter, IV, 499.
1838	ca. 12,000 (with suburbs)	Blondel, *Deux ans en Syrie et en Palestine*, p. 20.
In Beirut in 1808, 1810,	15,500	Guys, *Beyrouth et le Liban*, I, 8, 224.
1824–38	15–16,000	
1840	10,000	Armagnac, quoted by Chevallier, *La société du Mont Liban*, p. 52, n. 3.
1840	10,000	Jessup, I, 265.
1840	10,000	Urquhart, *The Lebanon*, II, 190.

(Table 1 continued)

Year	Total	Source
1842	10,000	Houry, *De la Syrie*, p. 49.
1843	12,000 (without suburbs)	Wilson, quoted by Ritter, IV, 449.
ca. 1846	19,120	Guys, *Esquisse*, table: "Pachalik de Seyde."
1847	27,500 (with suburbs)	Rafalovitch, quoted by Smilianskaya, *al-Harakat al fallahiyya*, p. 17.
1850	50,000[b]	Urquhart, II, 190.
1850	20,000	*Palestine and Syria* (Baedeker, 1876), p. 441; (Baedeker, 1894), p. 286.
1851–52	over 40,000	Velde, *Narrative of a Journey*, I, 61.
1856	22,000	Jessup, I, 265.
1857–58	50,000	Farley, *The Resources of Turkey*, p. 225.
1860	46,200	Etat-major du Corps Expéditionnaire Français en Syrie, quoted by Samné, *La Syrie*, p. 252.
1860	20,000	Hoche, p. 583.
ca. 1860	40,000 (with suburbs)	Thomson, *The Land and the Book* (1860), p. 37, quoted by Smilianskaya, p. 17.
1861 ca.	73,000[c]	F.O. 195/667, Moore-Russell, No. 41, Beirut, 21–11–1861, in Moore-Bulwer, No. 51, Beirut, 22–11–1861.
1861	60,000	Jessup, I, 238.
1863	60,000	Affaires Etrangères, Correspondance Commerciale, Beyrouth, 7, f. 401 (Outrey), quoted by Chevallier, *La société du Mont Liban*, p. 292.
1863	70,000	Jessup, I, 265.
1865	80,000	Affaires Etrangères, Correspondance Commerciale, Beyrouth, 8, f. 86 (Bernard des Essards), quoted by Chevallier, *La société du Mont Liban*, p. 292.
1869–71	ca. 72,000	Burton, *The Inner Life of Syria*, p. 15.
1870	ca. over 50,000	Burns, *Help-Book for Travellers*, p. 114.
1876	80,000[d]	*Palestine and Syria* (Leipzig, 1876), p. 441.

(Table 1 continued)

Year	Total	Source
1875–80	ca. 80,000	Lortet, *La Syrie d'aujourd'hui*, p. 74.
1881	75,000	*Da'irat al-ma'arif*, V, 752.
1882	ca. 80,000	Vaux, *La Palestine*, p. 27.
1883–85	90,000	Hoche, p. 584.
1885	100,000	Smilianskaya, p. 17, giving no source.
1886	80,000	Thomson, *The Land and the Book* (1886), p. 49.
1889	ca. 107,400	Khuri, *al-Jami'a*, p. 28.
1893–94	ca. 115–120,000	*Salname wilayat Bayrut 1311–1312*, p. 383.
1895	120,000	Vital Cuinet, *Syrie, Liban et Palestine: Géographie administrative, statistique, descriptive et raisonnée* (Paris, 1896), p. 53.
1895	120,000	Chevallier, *La société du Mont Liban*, p. 292.
1898	80,000	*L'Orient à vol d'oiseau*, p. 323.
1900	ca. 120,000	F.O. 195/2075.
1908	150,000[e]	*Salname wilayat Bayrut 1326*, p. 227.
1912	190,000[f]	*Palestine and Syria*, 5th ed. (Baedeker, 1912), p. 281.
1913	150,000	*A Handbook of Syria (Including Palestine)*, p. 393.
1913	ca. 200,000	Leary, *Syria*, p. 30.
1913	ca. 155,000	Thomson, *The Land and the Book* (1913), p. 19.
1915	200,000	Ruppin, quoted by Smilianskaya, p. 19.
1917	130,000	Adib Pacha, *Le Liban après la Guerre* (Cairo, 1917), quoted by Samné, p. 278.
n.d., ca. 1920	180,000	*A Handbook of Syria* (Including Palestine), p. 175; says the latest official record was in 1914–15.
1920	124,000	Samné, p. 285.
1922	ca. 91,000	*La Syrie et le Liban en 1922*, p. 58.

a. Estimates for the first half of the nineteenth century that include the suburbs are noted; the rest do not specify whether they include the suburbs. During the nineteenth century the suburbs gradually merged with the city.

(Table 1 continued)

b. Quoting figures of a census that, if added up, would give a total of 4,371 houses and 15,619 men.

c. Three quarters of the population: 50,000–60,000.

d. Official statistics of 1874 would give a much lower number: families, 5,023.

e. Including Lebanese and foreigners; 62,279 without them.

f. Including a garrison of 2,000 infantry and cavalry.

Table 2.   Estimated percentages of Muslims and Christians in Beirut

Year	Muslims	Christians
1838	45 %	45 %
1846	47	47
1860–61	38	58
1881	33	57
1882	29	58
1889	30	64
1889	31	66
1895	30	63
1908	47	48
1912	34	54
1917	30	60
1920	37	66
1922	39	45

Source: Percentages are drawn from sources in Table 1 that provide popula-tion estimates by community.

Table 3. Estimated percentages of the three major Christian sects in Beirut

Year	Greek Orthodox	Maronites	Greek Catholics
1838	26%	10%	8%
1846	23	9	7
1860–61	29	21	7
1881	28	21	8
1882	20	25	12.5
1889	27	16	8
1889	28	26	8
1895	29	23	7
1908	23	17	6
1912	23	21	7
1917	29	23	7
1920	29	26	7

Source: Percentages are drawn from sources in Table 1 that provide population estimates by sect.

Table 4. Traffic in the port of Beirut

Year	Steam ships	Sailing ships	Total tonnage	Tonnage increase/previous year	Tonnage decrease/previous year	Causes
1895	–	–	805,520	–		
1896	–	–	906,781	101,261		
1897	–	–	841,953	–	841,828	Greek-Turkish war
1899	682	2,614	833,777	–		
1900	694	2,418	855,489	21,712		
1901	769	2,663	984,811	129,322		
1902	715	2,637	1,010,408	25,579		
1903	813	2,776	1,085,240	74,832		
1904	902	2,272	1,182,699	97,459		
1905	861	1,845	1,198,071	15,372		
1906	858	2,238	1,292,024	93,953		
1907	1,087	2,381	1,456,919	164,895		
1908	1,101	2,190	1,481,167	24,248		
1909	1,171	1,842	1,679,341	198,174		
1910	1,143	2,294	1,732,854	55,513		
1911	1,073	2,109	1,598,485	–	134,369	Italian-Turkish war, cessation of service to Syria by Dutch Co. and Russian Co.
1912	805	1,588	1,304,123	–	294,362	Italian-Turkish war, 2 months' strike of licensed maritime personnel, loss of 2 ships by American-Hadj Daoud Co.
1913	1,024	1,826	1,799,414	495,291		End of Italian-Turkish hostilities (but still some effects of Balkan war and French strike)

Source: Annual reports, Compagnie de Gestion et d'Exploitation du Port du Beyrout.

Selected Bibliography

Unpublished Official Documents

Egypt. National Archives of Egypt, Dar al-Watha'iq, Cairo. Series: Mahafidh al-Sham 1246 H/1830–1257 H/1840 (archives of the period of Muhammad 'Ali's rule over Syria, 1830–1840). Folders 'Abidin Nos. 231 (1247 H), 232, 233, 234, 235, 236, 237 (1248 H), 247 (1249 H), 250 (1250 H), 253 (1252 H), 255 (1253 H), 258 (1255 H), 259 (1256 H), 260 (1256 H).

Great Britain. Public Record Office, Foreign Office Archives, London. Series F.O. 195: Vols. 103, 127, 171, 187, 194, 221, 234, 235, 250, 251, 260, 320, 351, 382, 390, 437, 479, 483, 484, 486, 490, 519, 557, 647, 648, 655, 656, 657, 658, 677, 700, 727, 760, 787, 866, 903, 927, 994, 1027, 1047, 1067, 1069, 1076, 1113, 1153, 1154, 1201, 1202, 1262, 1263, 1264, 1368, 1369, 1410, 1447, 1480, 1510, 1548, 2581, 1603, 1613, 1648, 1683, 1723, 1761, 1801, 1843, 1886, 1899, 1937, 1980, 2024, 2097, 2117.

Series F.O. 226: Vols. 68–90, 92–96, 98–101, 111, 116, 122, 125, 128, 130, 152, 158.

Series F.O. 78: Vols. 186–191, which contain little information on Beirut; Vols. 1519 (1860) and 1557 (1860).

Series: F.O. 406: Vol. 10 (1860)

France. Les Archives du Ministère des Affaires Etrangères, Paris. Series: Consular and commercial correspondence, 1793–1901, Beirut: Vols. 7 (1854–63), 8 (1864–67), 9 (1868–March 1888), 10 April 1888–1894), 11 (1895–96), 12 (1897–1901).

Series: Political Correspondence up to 1871. Turkey: Consular documents. Beirut: Vols. 12 (Jan.–Sept. 1860), 13 (Aug. 1863–Sept. 1864), 16 (Oct. 1864–July 1865), 17 (Aug. 1865–Dec. 1866).

Lebanon. Archives de la Direction Générale des Antiquités du Liban (A.D.A.), Beirut. Official Documents.

United States. United States Consuls, Washington, D.C. Series: Dispatches from the U.S. consuls in Beirut, 1836–1906. Vols. I (1838)–IV (Feb. 9, 1981–Dec. 31, 1863).

Unpublished Private Documents

France. Photographs of Beirut in the nineteenth century, Paris. Private collection of Fuad Debbas.

———— Records of the Bayhum family, Paris. Put at my disposal by Dominique Chevallier, who acquired them from Louis Massignon.

Lebanon. Archives de la Compagnie du Port, des Quais et Entrepôts de Beyrouth (A.P.), Beirut.

———— Archives de la Direction Générale des Antiquités du Liban (A.D.A.), Beirut.

———— Greek Orthodox Archbishopric, Beirut. List of Greek Orthodox in Beirut.

———— Archives of al-Mahkama al-Shar'iyya al-Sunniya, Beirut.

———— Information on the Bayhum family, Beirut. Put at my disposal by Afif and Jamil Bayhum.

———— Memoirs of Dimitri Debbas, Beirut. Put at my disposal by Selim and Antoine Debbas.

———— Papers of Musa and Alfred Sursock and family. Put at my disposal by Yvonne Lady Cochrane.

———— Papers of Musa Bustros and family, Beirut. Put at my disposal by Nicolas de Bustros.

———— Photographs of Beirut in the nineteenth century, Beirut. Archives of the American University of Beirut.

———— Records on Henry Heald and Company, 'Ayn Sa'ada. Put at my disposal by Mr. and Mrs. John Joly (Joly papers).

United States. Houghton Library, Harvard University, Cambridge, Mass. Records of the Presbyterian Mission, A.B.C. 16.8.1, vol. I: Syria (1831–1837).

Interviews

In Lebanon: Henri Abdelnour, Mahmoud Alaya, Peter Bachmann, Yvonne Badran, Afif Bayhum, Jamil Bayhum, Fouad E. Boustani, Nicolas de Bustros, Maurice Chehab, Yvonne Cochrane, Selim Dahdah, Youssef Daghir, Antoine Debbas, Selim Debbas, Bshara Dahan, Assad Germanos, T. G. Hadgithomas, Izzet Harb, Gebran Hayek, Hassan Hichi, Abdul Rahman Hout, Adel Ismail, Hassan Itani, Saad al-Din Itany, John Joly, Yvonne Joly, Ibrahim Khalaf, Samir Khalaf, Ossama Khalidy, Rashid Khalidy, Youssef Khuri, Nabil Kronfol, Ramez Kronfol, Youssef Lahoud, Malek Mahmasani, Anis Makdissi, Father McDermott, Alfred Naccache, Henri Naccache, Albert Naccache, Christiane Naccache, Mitri Nammar,

Salwa Nassar, Nakhle Nims, Henri Pharaon, Charles Rizk, Nohad Sal-
ame, Ghofrail Salibi, Iliyya Salibi, Kamal Salibi, Selim Shoucair, Abdul
Rahman Tabbara, Hassan Tamin, Alfred Tarazi, Emile Tarazi, Nagib
Tarazi, Philip Tawile, Suhair Yassin, Zeine Zeine, Leila Ziadeh, Constan-
tine Zreik.
In France: Dominique Chevallier, Fuad Debbas.
In England: Butrus Abu Manneh, David Briar, Derek Hopwood, Albert Hour-
ani, Roger Owen, Linda Schatkowsky.
In the United States: Charles Issawi; Paul Saba

Local Histories, Chronicles, and Memoirs

Abkarius, Iskandar ibn Ya'qub. *The Lebanon in Turmoil: Syria and the Powers in 1860*. Trans. J. F. Scheltema. New Haven: Yale University Press,
1920.
Abu Shaqra, Husayn Yusif wa 'Arif, *al-Harakat fi Lubnan*. Beirut, 1952.
al-'Aqiqi, Antun Zahir. *Thawra wa fitna fi Lubnan*. Ed. Yusif Ibrahim
Yazbik. Beirut: Matba' at al-Ittihad, 1939.
al-Rihla al-shamiyya li-sumuw al-amir al-jalil Muhammad 'Ali Pasha. Cairo:
al-Matba'a al-'Amiriyya, 1911.
Atiyah, Edward. *An Arab Tells His Story: A Study in Loyalties*. London:
John Murray, 1946.
al-Dibs, Yusif. *Tarikh Suriya*. Vol. 8. Beirut: al-Matba' a al-Kathulikiyya,
1893–1905.
al-Dimashqi, Mikha'il. *Tarikh hawadith al-Sham wa-Lubnan*. Ed. Louis
Cheikho. Beirut: al-Matba' a al-Kathulikiyya, 1957.
Kayat, Assaad Y. *A Voice From Lebanon*. London: Madden and Co., 1847.
Kerr, Malcolm H., ed. and trans. *Lebanon in the Last Years of Feudalism,
1840–1860: A Contemporary Account by Antun Dahir al-'Aqiqi and
Other Documents*. Beirut: American University in Beirut, 1959.
Khuri, Amin. *al-Jami'a aw dalil Bayrut li-'am 1889*. Beirut: al-Matba'a al-
Adabiyya, n.d.
Mishaqa, Mikha'il. *Kitab mashhad al-'iyan bi-hawadith Suriya wa Lubnan*.
Cairo, 1908.
Mudhakkirat Jirji Zaydan. Ed. Salah al-Din al-Munajjid. Beirut: Dar al-Kitab
al-Jadid, 1968.
al-Shidyaq, Tannus. *Akhbar al-a'yan fi jabal Lubnan*. Ed. Fu'ad Ifram al-Bus-
tani. Beirut: al-Matba'a al-Kathulikiyya, 1970.
al-Shihabi, Amir Haydar Ahmad. *Lubnan fi 'ahd al-umara' al-shihabiyyun*.
3 vols. Ed. Fu'ad Bustani, ed. Beirut: Publications de l'Université Liban-
aise, Section des etudes Historiques, 18, 1969.
_____*Tarikh Ahmad Pasha al-Jazzar*. Ed. Antunius Shibli and Ignatius 'Abdu
Khalifa. Beirut: Matba'a Antun, 1955.
Yahya, Salih ibn. *Tarikh Bayrut*. Ed. Francis Hours and Kamal Salibi et al.
Beirut: L'Institut de Lettres Orientales de Beyrouth, 4: Histoire et sociologie du Proche-Orient, XXXV, Dar al-Mashriq, 1969.

Western Observers

d'Arvieux, Chevalier. *Mémoires du Chevalier d'Arvieux*. With commentary by R. P. Jean Baptiste Labat. Paris: Charles-Jean-Baptiste Delespine, 1735.

Baedeker, K., ed. *Palestine and Syria: A Handbook for Travellers*. Leipzig: Karl Baedeker, 1876.

_____*Palestine and Syria: Handbook for Travellers*. 2nd rev. ed. Leipzig: Karl Baedeker, 1894.

_____*Palestine and Syria: With Routes through Mesopotamia and Babylonia and the Island of Cyprus. Handbook for Travellers*. 5th ed. Leipzig: Karl Baedeker, 1912.

Barrès, Maurice. *Une enquête au pays du Levant*. Paris: Plon, 1923.

Beaufort, Emily A., Viscountess Strangford. *Egyptian Sepulchres and Syrian Shrines, including a Visit to Palmyra*. New ed. London: Macmillan, 1874.

de Belgiojoso, Princesse. *Asie Mineure et Syrie: Souvenirs de voyage*. Paris: Michel Levy Frères, 1858.

"Beyroot and Vicinity," *Missionary Herald*, 32 (1936).

Blondel, Edouard. *Deux ans en Syrie et en Palestine (1838–1839)*. Paris: P. Dufart, 1840.

Bonnelière, l'Abbé F. Souvenirs de mon pèlerinage en terre sainte. Paris: Perisse Frères, n.d.

Browne, W. G. *Travels in Africa, Egypt, and Syria, from the Year 1792 to 1798*. London: Cadell and Davies, 1799.

Burckhardt, John L. *Travels in Syria and the Holy Land*. London: John Murray, 1822.

Burns, Rev. Jabez. *Help-Book for Travellers to the East: Including Egypt, Palestine, Turkey, Greece and Italy*. London: Cook's Tourist Office, 1870.

Burton, Isabel. *The Inner Life of Syria, Palestine, and the Holy Land: From My Private Journal*. New ed. London: Kegan Paul, Trench, 1884.

Carne, John. *Syria, The Holy Land, Asia Minor, etc., Illustrated*. London: Fisher, 1836–1838.

Castlereagh, Viscount M. P. *A Journey to Damascus: Through Egypt, Nubia, Arabia, Petrae, Palestine, and Syria*. London: Henri Colburn, 1847.

Charmes, Gabriel. *Voyage en Syrie*. Paris, 1891.

Churchill, Charles H. *The Druzes and the Maronites under Turkish Rule: From 1840 to 1860*. New York: Arno Press, 1973.

Churchill, Colonel Charles Henry. *Mount Lebanon: A Ten Year's Residence From 1842–1852*. 3 vols. London: Saunders and Otley, 1853.

Cuinet, Vital. *Syrie, Liban et Palestine: Géographie administrative, statistique, descriptive et raisonnée*. Paris: Ernest Leroux, 1896.

Delaroière, M. *Voyage en Orient*. Paris: Delecourt, 1836.

Egerton, Lady Francis. *Journal of a Tour in the Holy Land: In May and June, 1840*. London: Harrison, 1841.

Farley, Lewis. *The Resources of Turkey: Considered with Special Reference to the Profitable Investment of Capital in the Ottoman Empire*. London:

Longman, Green Longman, 1863.

———— Two Years in Syria. London: Saunders and Otley, 1859.

Flaubert, Gustave. Voyage en Orient (1849-1851). Paris: Librairie de France, 1925.

Frankland, Charles Colville. Travels to and from Constantinople in 1827 and 1828. 2nd ed. London: Henry Colburn and Richard Bentley, 1830.

Guys, Henri. Beyrouth et le Liban: Relation d'un sejour de plusieurs années dans ce pays. Paris: Comptoir des Imprimeurs, 1850.

———— Esquisse de l'état politique et commerciale de la Syrie. Paris: Chez France, 1862.

A Handbook of Syria (Including Palestine). Prepared by the Geographical Section of the Naval Intelligence Division, Naval Staff Admiralty. London: His Majesty's Stationary Office, n.d.

Hoche, Jules. Le pays des croisades. Paris: Corbed, 1883-1885.

Houry, C. B. De la Syrie considérée sous le rapport du Commerce. Paris, 1842.

Jessup, Henri Harris. Fifty-Three Years in Syria. 2 vols. New York: Fleming H. Revell, 1910.

Jobin, M. l'Abbé. La Syrie en 1860 et 1861: Lettres et documents. Paris: Librairie F. Leport, 1880.

Jouplain, M. La question du Liban. Paris: Rousseau, 1908.

Kelman, John. From Damascus to Palmyra. London: Adam and Charles Black, 1908.

de Laborde, Léon. Voyage de la Syrie. Paris, 1837.

de Lamartine, Alphonse. Voyage en Orient. Paris: Hachette, 1875.

Laorty-Hadji. La Syrie, la Palestine; et la Judée: Pèlerinage à Jérusalem et aux lieux saints. 9th ed. Paris: Bolle-Lasalle, 1854.

Leary, Lewis Gaston. Syria: The Land of Lebanon. New York: McBride, Neast, 1913.

Lortet, Le Dr. La Syrie d'aujourd'hui: Voyages dans la Phénicie, le Liban et la Judée 1875-1880. Paris: Librairie Hachette, 1884.

MacGregor, John. Commercial Statistics. London: Whittaker, 1947.

de Malherbe, Raoul. L'Orient, 1718-1845. Paris: Gide, 1846.

Michaud et Poujoulat. Correspondance d'Orient 1830-1831. VII. Bruxelles: J. P. Meline, 1835.

Murray, John. Handbook for Travellers in Syria and Palestine: Geography, History, and Inhabitants. London: 1858, 1868, 1875 and 1882.

de Nerval, Gerard. Voyage en Orient. Paris: Juilliard, 1964.

L'Orient á vol d'oiseau: Carnet d'un Pélerin. Paris: Imprimerie des Orphelins Apprentis d'Auteuil, 1902.

Paton, Andrew A. The Modern Syrians from Personal Notes; 1841, 1842 and 1843. London: Longman, Brown, Green and Longman, 1844.

Patterson, James Laird. Journal of a Tour in Egypt, Palestine, Syria and Greece. London: C. Dolman, 1852.

Paxton, J. D. Letters on Palestine and Egypt: Written during Two Years' Residence. Lexington: A. T. Skilman, 1839.

Pococke, Richard. *A Description of the East, and Some Other Countries.* London: Bowyer, 1745.

Porter, Rev. J. L. *Five Years in Damascus.* London: John Murray, 1855.

Poujade, M. Eugène. *Le Liban et la Syrie, 1845–1860.* Paris: Michel Lévy Frères, 1867.

Sandys, George. *A Relation of a Journey Begun An. Dom. 1610.* 2nd ed. London: W. Barett, 1621.

de Saulcy, L. F. Caignard. *Carnets de voyage en Orient 1815–1869.* Paris: Presses Universitaires de France, 1955.

Spencer, Rev. J. A. *The East: Sketches of Travels in Egypt and the Holy Land.* London: John Murray, 1850.

Taylor, Baron I. *La Syrie, la Palestine et la Judée: Pèlerinage à Jérusalem et aux Lieux Saints.* Paris: Lemaitre, 1860.

Thomson, W. M. *The Land and the Book.* Rev. ed. London: Thomas Nelson, 1913.

de Tott, Baron. *Mémoires du Baron de Tott, sur les Turcs et les Tartares.* Amsterdam, 1785.

Urquhart, David. *The Lebanon (Mount Souria): A History and a Diary.* London: Thomas Coutley Newby, 1860.

de Vaux, Ludovic. *La Palestine.* Paris: Ernest Leroux, 1883.

Véga. *An pays de la lumière: Notes et impressions d'un voyage en Syrie, en Galilée et à Jérusalem.* 2nd ed. Paris: Fischbacher, 1912.

de Vogüe, Eugène-Melchior. *Syrie, Palestine, Mont Athos: Voyage aux pays du passé.* Paris: Librairie Plon, 1924.

Volney, C. F. *Travels through Syria and Egypt, in the years 1783, 1784 and 1785.* Trans. G. G. J. and J. Robinson. New York, 1788.

Les voyages du Seigneur de Villamont. Rev. ed. Lyon: Claude Lariot, 1607.

Wortabet, Gregory. *Syria and the Syrians: or Turkey in the Dependencies.* London: James Madden, 1856.

Unpublished Theses

Abu-Manneh, Butrus. "Some Aspects of Ottoman Rule in Syria in the Second Half of the Nineteenth Century: Reform, Islam and Caliphate." Ph.D. dissertation, St. Antony's College, Oxford, 1971.

al-Husami, Ratib, "Tijarat Bayrut wa mahall Bayhum al-tijari." M.A. thesis, American University of Beirut, 1942.

Farag, Nadia. "*al-Muqtataf* 1876–1900: A Study of the Influence of Victorian Thought on Modern Arabic Thought." Ph.D. dissertation, St. Antony's College, Oxford, 1969.

Fontaine, Jean. "Le désaveu chex les écrivains Libanais Chrétiens de 1825 à 1940." Thèse de doctorat de 3e cycle, Faculté des Lettres de Paris (Sorbonne).

Labaki, Boutros. "Sériciculture et commerce extérieur: Deux aspects de l'impact européen sur l'économie du Liban et de son environnement arabe en fin de periode ottomane (1840–1914)." Thèse de doctorat de 3e cycle, Ecole Pratique des Hautes Etudes, Paris, 1974.

Naff, Alixa. "A Social History of Zahle, the Principal Market Town in Nineteenth-Century Lebanon." Ph.D. dissertation, University of California, Los Angeles, 1972.

Notes

1. Introduction

1. Charles Issawi, "Economic Change and Urbanization in the Middle East," in *Middle Eastern Cities: A Symposium on Contemporary Middle Eastern Urbanization*, ed. Ira M. Lapidus (Berkeley: University of California Press, 1969), pp. 102–121. The growth of seaports in the nineteenth century is also noted in Iliya F. Harik, "The Impact of the Domestic Market on Rural-Urban Relations," *Rural Politics and Social Change in the Middle East*, ed. Richard Antoun and Iliya Harik (Bloomington: Indiana University Press, 1972), p. 349.

2. Gideon Sjoberg, *The Preindustrial City: Past and Present* (Illinois: The Free Press, 1960). Among those who see a close relationship between urbanization and industrialization is Eric E. Lampard, "Urbanization and Social Change, on Broadening the Scope and Relevance of Urban History," *The Historian and the City*, ed. Oscar Handlin and John Burchard (Cambridge, Mass.: MIT Press, 1966), pp. 225–247; "The History of Cities in the Economically Advanced Areas," *Economic Development and Cultural Change*, 3 (January 1955), 81–136; Lampard, "Historical Aspects of Urbanization," *The Study of Urbanization*, ed. Philip M. Hauser and Leo F. Schnore (New York: Wiley, 1965), pp. 519–554. See also Kingsley Davis and Hilda Hertz Golden, "Urbanization and the Developments of Pre-Industrial Areas," *Economic Development and Cultural Change*, 3 (October 1954), 6–24; Bert F. Hoselitz, "Generative and Parasitic Cities," *Economic Development and Cultural Change*, 3 (April 1955), 278–294.

3. Leila Fawaz, "Le développement de Beyrout au XIXe et au debut du XXe siecle," ed. Abdelwahab Boudhiba and Dominique Chevallier, *La ville arabe dans l'Islam: Les espaces sociaux de la ville histoire et mutations*, Actes du Colloque de Tunis, March 12–18, 1979 (Tunis: Centre d'Etudes et de Recherches Economiques et Sociales, 1982), part 2, chap. 8.

4. The readings on migration and urbanization are extensive. The follow-

ing were particularly useful about migrants' urban adjustment: Myron Weiner, *Sons of the Soil: Migration and Ethnic Conflict in India* (Princeton: Princeton University Press, 1978); Fuad I. Khuri, "Sectarian Loyalty among Rural Migrants in Two Lebanese Suburbs: A Stage between Family and National Allegiance," *Rural Politics and Social Change in the Middle East*, pp. 198–213; F. I. Khuri, "Rural-Urban Migration in Lebanon: Motivation and Adjustments," *Cultural Resources in Lebanon* (Beirut: Librairie du Liban, 1969), pp. 135–146; F. I. Khuri, *From Village to Suburbs: Order and Change in Greater Beirut* (Chicago: University of Chicago Press, 1975); J. Abu-Lughod, "Migrant Adjustment to City Life: The Egyptian Case," *The American Journal of Sociology*, 67 (July 1961), 22–32; J. Abu-Lughod, "Varieties of Urban Experience: Contrast, Coexistence and Coalescence in Cairo," in *Middle Eastern Cities*, pp. 159–187.

5. See Moshe Ma'oz, *Ottoman Reform in Syria and Palestine 1840–1861: The Impact of the Tanzimat on Politics and Society* (Oxford: Clarendon Press, 1968); M. Ma'oz, "The Impact of Modernization on Syrian Politics and Society during the Early *Tanzimat* Period," in *Beginnings of Modernization in the Middle East*, ed. W. R. Polk and R. L. Chambers (Chicago: University of Chicago Press, 1968), pp. 334–349.

2. The Legacy of the Past

1. Said Chehabe Ed-Dine, *Géographie humaine de Beyrouth: Avec une étude sommaire sur les deux villes de Damas et de Baghdad* (Beirut: Imprimerie Calfat, 1960), chap. 1; Helmut Ruppert, *Beirut: Eine westlich gepragte Stadt des Orient* (Erlangen, 1969), pp. 10–11.

2. W. B. Fisher, *The Middle East: A Physical, Social and Regional Geography* (London: Methuen, 1971), p. 422; Ruppert, *Beirut*, p. 10; Chehabe Ed-Dine, *Géographie humaine de Beyrouth*, p. 221; René Mouterde, "Une ville remplit son site: Beyrouth," *Méditerranee*, 4.3 (1963), 37–39.

3. The quotes are respectively from Baron Ludovic de Vaux, *La Palestine* (Paris: Ernest Leroux, 1887), p. 27; *L'Orient à vol d'oiseau: Carnet d'un pèlerin: Hellenisme aramaisme et semitisme* (Paris: Orphelins-Apprentis d'Auteuil, 1902), p. 324; Emily A. Baufort, Viscountess Strangford, *Egyptian Sepulchres and Syrian Shrines, Including a Visit to Palmyra* (London: Macmillan, 1874), p. 103.

4. Henri Harris Jessup, *Fifty-Three Years in Syria* (New York: Fleming H. Revell, 1910), I, 26, 278; Isabel Burton, *The Inner Life of Syria, Palestine, and the Holy Land: From my Private Journal* (London: Kegan Paul, Trench and Co., 1884), p. 15; James Laird Patterson, *Journal of a Tour in Egypt, Palestine, Syria and Greece: With Notes and an Appendix on Ecclesiastical Subjects* (London: C. Dolman, 1852), p. 326. A description of Beirut as the Egyptians found it is available in N.A.E., 231/7, 66:3, 1247/1831.

5. Du Mesnil du Buisson, "Les anciennes défenses de Beyrouth," *Syria*, 2 (1921). 235–257, 317–327; *Awraq Lubnaniyya*, I. 4 (1955), 173–174, II.2,

55–56, II.6, 278–282, III.3, 133–134; Edouard Blondel, *Deux ans en Syrie et en Palestine, 1838–1839* (Paris: P. Dufart, 1840), p. 72; J. D. Paxton, *Letters on Palestine and Egypt: Written during Two Years' Residence* (Lexington: A. T. Skilman, 1839), p. 17.

6. Blondel, *Deux ans en Syrie*, pp. 11ff; Henry Guys, *Beyrout et le Liban: Relation d'un séjour de plusieurs années dans ce pays* (Paris: Comptoir des Imprimeurs, 1850), I, 18; Gerard de Nerval, *Voyage en Orient* (Paris: Julliard, 1964), I, 396.

7. Michaud et Poujoulat, *Correspondance d'Orient 1830–1831* Bruxelles: J. P. Meline, 1835), VII, 70. The contrast between the austerity of the houses as they appear to the passer-by and their actual openness, built as they are around an internal courtyard, is pointed out in Dominique Chevallier, "Signes de Beyrouth en 1834," *Bulletin d'études orientales*, 25 (1972), pp. 226–227; Dominique Chevallier, "La ville arabe: Notre vision historique," in Dominique Chevallier et al., *L'espace social de la ville arabe* (Paris: Maisonneuve et Larose), 1979), pp. 8ff.

8. Guys, *Beyrout et le Liban*, I, 19–22; Lortet, *La Syrie d'aujourd'hui: Voyages dans la Phénicie, le Liban, et la Judée* (Paris: Hachette, 1884), p. 73; Blondel, *Deux ans en Syrie*, p. 13; Gustave Flaubert, *Voyage en Orient (1849–1851)* (Paris: Librairie de France, 1925), p. 135; Nerval, *Voyage en Orient*, I, 395.

9. Buisson, "Les anciennes défenses de Beyrouth," pp. 235ff; Guys, *Beyrout et le Liban*, I, 20–22, 29, 31; *Magazin Pittoresque*, 1840, p. 389; Baron I. Taylor, *La Syrie, la Palestine et la Judée: Pèlerinage à Jerusalem et aux Lieux Saints* (Paris: Lemaitre, 1860), p. 29; Alphonse de Lamartine, *Voyage en Orient* (Paris: Hachette, 1875), I, 135–137; David Urquhart, *The Lebanon: Mount Souria. A History and a Diary* (London: Thomas Cautley Newby, 1860), II, 150, 193; Rev. J. A. Spencer, *The East: Sketches of Travels in Egypt and the Holy Land* (London: John Murray, 1850), p. 481; Patterson, *Journal*, p. 236. Flaubert, *Voyage en Orient*, p. 135; Van de Velde, *Narrative of a Journey through Syria and Palestine: In 1851 and 1852* (Edinburgh: William Blackwood, 1854), pp. 52, 68, 395.

10. *L'Orient à vol d'oiseau*, pp. 324–325; Urquhart, *The Lebanon*, II, 255–256; Lortet, *La Syrie*, p. 69; Lewis Gaston Leary, *Syria: The Land of Lebanon* (New York: McBridge, Neast, 1913), p. 30; Lamartine, *Voyage en Orient*, I, 385–387, 393–397, 420; M. Delaroière, *Voyage en Orient* (Paris: Debecourt, 1836), p. 46; Patterson, *Journal*, p. 326; Burton, *The Inner Life of Syria*, pp. 212–213.

11. Volney, *Voyage en Egypte et en Syrie*, ed. Jean Gaulmier (Paris: Mouton, 1959), p. 290.

12. The review of Beirut's history from ancient times to the nineteenth century is based primarily on "Bayrut," *Da'irat al-ma'arif*, ed. Bustros al-Bustani (Beirut: al-Ma'arif), V (1881), 744–753; *Beirut—Crossroads of Culture* (Beirut: Librairie du Liban, 1970); Louis Cheikho, *Bayrut: Tarikhuha wa-atharuha* (Beirut: Catholic Press, 1925); Du Mesnil Du Buisson, "Les anciennes défenses de Beyrouth"; Du Mesnil Du Buisson, "Recherches archeologiques a

Beyrouth, la légende de Saint Georges," *Bulletin de la Société Française de Fouilles Archeologiques*, 6 (1924–25), 81–130; Philip K. Hitti, *Lebanon in History from the Earliest Times to the Present*, 3rd ed. (New York: St. Martin's Press, 1967); A. H. Hourani, *Syria and Lebanon: A Political Essay*, Royal Institute of International Affairs (London: Oxford University Press, 1954; reprint, Beirut: Librairie du Liban, 1968), pp. 6–40; Samir Khalaf and Per Kingstad, *Hamra of Beirut: A Case of Rapid Urbanization* (Leiden: E. J. Brill, 1973), pp. 12–15; René Mouterde, *Regards sur Beyrouth, phénicienne, hellénistique et romaine* (Beirut: Imprimerie Catholique, 1966); *Religion in the Middle East*, ed. A. J. Arberry (Cambridge: The University Press, 1969), I and II: Salibi, *The Modern History of Lebanon*; Kamal S. Salibi, "The Buhturids of the Garb: Medieval Lords of Beirut and Southern Lebanon," *Arabica: Revue d'etudes arabes*, 7 (January 1961), 74–97; Salih ibn Yahya, *Tarikh Bayrut*, ed. Francis Hours and Kamal Salibi et al., L'Institut de Lettres Orientales de Beyrouth, 4: Histoire et sociologie du Proche-Orient, 35 (Beyrouth: Dar al-Mashriq, 1969).

13. Hitti, *Lebanon in History*, pp. 244–245.

14. Salibi, *The Modern History of Lebanon*, p. xvii. Salih ibn Yahya wrote in *Tarikh Bayrut*, p. 13, that after the Arab conquest, the Muslim population of Beirut began to increase and the Roman one to decline, until the majority of the population became Muslim. Salibi, *The Modern History of Lebanon*, is more correct to date to establishment of the first important Sunni communities in Beirut and other coastal towns to the period of Mamluk domination (1291–1516).

15. René Grousset, *Histoire des croisades et du royaume franc de Jérusalem*, III: *La monarchie musulmane et l'anarchie franque* (Paris: Librairie Plon, 1936), pp. 156–57.

16. One estimate is that the Jewish population of Beirut during the Crusades totaled sixty families: E. Rey, *Les colonies franques de Syrie au XIIe et XIIIe siècles* (Paris: Picard, 1883), p. 102.

17. W. Heyd, *Histoire du commerce du Levant au moyen-âge* (Leipzig: Otto Harrasowitz, 1885), II, 151, 320, 573, 685; Rey, *Les colonies franques de Syrie*, p. 213.

18. Heyd, *Histoire du commerce du Levant*, II, 4, 63, 417, 456, 460–61, 464, 468–97, 519, 524, 543, 549–50; Ira Marvin Lapidus, *Muslim Cities in the Later Middle Ages* (Cambridge: Harvard University Press, 1967), pp. 16, 18, 23–25.

19. Heyd, *Histoire du commerce du Levant*, II, 460. In the mid-fourteenth century, Beirut's population was quite dense. Cheikho, *Tarikh Bayrut*, p. 77, citing Jalal al-Din al-Sayyuti. Beirut's population diminished to about 10,000 after plagues in 1491 and 1492. Such estimates are approximate at best. Even if the figure 10,000 is in any way representative — we do not know on what it is based — we still do not know what Beirut's population was before the plagues mentioned. This uncertainty makes it impossible to evaluate how much a decline 10,000 stands for. A Western traveler of the mid-fourteenth century wrote that Beirut was "fairly well peopled," in Rudolph von

Suchem's *Description of the Holy Land, and the Way Thither,* p. 48.

20. Heyd, *Histoire du commerce du Levant,* II, 462.

21. Ghillebert de Lannoy, *Voyages et ambassades,* pp. 155–157, cited by Bertrandon de la Broquière, *Le voyage d'outemer* (Paris: Leroux, 1842), p. 30.

22. Salibi, "The Buhturids of the Garb"; Lapidus, *Muslim Cities in the Later Middle Ages,* p. 16.

3. The Mountain and the City

1. Salibi, *The Modern History of Lebanon,* introduction. For the administrative divisions of Syria by the Ottoman government, consult ibid.; Salibi, "Beirut Under the Young Turks, as Depicted in Memoirs of Salim 'Ali Salam (1868–1938)," *Les Arabes par leurs archives* (XVIe-XXe siècles), ed. Jacques Berque et Dominique Chevallier (Paris: Centre Nationale de la Recherche Scientifique, 1976), p. 15, n. 24; Moshe Ma'oz, *Ottoman Reform in Syria and Palestine,* pp. 31–34.

2. Salibi, *The Modern History of Lebanon,* chap. 1; Hitti, *Lebanon in History,* chaps. 15, 16; Hourani, *Syria and Lebanon,* pp. 24–25.

3. Salibi, *The Modern History of Lebanon,* pp. 90, 95; Charles H. Churchill, *The Druzes and the Maronites under the Turkish Rule: From 1840 to 1860* (New York: Arno Press, 1973), pp. 144–146, 155–156; Jessup, Fifty-Three Years in Syria, I, 168–170, 172–173, 177. See also the numerous reports on the events of 1860 in F.O. 195/655; F.O. 195–656; F.O. 406/10; U.S./3; U.S./4. The religious composition of the migrants of 1860 was collected from all the above sources and others, such as Chevallier, *La société du Mont Liban à l'époque de la révolution industrielle en Europe* (Paris: Librairie Orientaliste Paul Geuthner, 1971), p. 63.

4. F.O. 406/10, Moore-Bulwer, 29-8-1860, in Moore-Russell, No. 37, 31-8-1860; ibid., "Report by Mr. Graham on the Condition of the Christians in the Districts of Hasbeya and Rasheya," Damascus, 13-8-1860; F.O. 196/656, Dufferin, No. 34, 26-10-1860; F.O. 195/657, "Séance du 30 Octobre 1860," in Dufferin-Bulwer, No. 40, 3-11-1860; Mikha'il Mishaqa, *Kitab mashhad al-'iyan bi hawadith Suriya wa Lubnan* (Cairo, 1908), pp. 158–159; Jessup, *Fifty-Three Years in Syria,* I, 189.

5. F.O. 406/10, Bulwer-Russell, No. 476, Therapia, 1-8-1860. The other estimates are from Salibi, *The Modern History of Lebanon,* pp. 106–107; U.S./3, Johnson-Secretary of State, 27-6-1860; U.S./4, Johnson-Secretary of State, 14-7-1860; F.O. 406/10. Robson's Memorandum, in Dufferin-Russell, No. 9, 23-9-1860.

6. Salibi, *The Modern History of Lebanon,* introduction; Chevallier, *La société du Mont Liban;* John P. Spagnolo, *France and Ottoman Lebanon 1861–1914,* St. Antony's Middle East Monographs No. 7 (Oxford: Ithaca Press, 1977).

7. "Bayrut," *Da'irat al-Ma'arif,* p. 749; Guys, *Beyrout et la Liban,* I, 201; Georges Douin, *La mission du Baron de Boislecomte: l'Egypte et la Syrie en*

1833, Société Royale de Géographie d'Egypte, Publications spéciales (Le Caire: Imprimerie de l'Institut Français d'Archéologie Orientale, 1927), pp. 258–259; Chevallier, *La société du Mont Liban,* p. 186 and n. 2. Hitti, *Lebanon in History,* pp. 399–400, wrote that a first French consulate was established in Beirut in the seventeenth century. N.A.E. 236/161, 26 Safar 1248 H/1832, refers to a Mr. Shahun as the American consul of Beirut. A. L. Tibawi, *American Interests in Syria 1800–1901: A Study of Educational and Religious Work* (Oxford: Clarendon Press, 1966), pp. 75–76, mentioned that in 1834 the new American vice-consul in Beirut was a Levantine, Jasper Chasseaud. The records of the dispatches from the United States consuls in Beirut start only in 1836. F.O. 195/760, Eldridge-Erskine, No. 68, 27–12–1863, mentioned that a new Italian consulate-general had been established in Beirut.

8. These quotes are respectively from Guys, *Beyrout,* I, 8; F.O. 195/127, Moore-Ponsonby, No. 15, 20–8–1836; ibid., Moore-Ponsonby, No. 11, 22–6–1838; ibid., Moore-Ponsonby, 22–6–1838; French consular reports quoted by Chevallier, *La société du Mont Liban,* pp. 185–186; A.E., Correspondance commerciale, Beyrouth, 6, f, 398, dépêche de Lesparda, II, août 1852, quoted in Chevallier, *La société du Mont Liban,* p. 268, n. 1; Laorty-Hadji, *La Syrie, La Palestine et la Judée; pèlerinage à Jérusalem et aux lieux saints,* 9th ed. (Paris: Bolle-Lasalle, 1854), p. 28.

4. Population Growth

1. The quality of the cadastral surveys the Ottoman government made of its population in the early centuries of the Ottoman empire has been ascertained in the articles of Omer Lutfi Barkan and in M. A. Cook, *Population Pressure in Rural Anatolia 1450–1600* (London: Oxford University Press, 1972). The usefulness of Ottoman sources for demographic history as late as the nineteenth century is demonstrated also in the work of Kemal Karpat. It remains, however, that the study of the population of nineteenth-century Syria is difficult. The lack of censuses in nineteenth-century Syria and their problems are mentioned in Issawi, *The Economic History of the Middle East, 1800–1914: A Book of Readings* (Chicago: University of Chicago Press, 1966), p. 209; Issawi, "Middle East Economic Development, 1815–1914: The General and the Specific," *Studies in the Economic History of the Middle East: From the Rise of Islam to the Present Day,* ed. M. A. Cook (London: Oxford University Press, 1970), p. 397; Gabriel Baer, *Population and Society in the Arab East,* tr. from the Hebrew by Hanna Szoke (London: Routledge and Kegan Paul, 1964), pp. 2–4; Chevallier, *La société du Mont Liban,* pp. 31 and 53, n. 1. The problems of surveys of Syrian population in the nineteenth and early twentieth centuries is noted also by contemporaries: Guys, *Beyrout et le Liban,* I, 276; F.O. 78/191, from R. Gordon in Constantinople, No. 83, 26–10–1830; *A Handbook of Syria (Including Palestine),* prepared by the Geographical Section of the Naval Intelligence Division, Naval Staff Admiralty (London: His Majesty's Stationery Office, n.d.), p. 182. See also Chevallier, *La société du*

Mont Liban, p. 53, n. 1, quoting F.O. 195/196, Wood-Canning, 19-5-1842. An example of Ottoman awareness that their figures were approximate is *Salname wilayat Bayrut 1311-1312* (Ottoman Yearbook for the Vilayet of Beirut, 1893–1894; Vilayet mataba'a sinde, 1310), pp. 383, 397.

2. "Bayrut," *Da'irat al-ma'arif*, V, 752; *Palestine and Syria: A Handbook for Travellers* (Leipzig: Karl Baedeker, 1876), p. 441.

3. Urquhart, *The Lebanon*, II, 190.

4. After commenting on the difficulty of getting reliable statistics in Turkey, Guys asserted that his information on Mount Lebanon had been gathered at good sources and very carefully, but he did not provide much information on how he did that. Guys, *Beyrout et le Liban*, I, 278. Some explanation of his method is given in Henry Guys, *Esquisse de l'état politique et commerciale de la Syrie* (Paris: Chez France, 1862), p. 33. But there are no explanations or sources given for the figures Guys quoted for Beirut: Guys, *Beyrout et le Liban*, I, 8. For an analysis of Guys's statistics, see Chevallier, *La société du Mont Liban*, chap. 4.

5. Jessup, *Fifty-Three Years in Syria*, I, 25, 265, gave different figures for the population of Beirut in 1823 and 1825; W. M. Thomson, *The Land and the Book*, rev. ed. (London: Thomas Nelson and Sons, 1913), p. 19, mentioned that the population of Beirut was 5,000 people "fifty years ago." The problem is that the book ran through many editions and, since the first edition dates from 1858, the reference to 5,000 people "fifty years ago" probably means around the beginning of the nineteenth century.

6. In the 1830s, the French traveler M. Delaroière, *Voyage en Orient*, p. 45, was the only one to give a figure as low as 5,000–6,000 people for the population of Beirut. Since this was a figure commonly given by earlier travelers, he may have simply copied their estimates. The British consul-general in Beirut in 1861 wrote that three fourths of the population of Beirut amounted to 50,000–60,000 people: F.O. 195/677, Moore-Russell, No. 41, 21-11-1861, in Moore-Bulwer, No. 51, 22-11-1861. Such an estimate implies a total figure of about 73,000; this is higher than other estimates of the same period. The figures mentioned are not, then, to be taken at their face value and are more useful as gross rounded estimates than as exact figures.

7. *A Handbook of Syria (including Palestine)*, p. 183.

8. Carl Ritter, "Beirut," *Die Erkunde von Asien*, IV: *Phonicien, Libanon und gebirgigen Nordsyrien*, 2nd ed. (Berlin, 1854), p. 447, estimated realistically that around 1800–1820 Beirut had 7,000–8,000 inhabitants.

9. Guys, *Beyrout et le Liban*, I, 38; "Bayrut," *Da'irat al-ma'arif*, V, 750; Buisson, "Les anciennes défenses de Beyrouth," pp. 236, 317–27; René Dussaud, "Le peintre Montford en Syrie (1837–1838)," *Syria*, 1 (1920), 155–164; Urquhart, *The Lebanon*, II, 123–127; N.A.E., 236/116, 20 Safar 1248/1832; Lamartine, *Voyage en Orient*, pp. 143–144; Delaroière, *Voyage en Orient*, p. 46.

10. F.O. 195/127, Moore-Ponsonby, No. 7, 29-10-1835; ibid., Moore, "Report," 20-6-1837, and other reports; F.O. 226/68, "Reports," 20-6-1837; U.S. Consuls in Beirut 1836-1906, Vol. I: 25-3-1836 to 13-12-1850; Chas-

seaud-Forsyth, No. 4, 20–6–1837; Urquhart, *The Lebanon,* II, 190; Van de Velde, *Narrative of a Journey,* I, 60; Gregory M. Wortabet, *Syria and the Syrians; or Turkey in the Dependencies* (London: James Madden, 1856), II, 5; Thomson, *The Land and the Book* (1913), p. 19.

11. Henry Guys, *Beyrout et le Liban,* I, 50–52; Report on the Ottoman Board of Health established by the Egyptian government in 1835, F.O. 226/95, Moore-Rose, No. 2, 6–2–1847; F.O. 195/127, Moore-Ponsonby, No. 1, 26–8–1835; Thomson, *The Land and the Book* (1913), p. 19; Asad Rustum, "Bayrut fi 'ahd Ibrahim Pasha" (Beirut in the Period of Ibrahim Pasha), *al-Kulliya,* 13 (1927), 131–132; Fuad Salim Haddad, "The Development of Anasthesia in Lebanon 1800–1914, "*Middle East Journal of Anaesthesiology,* 3 (February 1971), p. 7; F.O. 195/171, Dr. John Robertson, Deputy Inspector General of Hospitals, Beirut, 16–3–1841, enclosure in a consular report of 19–3–1841.

12. F.O. 195/866, Eldridge-Lyons, No. 62, 22–6–1866; F.O. 195/1477, Eldridge-Wyndham, No. 44, 6–8–1833, and enclosure from the newspaper *Hadiqat al-akhbar,* 2–8–1883; F.O. 195/2075, Heathcote-O'Connor, No. 42, 13–6–1900; *ibid.,* Heathcote-O'Connor, No. 56, 16–8–1900.

13. Jessup, *Fifty-Three Years in Syria,* I, 207; F.O. 195/1447, Eldridge-Wyndham, No. 44, 6–8–1833; ibid., Eldridge-Wyndham, No. 47, 18–8–1883; F.O. 195/2075, Heathcote-O'Connor, No. 42, 13–6–1900.

14. F.O. 195/171, Dr. John Robertson, Beirut, 16–3–1841, in a consular report of 19–3–1841; Amin Khuri, *al-Jami 'a aw dalil Bayrut li'am 1889* (Directory for Beirut in 1889), 2nd ed. (Beirut: al-Matba'a al-adabiyya, n.d.), p. 28; Haddad, "The Development of Anasthesia in Lebanon 1800–1914," pp. 12–13.

15. Whether the spread of an epidemic in Beirut was checked by the existence of the quarantine center or by other causes is uncertain. One doctor, John Wortabet (son of an Armenian convert to Protestantism, Gregory Wortabet), wrote in 1891 that the purity of Beirut's water "conveyed in iron pipes to a distance of about eight miles" from the Dog River to Beirut since 1875 probably explained why the city had escaped an epidemic in 1883. The city escaped another epidemic in 1891, and Wortabet believed it was due also to the establishment of a cordon between Damascus and Beirut: John Wortabet, M.D., Corresponding Member of the Epidemiological Society of London and of the Medico-Chirugical Society of Edinburgh, March 17, 1891, in F.O. 195/1723, Trotter-White, No. 23, 22–4–1891. Other explanations were also given when Beirut escaped an epidemic. In F.O. 195/1447, Eldridge-Wyndham, No. 47, 18–8–1883, the British consul-general wrote: "If Beirut and Syria had been spared this year from a visitation of cholera, it is more due to the merciful interposition of Divine Providence than to the Administration of the Lazaret by the sanitation officials or the cordon and quarantines."

16. *al-Rihla al-shamiyya li sumuw al-amir al-jalil Muhammad 'Ali Pasha* (The Damascene trip by His Excellency the Prince Muhammad 'Ali Pasha; Cairo: al-Matba'a al-Miriyya, 1911), p. 35; Amir Haydar Ahmad al-Shihabi, *Lubnan fi 'ahd al-umara' al-Shihabiyyun* (Lebanon in the Period of the Shihab Emirs), ed. Fuad E. Bustany, new ed., Publications de l'Université Libanaise, Section des études historiques, 18 (Beirut, 1969), III, 564, 590, 631, 787–788,

790; Mikha'il al-Dimashqi, *Tarikh hawadith al-Sham wa Lubnan* (History of the Events of Damascus and Lebanon), ed. Louis Cheikho (Beirut: al-Matba'a al-Kathulikiyya, 1912), pp. 35, 48; Mikha'il Mishaqa, *Mashad al-'iyan*, p. 96; N.A.E., 232/40, 16 Ramadan 1247/1831; ibid., 232/56, 22 Ramadan 1247/1831; ibid., 232/81, 29 Ramadan 1247/1831; plague in Ras-Beirut: ibid., 232/75:2, 27 Ramadan 1247/1831; ibid., 232/123, 16 Shawwal 1247/1831; ibid., 233/39, 15 Dhu-l-Qa'da 1247/1831; ibid., 235/87, 12 Muharram 1248/1832; ibid., 235/196, end Muharram 1248–1832.

17. F.O. 195/127, Moore-Ponsonby, No. 1, 26–8–1835; ibid., Moore-Ponsonby, 1–9–1835; F.O. 226/95, Report on the state of the Ottoman quarantine establishment in Beirut, enclosed in Moore-Rose, No. 2, 6–2–1847; F.O. 195/12, Moore-Ponsonby, 18–8–1837; Chevallier, *La société du Mont Liban*, pp. 44–45; F.O. 195/127, Moore-Ponsonby, No. 9, 4–6–1838; U.S. Consul in Beirut, 1836, 1906, Vol. I, March 25, 1836–Dec. 13, 1850, Chasseaud-Forsythe, 7–7–1838; F.O. 195/171, Moore-Ponsonby, No. 6, 21–5–1840; ibid., Moore-Palmerston, No. 12, 29–5–1840. F.O. 226/95, report enclosed in Moore-Rose, No. 2, 6–2–1847. For 1841 and 1842, the references to plague do not specify that it hit Beirut but mention that, because of the unsettled state of the country, quarantine regulations were laxly observed and resulted in the appearance of plague "in this part of Syria." The remarks that follow refer to plague in Mount Lebanon. Plague in Beirut is mentioned specifically in F.O. 195/171, Robertson's report of 16–3–1841 in consular report 19–3–1841; and in ibid., Robertson-Dury, 3–4–1841.

18. F.O. 195/320, Rose-Palmerston, 26–10–1848; ibid., Rose-Palmerston, No. 15, 25–11–1848; F.O. 195/479, Moore-Redcliffe, No. 56, 15–10–1855; ibid., Tabet-Moore, 7–12–1855, in Moore-Redcliffe, No. 64, 8–12–1855; A.D.A., MSS 4796. F.O. 195/787, Wrench-Bulwer, No. 37, 21–6–1865; ibid., Eldridge-Bulwer, No. 42, 12–7–1865; Jessup, *Fifty-Three Years in Syria*, I, 289–290.

19. The quotes are respectively from F.O. 195/677, Moore-Russell, No. 41, 21–11–1861, in Moore-Bulwer, No. 51, 22–11–1861; Jessup, *Fifty-Three Years in Syria*, I, 289, and II, 437. See also F.O. 195/1447, Eldridge-Wyndham, No. 51, 27–8–1883; ibid., Eldridge-Wyndham, No. 59, 30–9–1883; Chevallier, *La société du Mont Liban*, pp. 44–45; A.D.A. MAA 1861: Cholera in Beirut, 3–8–1875.

20. F.O. 195/1447, Wassa Pasha-Eldridge, 8–8–1883, in Eldridge-Wyndham, No. 46, 12–8–1883; ibid., Eldridge-Wyndham, No. 59, 30–9–1883; Jessup, *Fifty-Three Years in Syria*, II, 544; F.O. 195/1723, Trotter-White, No. 23, 23–4–1891, and enclosure by John Wortabet, M.D., "Cessation of Cholera in Northern Syria"; ibid., Telegram from Trotter in Beirut, 12–10–1891; ibid., Trotter-Fane, No. 5, 26–1–1892.

21. Jessup, *Fifty-Three Years in Syria*, II, 634; F.O. 195/1980, Telegram from Hay in Beirut, 26/27–11–1897; ibid., 6–12–1897; F.O. 195/2056, Hay-O'Connor, 12–9–1899; F.O. 195-2075, Telegram from Heathcote in Beirut, 16/17–7–1900; ibid., 17–7–1900; ibid., 19–7–1900; ibid., Heathcote-O'Connor, No. 54, 20–7–1900; ibid., Heathcote-O'Connor, No. 56, 16–8–1900. It was mentioned in ibid., No. 54, that bubonic plague was

suspected. F.O. 195/2117; Sursock Papers, Georges to Alfred Sursock, Beyrouth, 21-10-1902.

22. Jessup, *Fifty-Three Years in Syria*, I, 283; N.A.E., 234/64, 15 Dhu-l-Hijja 1247/1831; F.O. 195/320, Moore-Rose, No. 15, 25-11-1848; in Rose-Palmerston, No. 53, 28-11-1848.

23. Chevallier, *La société du Mont Liban*, p. 45; Jessup, *Fifty-Three Years in Syria*, II, 444.

24. F.O. 195/1447, Eldridge-Wyndham, No. 44, 6-8-1883; ibid., Eldridge-Wyndham, No. 46, 12-8-1883; ibid., No. 47, Eldridge-Wyndham, 18-8-1883; F.O. 195/2075, Heathcote-O'Connor, No. 54, 20-7-1900. The cordon was referred to again in ibid., Heathcote-O'Connor, No. 56, 16-8-1900; ibid., Telegram Heathcote-British Ambassador, Constantinople, 19-7-1900. The immunity of Mount Lebanon from cholera is also mentioned in F.O. 195/320, Rose-Palmerston, 26-10-1848; F.O. 195/1723, Dr. Gregory Wortabet, "Cessation of Cholera in Northern Syria," in Trotter-White, No. 23, 22-4-1891.

25. F.O. 195/320, Rose-Palmerston, 26-10-1848; Jessup, *Fifty-Three Years in Syria*, I, 289; Guys, *Beyrout et le Liban*, I, 110-111.

26. F.O. 195/320, Rose-Palmerston, 26-10-1848; F.O. 195/320, Moore-Rose, No. 15, 25-11-1848, in Rose-Palmerston, No. 53, 28-11-1848; Chevallier, *La société du Mont Liban*, p. 45; F.O. 195/1723, Wortabet, "Cessation of Cholera in Northern Syria," in Trotter-White, No. 23, 22-4-1891; F.O. 195/2075, Heathcote-O'Connor, No. 54, 20-7-1900.

27. Jessup, *Fifty-Three Years in Syria*, I, 289. New School Muslims had a Shaykh issue a *fatwa* declaring that to flee from cholera was not against the Qur'an: ibid.

28. Chevallier, *La société du Mont Liban*, pp. 45, 197; Jessup, *Fifty-Three Years in Syria*, I, 289; F.O. 195/866, Eldridge-Lyons, No. 81, 30-10-1866; F.O. 195/1447, Eldridge-Wyndham, No. 47, 18-8-1883.

29. Haydar, *Lubnan*, new ed., III, 631, 776, 784, 800; F.O. 195/2056, Hay-O'Connor, 10-4-1899, etc.; Assaad Y. Kayat, *A Voice from Lebanon* (London: Madden, 1847), p. 105; F.O. 195/127, Moore-Ponsonby, No. 29, 28-11-1838; F.O. 195/437, Moore-Redcliffe, No. 2, 17-3-1854; F.O. 195/976, Eldridge-Elliot, No. 7, 30-1-1871; Jessup, *Fifty-Three Years in Syria*, I, 289. There were references also to earthquakes: U.S. Consuls in Beirut 1836-1906, Vol. I, 25-3-1836-3-12-1850, Chasseaud-Forsyth, No. 1, Beirut, 15-1-1837; F.O. 195/127, Moore-Ponsonby, No. 1, 9-1-1837. But the effects of the quakes were minor in Beirut.

30. F.O. 78/186, Blunt-Wellington, 18-5-1829; F.O. 195/976, Eldridge-Elliot, No. 7, 30-1-1871; F.O. 195/1154, Eldridge-Layard, No. 73, 4-7-1877; F.O. 195/171, "Consul" [on verso]-Ponsonby, No. 9, 31-10-1840.

31. Kayat, *A Voice from Lebanon*, pp. 267-269. Even an event like the change of regime in France had repercussions in Syria. The English consul in Beirut thus reported that it displeased the Christian inhabitants and it had affected negatively local French commercial interests: F.O. 226/101, Rose-Palmerston, No. 19, 2-4-1848. In 1827, rumor of a war between Turkey and

European powers caused Europeans and local Christians to flee Beirut for the Mountain: Captain Charles Colville Frankland, *Travels to and from Constantinople in 1827 and 1828*, 2nd ed. (London: Henry Colburn and Richard Bentley, 1830), I, 351–353.

32. F.O. 195/171, Moore-Ponsonby, No. 1, 1–2–1840. See also F.O. 195/127, Moore-Ponsonby, No. 1, 26–8–1835; F.O. 195/221, Rose-Canning, No. 47, 4–11–1843; Blondel, *Deux ans en Syrie*, p. 50; N.A.E., 250/519:4, 28 Dhu-l-Hijja 1250/1834; ibid., 250/519:5, 28 Dhu-l-Hijja 1250/1834; complaint of consular mistreatment because of conscription: ibid., 250/519:6, n.d., ibid., 251/321, 29 Jumada 1251/1835.

33. F.O. 193/1113, Eldridge-Elliot, No. 54, 13–11–1876; ibid., Eldridge-Elliot, 10–2–1876; ibid., Eldridge-Elliot, No. 11, 3–3–1876; F.O. 195/519, Moore-Redcliffe, No. 42, 18–8–1856; F.O. 195/351, Rose-Palmerston, 30–9–1850. Mazailler-Duhamel, Lattaquie, 29–6–1835, quoted by Rene Cattaui, *Le règne de Mohamed Aly d'après les archives Russes en Egypte*, II: *La Mission du Colonel Duhamel 1834–1837* (Première partie) (Roma: Nell'Instituto Poligra Rico Dello Stato, 1933), 294, 342; Mikha'il Mishaqa, *Mashad al-'iyan*, p. 25.

34. *Economic History of the Middle East, 1800–1914*, p. 209, estimated at about 3,200,000 the population of Palestine, Syria, and Lebanon by 1921–22, after losses from the war and changes of frontiers. Although the population increase of Syria in that period was probably less marked than that of Egypt, the population growth of Syria in the nineteenth century was a fact that was checked only by the heavy emigration that occurred between the 1860s and 1914: ibid., p. 210. See also ibid., pp. 220, 269–273; *A Handbook of Syria (including Palestine)*, pp. 175–192.

35. Chevallier, *La société du Mont Liban*, chaps. 2, 4; Dominique Chevallier, "Aspects sociaux de la question d'Orient: Aux origines des troubles agraires libanais en 1858," *Annales: Economies, Sociétés, Civilizations*, 14 (1959), 37–38; Youssef Courbage et Philippe Fargues, *La situation démographique au Liban*, Publications de l'Université Libanaise, Section des études philosophiques et sociales (Beyrouth: Imprimerie Catholique, 1974), II, 9–14; Toufic Touma, *Paysans et institutions féodales ches les Druzes et le Maronites du Liban du XVIIe siècle à 1914*, Publications de l'Université Libanaise, Section des études historiques, 20, (Beirut: Imprimerie Catholique, 1971), I, 221–223; *A Handbook of Syria* (including Palestine), pp. 182ff.

36. Guys, *Beyrout et le Liban*, I, 38, 225, 172; Michaud and Poujoulat, *Correspondance d'Orient*, VII, 67, 81; Lamartine, *Voyage en Orient*, I, 123–124, 203, 429; Viscount Castlereagh, *A Journey to Damascus: Through Egypt, Nubia, Arabia, Petrae, Palestine, and Syria* (London: Henri Colburn, 1847), p. 297; Spencer, *The East*, p. 481; Urquhart, *The Lebanon*, II, 275; Rev. J. L. Porter, *Five Years in Damascus* (London: John Murray, 1855), I, 3, 5; Haydar, *Lubnan*, new ed., III, 591ff., 656–657; Shaykh Tannus al-Shidyaq, *Akhbar al a'yan fi jabal Lubnan* (1859), ed. Fuad E. Bustany, new ed., Publications de l'Université Libanaise, Section des études historiques, 19, (Beirut: Imprimerie Catholique, 1970), II, 400.

37. Volney, *Voyage en Egypte et en Syrie*, p. 241. See also Haydar Ahmad al-Shihabi, *Tarikh Ahmad Pasha al-Jazzar*, ed. Antunius Shibli and Ignatius 'Abduh Khalifa (Beirut: Maktaba Antoine, 1955), pp. 50ff.

38. When al-Jazzar's oppression drove out most of the importers of Damascus, they went to Aleppo and to Mount Lebanon: Mikha'il al-Dimashqi, *Tarikh*, p. 13. When the Mishaqa family lost all their possessions at the hands of al-Jazzar in Tyre, they turned to Egypt and to Mount Lebanon: Mikha'il Mishaqa, *Mashhad al'iyan*, pp. 7–8. In the same way, Elias Edde, who was in the service of al-Jazzar, asked the pasha for permission to go to Beirut. But after he arrived in Beirut he took his family and fled to the Mountain: Haydar, *Tarikh Ahmad Pasha al-Jazzar*, p. 90. When the Atiyya brothers left Dayr al-Qamar to do business in 1797, they went to Egypt: Mikha'il Mishaqa, *Mashhad al-'iyan*, p. 50. Beirut appears to have been neither safe enough in the hands of al-Jazzar nor important enough for many merchants to do business there.

39. The Bustros papers mention that the family left Beirut seeking refuge at al-Khariba near Shwayfat in Mount Lebanon during Bonaparte's siege of Acre in 1797–98 (chap. 2) and refer to the fact that others did the same. Others had been discouraged from remaining in the city earlier. See, for example, Haydar, *Tarikh Ahmad Pasha al-Jazzar*, p. 103, for 1205 H/1791 A.D. See also Baron de Tott, *Mémoires du Baron de Tott, sur les Turcs et les Tartares* (Amsterdam, 1785), p. 89.

40. Le Baron de Boislecomte au Ministre, September 1, 1833, quoted by Georges Douin, *La mission du Baron de Boislecomte*, p. 252; Guys, *Beyrout et le Liban*, I, 201; William R. Polk, *The Opening of South Lebanon 1788–1840* (Cambridge: Harvard University Press, 1963), p. 72.

41. Bustros papers; Mikha'il Mishaqa, *Mashhad al-'iyan*, p. 72; Kamal S. Salibi, *The Modern History of Lebanon*, p. 24. The immigration in question seems to have occurred around 1810.

42. Paul Saba, "The Creation of the Lebanese Economy: Economic Growth in the Nineteenth and Early Twentieth Centuries," *Essays on the Crisis in Lebanon*, ed. Roger Owen (London: Ithaca Press, 1976), p. 5; Bustros papers; Tannus al-Shidyaq, *Akhbar al-a'yan*, new ed., pp. 438–439; Haydar, *Lubnan*, new ed., III, 779–780ff. In the edition used for Shidyaq's *Akhbar al-a'yan*, the raid is recorded as having taken place in 1826, while in the edition used for Haydar's *Lubnan*, the raid is attributed to 1825. See also note 31 above. The Bustros papers refer to losses incurred by merchants under 'Abdullah Pasha; N.A.E., 235/191, 29 Muharram 1249/1832, refers to "the enormous losses" incurred by the holders of the concession of customs.

43. Chevallier, *La société du Mont Liban*, chap. 13. esp. pp. 196–197; Dominique Chevallier, "Western Development and Eastern Crisis in the Mid-Nineteenth Century: Syria Confronted with the European Economy," *Beginnings of Modernization in the Middle East*, pp. 205–222; Smiliyanskaya, "Razlozhenie feodalnikh otnoshenii v Sirii i Livane v Seredine XIX v" (The Disintegration of Feudal Relations in Syria and Lebanon in the Middle of the Nineteenth Century), trans. in *Economic History of the Middle East, 1800–*

1914, pp. 234–247; I. M. Smiliyanskaya, *al-Harakat al-fallahiyya fi Lubnan*, trans. Adnan Jamus, ed. Salim Yusuf (Beirut: Dar al-Farabi, 1972), part I. Note that although Issawi, "Middle East Economic Development, 1815–1914: The General and the Specific," *Studies in the Economic History of the Middle East*, p. 405, seemed to doubt that there was a general impoverishment of Syria in the 1840s and 1850s, as depicted by Chevallier and Smilianskaya, he still believed that if a decline of levels of living had indeed taken place, it probably had done so in the towns.

44. Kayat, *A Voice from Lebanon*, p. 274.

45. Guys, *Beyrout et le Liban*, I, 227.

46. Mikha'il Mishaqa, *Mashhad al-'iyan*, pp. 144–145, 131, etc.; Adel Ismail, *Histoire du Liban du XVII siècle à nos jours*, IV: *Redressement et déclin du féodalisme libanais (1840–1861)* (Beirut: Harb Bijjani, 1958), p. 45.

47. F.O. 195/127, Moore-Ponsonby, No. 4, 3–4–1837; ibid., Moore-Ponsonby, No. 7, 16–6–1837; F.O. 226/68, "Report," 20–6–1837. N.A.E., 236/23, 4 Safar 1248/1832; ibid., 236/42, 8, Safar 1248/1892: 40 builders and 10 stone masons were requested from Beirut, the number of builders being larger than from any other town listed; ibid., 236/96, 17 Safar 1248/1832; ibid., 247/201, 22 Rabi' II 1249/1833. F.O. 195/127, Moore-Ponsonby, No. 1, 26–8–1835: 50 youths from Beirut were to go to work in public manufactures in the neighborhood of Tyre. Masons and builders from Beirut were sent also to work on Egyptian projects elsewhere: note 32 above; Haydar, *Lubnan*, new ed., III, 857.

5. Population Change

1. *Palestine and Syria: Handbook for Travellers* (Leipzig: Karl Baedeker, 1876), p. 441; *Palestine and Syria: With Routes through Mesopotamia and Babylonia and the Island of Cyprus. Handbook for Travellers*, 5th ed. (Leipzig: Karl Baedeker, 1912), p. 282.

2. Etienne de Vaumas, "La répartition confessionnelle au Liban et l'équilibre de l'Etat Libanais," *Revue de géographie Alpine*, 43, fasc. 3 (1955), 540. Said Chehabe-Ed-Dine, *Géographie humaine de Beyrouth*, p. 223; Baer, *Population and Society in the Arab East*, p. 113. Baer mentions that the Shi'i areas of south Lebanon and al-Biqa' were also included in Greater Lebanon.

3. Muhammad Taha al-Wali, *Tarkikh al-masajid wa-l-jawami' al-shar'iyya fi Bayrut*, part I (Beirut: Dar al-Kutub, 1973), pp. 21–24; Chevallier, *La société du Mont Liban*, p. 52; Dominique Chevallier, "Signes de Beyrouth en 1834," *Bulletin d'Etudes Orientales*, 25 (1972), 211.

4. *Les voyages du Seigneur de Villamont*, Chevalier de l'Ordre de Jierusalem Gentilhomme Ordinaire de la Chambre du Roy, rev. ed. (Lyon: Claude Lariot, 1607), p. 377: Turks, Moors, Christians of different denominations, and Jews live in Beirut: George Sandys, *A Relation of a Journey Begun An. Dom. 1610*, 2nd ed. (London: W. Barett, 1621), p. 212, mentions Christians, Jews and foreign merchants in Beirut.

5. *Memoires du Chevalier d'Arvieux* (Envoyé Extraordinaire du Roy à la Porte, Consul d'Alep, d'Alger, de Tripoli, et autres Echelles du Levant) contenant ses Voyages . . . recueillis de ses Mémoires originaux, et mis en order avec reflexions par le R. P. Jean Baptiste Labat (Paris: Charles-Jean-Baptiste Delespine, 1735), p. 343; Lettre du P. Poiresson au P. Provincial de Paris, chap. 3: "Etat du Pays," quoted by Le Père Antoine Rabbath, *Documents inédits pour servir à l'histoire du Christianisme en Orient* (Paris: A. Picart, 1907), I, 44.

6. Richard Pococke, *A Description of the East and some other Countries*, vol. II, part 1: *Observations on Palestine or the Holy Land, Syria, Mesopotamia, Cyprus and Candia* (London: W. Bowyer, 1745), p. 91; W. G. Browne, *Travels in Africa, Egypt, and Syria, From the Year 1792 to 1798* (London: T. Cadell Jr. and W. Davies Strand, T. N. Longman and O. Rees, Paternoster Row, 1799), pp. 376–377.

7. Volney, *Voyage en Egypte et en Syrie*, pp. 290, 241; Tott, *Memoires*, p. 89.

8. Asad Rustum, "Bayrut fi 'ahd Ibrahim Pasha al-Masri: wa a'mal al-amir Mahmud Nami fiha," *al-Kulliya*, 13 (1927), 130.

9. Jessup, *Fifty-Three Years in Syria*, I, 25; Michaud et Poujoulat, *Correspondance d'Orient*, VII, 69, who noted also the presence of a few Frenchmen; Sir A. Henry Layard, *Autobiography and Letters from his Childhood until his Appointment as H. M. Ambassador at Madrid*, ed. by William N. Brure, with a chapter on his parliamentary career by Sir Arthur Otway (London: John Murray, 1903), I, 251.

10. Delaroière, *Voyage en Orient*, p. 47; Blondel, *Deux ans en Syrie et en Palestine*, p. 20; Guys, *Beyrouth et le Liban*, I, 8–9.

11. John Carne, *Syria, the Holy Land, Asia Minor, etc., Illustrated* (London: Fisher, 1836–1838), II, 9.

12. Guys, *Esquisse*, table: "Pachalik de Seyde"; Urquhart, *The Lebanon*, II, 190.

13. Laorty-Hadji, *La Syrie*, p. 33; Taylor, *La Syrie*, p. 25; Tannus al-Shidyaq, *Akhbar al-a'yan*, new ed., p. 13; F.O. 195/390. Calvert-Redcliffe, No. 8, 24–6–1853. Antun Dahir al-'Aqiqi's manuscript mentioned that even if one excluded the refugees who came to Beirut in 1860, the Christians of Beirut were more numerous than its Muslims at that time: *Lebanon in the Last Years of Feudalism, 1840–1868: A Contemporary Account by Antun Dahir al-Aqiqi and Other Documents*, trans. Malcolm H. Kerr, American University of Beirut: Faculty of Arts and Sciences Publications, Oriental Series, No. 33 (Beirut: Catholic Press, 1959), p. 69.

14. 5,979 Muslim males as against 7,183 non-Muslim males. See Table 2. These official statistics were quoted in *Palestine and Syria* (Leipzig, 1876), p. 441.

15. F.O. 195/1027, Jago, "Ottoman Conservatism in Syria"; Lortet, *La Syrie d'aujourd'hui*, p. 74.

16. Jules Hoche, *Le pays de croisades* (Paris: Corbeil, 1883–1885), p. 583; Thomson, *The Land and the Book* (New York, 1886), p. 49; A. E. Krimsky,

Letters from Lebanon 1896–98), quoted in translation from the Russian in *al-Nahar*, May 5, 1975, p. 7. See also F.O. 195/1886, Drummond May-Currie, 24-8-1895, where it is mentioned that in Beirut "the Christians form a large majority of the population"; *L'Orient à vol d'oiseau*, p. 323.

17. Baedeker, *Palestine and Syria*, 5th ed. (Leipzig, 1912), p. 282; *A Handbook of Syria (Including Palestine)*, p. 393; *Salname wilayat Bayrut 1326* (Ottoman Yearbook for the Vilayet of Beirut, 1908), p. 227.

18. Haut Commissariat de la République Française en Syrie et au Liban, *La Syrie et le Liban en 1922* (Paris: Emile Larose, 1922), p. 58.

19. Georges Samné, *La Syrie* (Paris: Editions Bossard, 1920), p. 285; al-Wali, *Tarikh al-masajid wa-l-jawami'*, p. 116. The proportion of Shi'is in Beirut, which was insignificant in the nineteenth and early twentieth centuries, had grown to 6 percent of Beirut's population by the 1950s: Vaumas, "La répartition confessionnelle au Liban et l'équilibre de l'état Libanais," p. 547. The number of Shi'is in Beirut continued to grow after the 1950s and until the 1970s and early 1980s, when political insecurity in south Lebanon encouraged more and more of its heavily Shi'i population to move to the suburbs of Beirut and elsewhere. Shi'is have also come to Beirut and its suburbs from other areas of Lebanon. One of the rare studies with information on Shi'i settlement in greater Beirut is by Khury, *From Village to Suburbs*.

20. Chevallier, *La société du Mont Liban*, chaps. 4, 5; Courbage et Fargues, *La situation démographique du Liban*, II, 11, table I.1; F.O. 276/158, Dufferin-Kennedy, Beyrout, 1861; F.O. 406/10, Dufferin-Russell, No. 7, 14-9-1860, enclosed in Dufferin-Bulwer, 13-9-1860; F.O. 195/658, Dufferin-Bulwer, No. 120, 15-2-1861; F.O. 195/658, Dufferin-Bulwer, No. 126, 24-2-1861; U.S./4, Johnson-Secretary of State, 9-3-1861.

21. *Memoirs du Chevalier d'Arvieux*, p. 349; *Salname wilayat Bayrut 1326* (1908), p. 227; Jessup, *Fifty-Three Years in Syria*, I, 227.

22. *Salname wilayat Bayrut 1326* (1908), p. 227.

23. Salibi, *The Modern History of Lebanon*, p. 24.

24. F.O. 195/194, Rose-Bankhead, No. 1, 6-1-1842.

25. F.O. 195/194, Rose-Bankhead, No. 1, 6-1-1842; F.O. 226/90, Aberdeen-Rose, No. 5, Foreign Office, 6-6-1845; ibid., F.O. 226/94, to Aarif Agha, enclosed in a letter to Stratford Canning of 6-6-1846. F.O. 226/96, Thomson-Rose, 29-7-1847; F.O. 226/96, Rose-Cowley, 30-7-1847; F.O. 226/98, Wood-Palmerston, 1-7-1847; F.O. 226/98, Palmerston-Wood, No. 1, 4-8-1847; F.O. 226/98, Cowley-Rose, No. 25, Constantinople, 21-11-1847 and enclosure; F.O. 226/98, "Extract from a Memorandum respecting the persecuted Hasbeiya Protestants forwarded by the American Missionaries at Beirut," Beyrout, February, 1847. "Petition of the Hasbeyan Protestants to the Sublime Porte," in Wellesley-Rose, 27-4-1847; F.O. 195/351, Rose-Palmerston, No. 60, 13-12-1850; ibid., Rose-Stratford Canning, No. 47, 31-10-1850.

26. F.O. 226/83, Rose-Stratford Canning, No. 24, 30-4-1843; F.O. 195/221, Rose-Stratford Canning, No. 24, 30-4-1843.

27. F.O. 195/351, Rose-Stratford Canning, No. 47, 31-10-1850; ibid., Rose-Palmerston, No. 60, 13-12-1850.

28. There are discrepancies (but only four) between the number given under the village or town headings and the totals given at the end, apparently because names were added after the total was made. To the list I have added the districts of the different places mentioned, to show the variety of the areas from which the refugees came. The reconstruction of the districts is not complete because some of the places mentioned were too small to be on any of the maps I consulted. For a reconstruction of the districts, the following sources were consulted: Toufic Touma, *Paysans et institutions féodales*, II, 780–782, and maps; Chevallier, *La société du Mont Liban*, plate 5; F.O. 195/1980 (1897), "Carte des Kaimmakamiets el-Chouf et Mudiriet Deir el-Kamar."

29. F.O. 195/655, Moore-Eardley, 14–8–1860; ibid., Moore-Russell, No. 38, 31–8–1860.

30. F.O. 406/10, Report of 22–8–1860, in Moore-Russell, No. 38, 31–8–1860; ibid., F.O. 195/655, Moore-Bulwer, No. 33, 9–6–1860; Tibawi, *Modern History of Syria*, p. 129.

31. F.O. 195/656, Rev. Robson-Dufferin, Damascus, 1–10–1860; F.O. 195/657, Dufferin-Bulwer, 15–11–1860. Refugees from Hasbayya and Rashayya are also mentioned in ibid., Moore-Bulwer, 29–8–1860, in Moore-Russell, No. 37, 31–8–1860; ibid., "Report by Mr. Graham on the Conditions of the Christians in the Districts of Hasbeya and Rasheya," in Brant-Russell, No. 13, Damascus, 13–8–1860; F.O. 195/656, 4e séance, 15–10–1860, in Dufferin's dispatch, No. 34, 26–10–1860; F.O. 195/657, 7e séance, 30–10–1860, in Dufferin-Bulwer, No. 40, 3–11–1860; ibid., No. 57, Dufferin-Bulwer, 15–11–1860.

32. F.O. 406/10, Report, Beirut, 22–8–1860, in Moore-Russell, No. 38, 31–11–1860: "Long caravans from Damascus block up our streets." Jessup, *Fifty-Three Years in Syria*, I, 207, seems to base the 11,000 figure on the fact that as many names were added to the lists of the Anglo-American Relief Committee after the events of 1860 in Damascus. However, the 11,000 may have taken more than a month to arrive in Beirut. A British report of September 1860 estimated at 5,000 the number of Christian Damascenes who had left for Beirut; F.O. 195/656, Dufferin-Bulwer, No. 10, 21–9–1860. Later reports indicate that the flow to Beirut continued thereafter, as shown in the next notes and in the text. Jessup's figure may thus be more representative of the total number of Damascene refugees in Beirut than it is of the number of refugees who came in the course of a month. The arrival of 3,000 in one day is mentioned in F.O. 406/10, Fraser-Russell, No. 2, 8–8–1860.

33. Ibid., Fraser-Russell, No. 10, Damascus, 20–10–1860, and other reports; ibid., Dufferin-Bulwer, 26–10–1860; ibid., Dufferin-Dufferin-Bulwer, 1–11–1860, No. 21, 4–11–1860.

34. Selim Debbas and Antoine Debbas made Dimitri Debbas' memoirs available to me. They also provided me with all additional information I possess on the family and on its arrival and settlement in Beirut.

35. The house in question was located in the Bulad quarter of Damascus near Bab Tuma, where the Christian quarter was located.

36. Kamal Salibi, "The 1860 Upheaval in Damascus as Seen by al-Sayyid

Muhammad Abu'l-Su'ud al-Hasibi, Notable and Later *Naqib al-Ashraf* of the City," *Beginnings of Modernization in the Middle East*, p. 188, n. 19, pointed out that July 9 is the date generally accepted for the outbreak of hostilities in Damascus in 1860. Salibi adds that Hasibi gives the dates variously as July 7 and 11 and indicates that it was a Monday. In the same way, Dimitri Debbas mentions that it was on a Monday and specifies that it was in the afternoon, but the date he gives is June 27. F.O. 406/10, Robson's Memorandum, in Dufferin-Russell, No. 187, 23-9-1860, reported that trouble started about two o'clock p.m. on the July 9. N. Eliseeff, "Dimashk," *Encyclopaedia of Islam*, B. Lewis et al., new ed. (Leiden: E. J. Brill, 1965), II, 288, gives the date as July 12.

37. Bab al-Barid was at the western entrance of the Umayyad Mosque of Damascus: Salibi, "The 1860 Upheaval in Damascus," p. 194. See also Eliseeff's "Dimashk," monument 6 on the map facing p. 288.

38. Salibi, "The 1860 Upheaval in Damascus," p. 196, n. 76, notes that 'Abdallah ibn Sa'id al-Halabi lived from 1808 to 1870, was a prominent Damascene notable, and a leading scholar of Islam. For a biography of al-Halabi, Salibi cites al-Bitar, Hulyat, 2: 1008-1010. Shaykh 'Abdallah al-Halabi was singled out for attention and described as "a most influential Moslem" in F.O. 406/10, Dufferin-Bulwer, 26-10-1860, in Dufferin-Russell, No. 20, 26-10-1860. Robson's Memorandum, in Dufferin-Russell, No. 187, 23-9-1860, related a rumor that Shaykh 'Abdallah al-Halabi had incited the mob to attack Christians. Both Hasibi and Dimitri Debbas mention that the Christians were brought to the house of the Shaykh for protection. Yet he was one of the 230 Muslim notables arrested after the events of July 1860 in Damascus.

39. F.O. 406/10, Brant-Bulwer, Damascus, 16-8-1860, in Brant-Russell, No. 15, Damascus, 25-8-1860; ibid., Fraser-Russell, No. 2, 8-8-1860; ibid., Brant-Bulwer, 16-8-1860, in Brant-Russell, No. 15, Damascus, 25-8-1860.

40. After fighting the French conquest of Algeria and his ensuing exile from Algeria, Emir 'Abd al-Qadir had settled in Damascus where he rescued a great number of Christians during the events of July 1860. As for the district of the Maydan, it was located at the extreme southern limits of the city of Damascus. In the medieval and early modern periods, it consisted of a three-kilometer area of cereal warehouses and Mamluk mausoleums: Elisseeff, "Damashk," p. 287. By the time of the incidents of 1860, it was traditionally known for its troublemaking mob: Salibi, "The 1860 Upheaval in Damascus," p. 195, n. 67.

41. The same distinction is made in Salibi, "The 1860 Upheaval in Damascus," p. 196; F.O. 406/10, Bulwer-Russell, No. 476, Therapia, 1-8-1860.

42. Madrasat Thalathat Aqmar, or College of the Three Doctors, was named after Saint Basil the Great, Saint Gregory the Theologian, and Saint John Chrysostom. It was located in the Ashrafiyya quarter of Beirut in the eastern quarter of town and enjoyed a high reputation.

43. The house in question was located in the eastern section of Beirut, in

the elegant part of the Ashrafiyya quarter of town.

44. Jessup, *Fifty-Three Years in Syria*, I, 182, 186, 190, 207, 238. U.S./4, Johnson-Secretary of State, 27–6–1860; F.O. 407/10, Report of the Anglo-American Relief Committee in Beirut, in Moore-Russell, No. 38, 31–8–1860.

45. Jessup, *Fifty-Three Years in Syria*, I, 191; 406/10, Fraser-Russell, No. 1, 2–8–1860; ibid., "Report by Mr. Graham on the Condition of the Christians in the Districts of Hasbeya and Rasheye," in Brant-Russell, No. 13, Damascus, 13–8–1860; F.O. 195/655, Moore-Bulwer, No. 41, 26–6–1860; U.S./4, Johnson-Secretary of State, 27–6–1860, 14–7–1860, 28–7–1860.

46. Churchill, *The Druzes and the Maronites*, p. 198. See also F.O. 195/655, Moore-Russell, No. 19, 5–7–1860; ibid., Moore-Russell, No. 20, 13–17–1860.

47. F.O. 195/656, "Notification to the Christians of Damascus residing at Beirut," in Dufferin-Bulwer, No. 10, 21–9–1860; F.O. 195/657, No. 10, 21–9–1860; F.O. 195/657, "7e séance. Séance du 30 octobre 1860," in Dufferin-Bulwer, No. 40, 3–11–1860; F.O. 406/10, Dufferin-Abro Effendi, 19–1–1860, in Dufferin-Russell, No. 8, 21–9–1860; ibid., "Notes of a Conversation with Fuad Pasha by Major Fraser at Damascus, 3–9–1860," in Fraser-Russell, No. 7, Damascus, 3–9–1860.

48. F.O. 195/866, Rogers-Lyons, No. 17, 12–8–1867. An earlier dispatch had referred to a rumor about a massacre of Christians spreading in Damascus and even in Beirut and causing panic among Damascene Christians: ibid., Eldridge-Lyons, No. 13, 31–3–1867. Note, interestingly, that as in 1860 well-to-do and "well-disposed" Muslims were described as taking steps on their own to prevent a recurrence of sectarian trouble: ibid., Rogers-Lyons, No. 17, 12–4–1867.

6. The Foreign Entrepreneurs

1. L. Girard, "Transport," *The Cambridge Economic History*, VI: *The Industrial Revolution and After: Income, Population and Technological Change*, part I, ed. H. J. Habakkuk and M. Postan (Cambridge: The University Press, 1966), pp. 246–249; *Economic History of the Middle East*, p. 207; Charles Issawi, "British Trade and the Rise of Beirut, 1830–1860," *The International Journal of Middle Eastern Studies*, 7 (January 1977), 97; Chevallier, *La société du Mont Liban*, pp. 183–184; John Kelman, *From Damascus to Palmyra*, (London: Adams and Charles Black, 1908), pp. 8–9; J. Lewis Farley, *The Resources of Turkey: Considered with Special Reference to the Profitable Investment of Capital in the Ottoman Empire* (London: Longman, Green, Longman, 1863), p. 209; A. P., Dossier 1906; F.O. 195/127, Moore-Ponsonby, No. 4, 9–2–1839; ibid., 195/260, "Notice sur le service de paquettes à vapeur de l'administration des postes de France," Wallis-Rose, in Rose Aberdeen, No. 73, 28–12–1845; ibid., 195/557, Moore-Redcliffe, No. 13, 6–3–1857, and enclosure.

2. Chevallier, *La société du Mont Liban*, pp. 188–189.

3. Boutros Labaki, "Sériciculture et commerce extérieur: Deux aspects de l'impact europeen sur l'économie du Liban et de son environnement arabe en fin de période ottomane (1840–1914)" (Thèse de Doctorat, Paris, Ecole Pratique des Hautes Etudes, 1974), chap. 5; Issawi, "British Trade and the Rise of Beirut," pp. 94–95; Chevallier, *La société du Mont Liban*, pp. 196–197.

4. Chevallier, *La société du Mont Liban*, pp. 189–199; Chevallier, "Western Development and Eastern Crisis," pp. 210–217; Issawi, "Middle East Economic Development, 1815–1914," *Studies in the Economic History of the Middle East*, p. 403; *Economic History of the Middle East*, pp. 208–209; Issawi, "British Trade and the Rise of Beirut," pp. 94–95.

5. A. Ruppin, *Syrien als Wirthschaftsgebiet* (Berlin, 1917), pp. 132ff.

6. Labaki, "Sériciculture," pp. 186–187, 377–378, 387.

7. Smiliyanskaya, in *Economic History of the Middle East*, pp. 227ff.; Labaki, *Sériciculture*, pp. 38–39, 343, 380ff; E. Weakley, "Report on the Conditions and Prospects of British Trade in Syria," *Great Britain*, Accounts and Papers, 87 (1911), quoted in *Economic History of the Middle East*, pp. 280–281; Saba, "The Creation of the Lebanese Economy," p. 18; F.O. 195/221, Aberdeen-Rose, No. 22, 5-3-1843; Chevallier, "Western Impact and Eastern Crisis," pp. 214–215; Dominique Chevallier, "Lyon et la Syrie en 1919: Les bases d'une intervention," *Revue historique*, 224 (October-December 1960), 285–287.

8. Haydar, *Lubnan*, new ed., II and III; *Memoires de Chevalier d'Arvieux*, pp. 334–338; Guys, *Beyrout et le Liban*, I, 55, 170, 225; Smiliyanskaya, in *Economic History of the Middle East*, p. 229; Gaston Ducousso, *L'industrie de la soie en Syrie* (Paris: Librairie Maritime et Coloniale Challamel, 1918), pp. 53–60.

9. Chevallier, "Lyon et la Syrie en 1919," pp. 287–289; Ducousso, *L'industrie de la soie*, pp. 64–74; Labaki, "Sériciculture," pp. 23–30; Weakley, "Report," pp. 280–281.

10. Chevallier, "Lyon et la Syrie"; Chevallier, *La société du Mont Liban*, chap. 14; Smiliyanskaya, in *Economic History of the Middle East*, p. 343; Ducousso, *L'industrie de la soie*, pp. 123–128, 133; Labaki, "Sericiculture," pp. 80–81; Isma'il Haqqi, *Lubnan: Mabahith 'ilmiyya wa ijtima'iyya*, ed. Fu'ad Ifram al-Bustani (Beirut: al-Matba'at al-Kathulikiyya, 1970), II, 439.

11. Haqqi, *Lubnan*, II, 439–440; D. S. Landes, *Bankers and Pashas: International Finance and Economic Imperialism in Egypt* (New York: Harper Torchbooks, 1958), pp. 195–196, for information on Pastre Frères; Labaki, "Sériciculture," p. 88; Chevallier, *La société du Mont Liban*, pp. 210–221; Chevallier, "Lyon et la Syrie," pp. 292–293; Dominique Chevallier, "Aspects sociaux de la question d'Orient: Aux origines des troubles agraires Libanais en 1858," *Annales*, 14 (1959), p. 53.

12. Ducousso, *L'industrie de la soie*, pp. 125, 127; F.O. 195/1581, Eyres-White, No. 19, 3-5-1887; Noël Verney and George Dambmann, *Les puissances étrangères dans le Levant en Syrie et en Palestine* (Paris: Guillaumin, 1900), p. 648; Chevallier, "Lyon et la Syrie," p. 292.

13. Chevallier, "Lyon et la Syrie," pp. 292–293.

14. Labaki, "Sériciculture," pp. 44–45. On the Ottoman Bank: F.O. 195/460, 1854–57; F.O. 196/519, Moore-Redcliffe, No. 59, 5–10–1856.

15. Chevallier, *La société du Mont Liban*, pp. 233–237; Chevallier, "Lyon et la Syrie," pp. 295–296; Chevallier, "Aspects sociaux de la question d'Orient," p. 53; Smiliyanskaya, *al-Harakat al-fallahiyya fi Lubnan*, chap. 1, Smiliyanskaya, in *Economic History of the Middle East*, p. 234.

16. Hourani, "Lebanon from Feudalism to Modern State," *Middle Eastern Studies*, 2 (April 1966), 256–263; Chevallier, *La société du Mont Liban*; Chevallier, "Aspects sociaux de la question d'Orient."

17. R. Tresse, "Histoire de la route de Beyrouth à Damas (1857–1892)," *La Géographie*, 64 (1936), 227–229; Charles Issawi, "Assymetrical Development and Transport in Egypt, 1800–1914," *Beginnings of Modernization in the Middle East*, p. 396; Roger le Tourneau, *Les villes musulmanes de l'Afrique du Nord* (Alger: La Maison des Livres, 1957), p. 75; Richard W. Bulliet, *The Camel and the Wheel* (Cambridge: Harvard University Press, 1975), chap. 1; F.O. 195/127, Moore-Ponsonby, 22–6–1838: robbery of muleteers traveling from Damascus to Beirut at Wadi al-Qurn; F.O. 195/727, Moore-Russell, No. 1, 30–1–1862, in Moore-Bulwer, No. 5, 31–1–1862: several robberies in Wadi al-Qurn; Haydar, *Lubnan*, new ed., III, 580, 583, on the insecurity of roads.

18. Tresse, "Histoire de la route de Beyrouth à Damas," p. 235; A.P., General de Dumast, "Une réalisation française au Levant, le port de Beyrouth," communication à l'Académie de Marine, Paris, 25–1–1857; J. Lewis Farley, *Two Years in Syria*, 2nd ed. (London: Saunders and Ottley, 1859), p. 34.

19. F.O. 195/760, Moore-Russell, No. 9, 15–1–1863, in Moore-Erskine, No. 8, 23–1–1863; A. P., Baron Maxime de Dumast, "Le port de Beyrouth: Développement historique," Conférence donnée au Centre d'Etudes Géographiques du Proche et du Moyen Orient," 23–11–1951, et au Rotary Club de Beyrouth, 17–1–1952, mentions that the Beirut-Damascus road was 110 kilometers long. Eleuthère Eleftériadès, *Les chemins de fer en Syrie et au Liban: Etude historique financière et économique* (Beirut: Imprimerie Catholique, 1943), p. 39, specifies that the Beirut-Damascus road was 111 kilometers long; Tresse, "Histoire de la route de Beyrouth à Damas," p. 236, that the road was to be 112 kilometers long.

20. Lortet, *La Syrie d'aujourd'hui*, p. 88. Eleftériadès, *Les chemins de fer*, pp. 39–40; F.O. 195/927, Eldridge-Elliot, No. 41, 11–11–1869: mounted couriers ensured communication between Damascus and Beirut until 1863; when a regular stagecoach began to run daily on the new road, and the British, French, and Italian consulates made arrangements with the Compagnie Ottomane de la Route de Beyrouth à Damas for the correspondence of the Baghdad mail as well as all correspondence between Beirut and Damascus.

21. F.O. 195/866, Eldridge-Lyons, No. 59, 9–6–1866; Tresse, "Histoire de la route de Beyrouth à Damas," pp. 238–239, 249; Eleftériadès, *Les chemins de fer*, pp. 39–43 and annexe 1; F.O. 195/927, Eldridge-Elliot, No. 16, 27–4–1869; Lortet, *La Syrie d'aujourd'hui*, p. 88.

22. Eleftériadès, *Les chemins de fer*, pp. 40, 42; Labaki, "Sériciculture," p. 104; F.O. 195/760, Rogers-Erskine, Damascus, 15–1–1863; F.O. 195–1447,

Eldridge-Dufferin.

23. Eleftériadès, *Les chemins de fer*, p. 43; M. Hecker, "Die Eisenbahnen in der asiatischen Türkei," *Avec für Eisenbahnwesen* (Berlin), 37 (1914), 789ff, as quoted in translation in *Economic History of the Middle East*, p. 250.

24. F.O. 195/1683, Eyres-White, No. 57, 29-10-1890. On the Haifa-Damascus railway, see F.O. 195/1761, Hallward-Ford, No. 52, 31-8-1892; ibid., Hallward-Ford, No. 71, 15-12-1892, and other reports.

25. Eleftériadès, *Les chemins de fer*, pp. 43–45; Hecker, *Economic History of the Middle East*, p. 251.

26. Lewis Gaston Leary, *Syria: The Land of Lebanon* (New York: McBride, Neast, 1913), p. 60.

27. A.P., Dumast, "Le Port de Beyrouth: Développement Historique," and "Une réalisation française au Levant, le Port de Beyrouth"; Jacques de Monicault, *Le Port de Beyrouth et l'économie des pays du Levant sous mandat français* (Paris: Librairie Technique et Economique, 1936), pp. 20–21.

28. A.P., Dumast, "Le Port de Beyrouth: Développement historique," and "Une réalisation française au Liban." Salim Malhama, the first Ottoman subject to be on the port company's administrative council, was the father of Halim Malhama, president of the company in the 1950s.

29. Ibid.

30. Leary, *Syria*, p. 30.

31. Vaux, *La Palestine*, 27; *L'Orient à vol d'oiseau*, p. 323; Rev. Jabez Burns, *Help-Book for Travellers to the East: Including Egypt, Palestine, Turkey, Greece and Italy* (London: Cook's Tourist Office, 1870), pp. 114–116; Hoche, *Le pays des croisades*, II, 583; Kelman, *From Damascus to Palmyra*, p. 11; Lortet, *La Syrie d'aujourd'hui*, p. 66; *L'Orient à vol d'oiseau*, p. 325.

32. Heyd, *Histoire du commerce du Levant*, I, 174, 320; II, 573, 658–686, 700; Nicola A. Ziadeh, *Urban Life in Syria: Under the Early Mamluks* (Beirut: American Press, 1953), p. 132; *Palestine Under the Moslems: A Description of Syria and the Holy Land from A.D. 650 to 1500* (Beirut: Khayat's, 1965), p. 410, quoting Idrisi; Rey, *Les colonies franques de Syrie*, p. 213.

33. Ghillebert de Lannoy, cited by La Broquière, *Voyage d'outremer*, p. 30.

34. René Ristelhueber, *Traditions françaises au Liban* (Paris: Felix Alcan, 1918), p. 60.

35. Landes, *Bankers and Pashas*, pp. 90–91; D. C. M. Platt, *The Cinderella Service: British Consuls since 1825* (London: Longmans, 1971), pp. 136ff.; Chevallier, *La société du Mont Liban*, p. 207. The Young Turks abrogated the capitulations for Italians in 1911 and then unilaterally on September 9, 1914: Feroz Ahmad, *The Young Turks: The Committee of Union and Progress in Turkish Politics 1908-1914* (Oxford: Clarendon Press, 1969), pp. 96, 157. At the Lausanne Conference in 1922 and then again under Ataturk, the capitulations and other privileges to foreigners in Turkey were abolished entirely. In Egypt they remained in force until 1937.

36. Ristelhueber, *Traditions françaises au Liban*, pp. 93–94, 97, 128–130; Michel Chebli, *Une histoire du Liban à l'époque des emirs (1635-1841)*

(Beyrouth: Imprimerie Catholique, 1955), p. 53; Ralph Davis, *Aleppo and Devonshire Square: English Traders in the Levant in the Eighteenth Century* (London: Macmillan, 1967), pp. 28–29; *Mémoires du Chevalier d'Arvieux*, pp. 334, 343, 338; Ducousso, *L'industrie de la soie*, pp. 55–56.

37. Hitti, *Lebanon in History*, p. 400; Ristelhueber, *Traditions françaises au Liban*, pp. 134ff.; Chebli, *Une histoire du Liban*, pp. 56–64; *Mémoires du Chevalier d'Arvieux*, p. 344; Douin, *La mission du Baron de Boislecomte*, p. 252; Guys, *Berout et le Liban*, I, 201; F.O. 195/1113, Eldridge-Elliot, No. 2, 17-1-1876; ibid., enclosure, Black-Eldridge, 20-12-1875; Ratib al-Husami, "Tijarat Bayrut wa mahall Bayhum al-tijari" (Beirut's trade and the Bayhum's commercial house; M.A. thesis, American University of Beirut, 1942), pp. 53–54.

38. Guys, *Beyrout de le Liban*, I, 13–14; F.O. 195/221, Rose-Aberdeen, No. 22, 5-3-1843, and enclosures; F.O. 194/194, p. 310ff.; Husami, "Tijarat Bayrut," pp. 53–55; Delaroière, *Voyage en Orient*, p. 49.

39. F.O. 195/127, Moore-Ponsonby, 19-6-1837 and 20-6-1837; F.O. 226/79, Rose-Aberdeen, No. 49, 6-7-1842; F.O. 226/92, Wood-Rose, Damascus, 22-4-1845; F.O. 226/94, Rose-Stratford Canning, No. 6, 1846; F.O. 195/725, Traduction d'une lettre vizirielle au gouverneur, 8 Zilkade 1277, in Moore-Bulwer, No. 7, 21-2-1862; F.O. 195/1153, Eldridge-Jocelyn, No. 20, 3-3-1877; F.O. 195/1369, Eldridge-Dufferin, No. 60, 19-12-1881.

40. F.O. 226/83, Rose-Stratford Canning, No. 24, 30-4-1843; ibid., Rose-Stratford Canning, No. 7, 12-3-1844; F.O. 226/85, Rose-Aberdeen, No. 7, 12-3-1844; F.O. 226/90, unsigned (probably Rose)-Aberdeen, No. 59, 7-11-1845; F.O. 226/101, Rose-Palmerston, No. 40, 26-9-1848; F.O. 195/221, Moore-Stratford Canning, No. 1, 19-1-1843; ibid., Rose-Aberdeen, No. 72, 8-11-1843; F.O. 195/234, Rose-Stratford Canning, No. 1, 6-1-1844; F.O. 195/519, Moore-Redcliffe, 1-3-1848; F.O. 195/657, Dufferin-Bulwer, No. 45, 9-11-1860; ibid., Dufferin-Fraser, 28-11-1860 in Dufferin-Bulwer, No. 69, 28-11-1860; F.O. 195/1369, Eldridge-Dufferin, No. 55, 1-12-1881; ibid., Dickson-Dufferin, No. 40, 28-7-1881; F.O. 195/1447, Eldridge-Wyndham, No. 7, 31-1-1883; ibid., Eldridge-Dufferin, No. 62, 20-10-1883.

41. Véga, *Au pays de la lumière: Notes et impressions d'une voyage en Syrie, en Galilée et à Jérusalem*, 2nd ed. (Paris: Fischbacher, 1912), pp. 70–75; Chevallier, "Lyon et la Syrie," pp. 280–281; K. T. Khairallah, "La Syrie," *Revue du monde musulman*, 19 (June 1912), 55–56; *L'Orient à vol d'oiseau*, pp. 333–337; Burton, *The Inner Life of Syria*, pp. 287–288; F.O. 226/85, Rose-Moore, No. 7, 4-12-1844, with a list of Latin convents, colleges, and schools in Mount Lebanon and Beirut under French protection in 1844.

42. Labaki, "Sériciculture," pp. 40, 96, 224–225.

43. Hoche, *Le Pays des croisades*, II, 584. See also *L'Orient à vol d'oiseau*, p. 325; Vaux, *La Palestine*, p. 486; Véga, *Au pays de la lumière*, pp. 70–75.

44. F.O. 195/1683, Trotter-White, No. 36, 25-6-1890.

45. Ralph Davis, *Aleppo and Devonshire Square*, pp. 26–42; Issawi, "British Trade and the Rise of Beirut," pp. 91–92.

46. F.O. 195/127, Moore-Ponsonby, No. 1, 26-8-1835; ibid., Moore-Ponsonby, No. 3, 13-2-1836; ibid., Moore-Ponsonby, No. 8, 7-4-1836; ibid., Moore-Ponsonby, No. 7, 27-2-1839, and other reports; F.O. 197/700, "For the Census of the Population of the United Kingdom appointed to be taken in April 1861," in Moore's dispatch No. 6, 6-4-1861; F.O. 195/221, Assaad Pasha-Moore, 7th Moharrem 1260, received 27-1-1844; F.O. 195/1613, Eldridge-White, No. 15, 2-5-1888; ibid., Eldridge-White No. 22, 4-6-1888; F.O. 195/1648, Eldridge-White, No. 7, 7-3-1889; F.O. 195/351, "Translation of a Circular Letter from His Excellency Wameck Pasha to Her Britannic Majesty's Acting Consul-General at Beirut," received February 21, 1850, in No. 7, Moore-Stratford Canning, 1-3-1850; Dodge, *The American University at Beirut*, p. 11.

47. Urquhart, *The Lebanon*, II, 190ff.; *Palestine and Syria*, ed. Baedeker (1894), p. 286; Leary, *Syria*, p. 33; F.O. 195/1937, Drummond Hay-Currie, No. 31, 22-4-1896; ibid., Drummond Hay-Currie, No. 33, 30-4-1896, and enclosure; Martindale-Drummond Hay, 27-4-1896; ibid., Drummond Hay-Herbert, No. 45, 23-6-1896.

48. Farley, *The Resources of Turkey*, pp. 214, 219; F.O. 195/519, Moore-Ponsonby, No. 59, 5-10-1856, and enclosures; F.O. 195/700, list of British subjects in 1861 in Moore's No. 6, 6-4-1861. The first manager of the Ottoman Bank in Beirut was Malcolm Lainz Meason from Edinburgh. In 1861, the manager of the bank was Charles William Buchanan from Gloucester, with George Hand from Scottlethorp as accountant; Joly papers, "Notes from Bankers' Almanac editions." The almanac started in 1836. Before 1886, for several years, Dutchesne, Stussy and Company and the Ottoman Bank were listed. In 1872 the Bankers' Almanac named the Chas Heald and Company, probably an error (it should have been Henry Heald).

49. For example, F.O. 195/787, Eldridge-Bulwer, No. 21, 19-3-1864, and enclosure; F.O. 195/1369, Dickson-Dufferin, No. 41, 30-7-1881, and enclosure; F.O. 195/1410, Eldridge-Dufferin, No. 3, 13-1-1882; F.O. 195/1447, Eldridge-Wyndham, No. 29, 30-5-1883, and enclosures; F.O. 195/127, Moore-Ponsonby, 26-8-1835, and other reports; F.O. 195/1201, Eldridge-Layard, No. 30, 25-3-1878, and enclosure; F.O. 195/727, Moore-Bulwer, No. 11, 7-3-1862; F.O. 195/700, List of British subjects in Moore's dispatch No. 6, 6-4-1861; F.O. 195/1480, Eldridge-Dufferin, No. 9, 18-4-1884; F.O. 195/1937, Drummond Hay-Currie, No. 1, 6-1-1896, and enclosure; F.O. 195/1410, Eldridge-Dufferin, No. 67, 16-9-1882; F.O. 195/195, Moore-Stratford Canning, No. 26, 27-9-1847; F.O. 195/260, enclosure in Rose's dispatch No. 10, 1846; F.O. 195/260, Rose-Aberdeen, No. 8, 13-2-1846, and enclosures; F.O. 226/96, Rose-Cowley, No. 33, 18-7-1847; F.O. 195/727, Moore-Bulwer, No. 7, 21-2-1862, and enclosure.

50. F.O. 195/1480, Memorial of British Residents in Beirut to Granville, July 8/13, 1883, in Eldridge-Granville, No. 7, 16-1-1884; F.O. 195/1410, Eldridge-Dufferin, No. 28, 19-5-1882, and enclosure; F.O. 195/994, 1872; F.O. 195/1201, Eldridge-Layard, No. 30, 25-3-1878; F.O. 195/1447, Eldridge-Wyndham, No. 22, 18-4-1883; F.O. 195/1480, Eldridge-Dufferin, No. 9,

18-4-1884; F.O. 195/1937, Drummond Hay-Currie, No. 1, 6-1-1896, and enclosure; F.O. 195/1843, Telegram from Eyres, August 7/8, 1894; ibid., Eyres-Currie, No. 28, 8-8-1894, and other reports; F.O. 195/221, William and Robert Black and Company and Henry Heald and Company-Rose, 4-3-1843; F.O. 195/727, Moore-Bulwer, No. 11, 7-3-1862; ibid., Moore-Bulwer, No. 12, 22-3-1862, and enclosures of 20-3-1862; F.O. 195/760, Eldridge-Bulwer, No. 39, 21-8-1863, and enclosure.

51. Black and Company involved in trade of cotton: F.O. 195/787, Eldridge-Bulwer, No. 21, 19-3-1864, and enclosures. Black and Company as agents for the enrollment of the drivers for the Land Transport Corps: F.O. 195/479, Moore-Redcliffe, No. 59, 5-11-1855. W. and R. Black and Company as representatives of Lancaster, Watson and Kinnear: F.O. 195/221, Rose-Aberdeen, No. 22, 5-3-1843. J. Black and Company, one of two British houses in the export of tobacco: F.O. 195/1201, No. 30, 25-5-1878; exporting tobacco from Latakia: ibid., No. 30, 2nd enclosure. On Black and Company, see also F.O. 195/479, Moore-Redcliffe, No. 59, 5-11-1855; F.O. 195/760, Wrench-Bulwer, 18-4-1863; ibid., Eldridge-Bulwer, No. 43, 15-9-1863; ibid., enclosure, in Eldridge-Bulwer, No. 61, 28-11-1863; F.O. 195/787, Black-Eldridge, 24-2-1864, in Eldridge-Russell, 1-3-1864, in Eldridge-Bulwer, No. 21, 19-3-1864; ibid., Moore, March 1864 and chart.

52. Farley, *Two Years in Syria*, p. 53.

53. Ibid.

54. Joly papers, Beatrice McCandlish Smith-Norman Joly, 26-3-1958, and other correspondence; F.O. 195/760, Henry Heald and Company, M. Bustros and Nephews, P. Pon M. Schmeil and Company, F. Zalzal and Sons-Eldridge, 17-12-1863. All those signing were agents for Liverpool steamers.

55. Joly papers, Beatrice McCandlish Smith-Norman Joly, 26-7-1958.

56. Joly papers, Norman Joly-Chivers, 1-5-1958.

57. Farley, *Two Years in Syria*, pp. 48, 52; F.O. 195/127, Moore-Ponsonby, No. 1, 9-1-1837; F.O. 226/101, Rose-Palmerston, 2-4-1848.

58. Issawi, "British Trade and the Rise of Beirut," p. 98, quoting F.O. 78/580, 78/661A, 78/802, 78/912. In 1846, The Ionian islands were returned to Greece. This reduced considerably the number of persons entitled to British protection in the Ottoman empire: Platt, *The Cinderella Service*, p. 144.

59. F.O. 195/1723, 1891, "Statement on the Number of British Subjects in the District of Her Majesty's Consulate General in Syria"; F.O. 226/95, "Subscriptions for Ireland," 23-2-1847; F.O. 226/99, "Copy of an Address from the English Residents of Beyrout and Mount Lebanon to Colonel Rose," 27-11-1848; Joly papers, Beatrice McCandlish Smith-Norman Joly, 1-11-1958; F.O. 195/700, Moore's "Report on the Trade of Beyrout in 1860," 24-1-1861, in Moore's No. 6, 6-4-1861.

60. F.O. 195/760, Moore-Russell, No. 2, 20-1-1863, in Moore-Erskine, No. 8, 23-1-1863; F.O. 195/557, Moore-Clarendon, No. 14, 8-4-1857, and enclosure undersigned-Wood, 2-4-1857. The signatures were W. M. Thomson, G. H. Calhoun, William Austin Benton, Wm. W. Eddy, David M.

Wilson, J. Edwards Ford, William Bird, Edward Aiken, Henri Harris Jessup, and Daniel Bliss.

61. Issawi, "British Trade and the Rise of Beirut," pp. 94, 98. Farley, *Two Years in Syria*, pp. 53–54, enumerated the British in Beirut. After mentioning the consul, vice-consul, Black, Heald, and Riddell, he added: "Besides these there are four or five other merchants and their families and clerks, and a lady who keeps a preparatory school for children. A physician of considerable eminence, Dr. Smith, has established his residence in Beyrout."

62. F.O. 195/700, enclosure in Moore's No. 6, 6–4–1861; F.O. 195/1480, Memorialists to Granville, in Eldridge-Granville, No. 7, 16–1–1884; F.O. 195/1683, Eyres-White, No. 58, 11–11–1890.

63. F.O. 195/2056, Drummond Hay-O'Connor, 8–4–1899.

64. F.O. 195/760, Moore-Russell, No. 2, 20–1–1863, in Moore-Erskine, No. 8, 23–1–1863; Farley, *The Resources of Turkey*, p. 214; Guys, *Beyrout et le Liban*, I, 233; Ratib al-Husami, "Tarikh Bayrut," p. 53.

65. Douin, *La mission du Baron de Boislecomte*, p. 256; F.O. 195/221, Rose-Aberdeen, 5–3–1843; Guys, *Beyrout et le Liban*, I, 200ff.; Labaki, "Sériciculture," pp. 92–93.

66. Farley, *The Resources of Turkey*, pp. 214–216; Farley cited by Zeine N. Zeine, *The Emergence of Arab Nationalism: With a Background Study of Arab-Turkish Relations in the Near East* (Beirut: Khayat, 1966), p. 43; F.O. 195/1113, Black and Company-Eldridge, 20–12–1875, in Eldridge-Elliot, No. 2, 17–1–1876.

7. The Local Entrepreneurs

1. Issawi, "British Consular Views on Syria's Economy in the 1850's–1860's," *American University of Beirut Festival Book*, Centennial Publications (Beirut: American University, 1967), p. 120; Charles Issawi, "Economic Development and Political Liberalism in Lebanon," *Politics in Lebanon*, ed. Leonard Binder (New York: John Wiley, 1966), pp. 71–72; Issawi, "British Trade and the Rise of Beirut," pp. 98–100; *Economic History of the Middle East*, p. 207, n. 3.

2. Platt, *The Cinderella Service*, pp. 138–141; Chevallier, *La société du Mont Liban*, pp. 207–228; Landes, *Bankers and Pashas*, pp. 90–98.

3. All the cavasses at the British consulate-general were Beiruti Muslims in 1877; F.O. 195/1153, Eldridge-Jocelyn, No. 18, 26–2–1877.

4. F.O. 195/727, Moore-Bulwer, No. 7, 21–2–1822, and enclosure, C. P. Lascaridi-Moore, 18–2–1862; example of Nicolas Sursock and Brothers of Beirut, under Greek protection for twenty years, who claimed in 1862 to be Ottoman subjects — with Ottoman support — to avoid appearing in front of the Hellenic Tribunal of Beirut in relation to a law suit between them and C. P. Lascaridi, naturalized British subjects of Lascaridi and Company of Marseilles, with whom the Sursocks had been in business since the 1830s.

5. Guys, *Beyrouth et le Liban*, I, 204ff.; C. B. Houry, *De la Syrie considérée sous le rapport commercial* (Paris: Arthur Bertrand, 1842), p. 52; F.O. 195/235, Rose-Stratford Canning, No. 43, 26–9–1843.

6. Guys, *Beyrouth et le Liban*, I, 208–209; Chevallier, "Aspects sociaux de la question d'Orient," p. 51.

7. Guys, *Beyrout et le Liban*, I, 208; Guys, *Esquisse*, pp. 110, 139ff.; Chevallier, *La société du Mont Liban*, pp. 203, 208; F.O. 195/235, Rose-Stratford Canning, No. 43, 26–9–1843, and enclosures; F.O. 195/965, Eldridge-Elliot, No. 38, 12–10–1870; F.O. 226/116, Rose's dispatch No. 6, 18–11–1852; F.O. 195/1153, Eldridge-Derby, No. 17, 25–4–1877.

8. F.O. Rose-Stratford Canning, No. 43, 29–9–1843; F.O. 195/760, Wrench-Bulwer, No. 23, 16–5–1863.

9. F.O. 195/235, "Translation of a Letter from Assaad Pasha to Colonel Rose, received 17th Feb. 1843," in Rose-Stratford Canning, No. 43, 26–9–1843.

10. F.O. 195/1113, Eldridge-Elliot, No. 37, 6–7–1876; F.O. 195/1581, Eyres-White, No. 3, 27–1–1887, and enclosure; F.O. 195/2056, Hay-O'Connor, No. 60, 24–7–1899; ibid., Hay-O'Connor, No. 97, 15–2–1899 and enclosure; F.O. 195/1980, Drummond Hay-Currie, No. 40, 10–7–1897. F.O. 195/1369, Eldridge-Dufferin, No. 60, 19–12–1881; ibid., Trotter-White, No. 4, 1–2–1891; ibid., Trotter-White, No. 16, 6–4–1891; F.O. 195/1761. Hallward-Clare Ford, No. 64. 8–11–1892.

11. F.O. 195/1113, Eldridge-Elliot, No. 37, 6–7–1876. Salloum Bassoul was fourth dragoman at the British consulate-general in 1886: F.O. 195/866, Eldridge-Lyons, 5–10–1866.

12. Farley, *Two Years in Syria*, pp. 54–55. Farley mentioned that the two hotels of Beirut were called Belle Vue. Most travelers, however, called only the other hotel (owned by a Greek) Belle Vue. Ottoman pashas stayed at the Bassoul Hotel, as I was told during interviews in Beirut.

13. Ibid., Buisson, "Les anciennes défenses de Beyrouth," p. 236; Burton, *The Inner Life of Syria*, p. 15; Ducousso, *L'industrie de la soie*, p. 233.

14. Mesnil du Buisson, "Les anciennes défenses de Beyrouth," p. 322, citing *al-Mashriq*, 15–3–1903.

15. F.O. 195/1153, Eldridge-Layard, No. 48, 10–5–1877.

16. Ibid.

17. Ibid.

18. F.O. 195/419, Moore-Redcliffe, No. 2, 10–1–1855.

19. Guys, *Voyage en Syrie: Peinture des moeurs musulmanes, chrétiennes et israélites* (Paris: J. Rouvier, 1855), pp. 19–20; Chevallier, *La société du Mont Liban*, pp. 206–207. See also F.O. 195/260, Rose-Aberdeen, No. 8, 13–2–1846, and enclosures; Raoul de Malherbe, *L'Orient 1718–1845* (Paris: Gide, 1913), pp. 6ff.

20. I am indebted to Yvonne Lady Cochrane for information on the Sursocks and for access to the private papers of Musa and Alfred Sursock and their family.

21. N.A.E. 236/161, 26 Safar 1248/1832 refers to Dimitri Sursock; ibid.,

235/175, 27 Muharram 1248/1832 to Abu 'Awn Sursock; F.O. 195/727, Moore-Bulwer, No. 7, 21-2-1862, and enclosure C. P. Lascaridi-Moore, 18-2-1862; F.O. 195/510, Meshaka-Moore, 1-10-1856, in ibid., Moore-Redcliffe, 7-10-1856; F.O. 195/787, Eldridge-Stuart, No. 22, 21-3-1865, and enclosures: Eldridge-Khourshid Pasha, 3-3-1865, and Khourshid Pasha-Eldridge, 13-3-1865; D. A. Skalon, *Puteshestvie po Vostoku i Sviatoi Zemle v svite Velikogo Kniazia Nikolaia Nikolaevicha v 1872 godu* (Travels through the East and the Holy Land in the Suite of Grand Duke Nikolai Nikolaevich in 1872), 2nd ed. (St. Petersburg: Berezovskogo, 1892), p. 112. I am indebted to Lady Cochrane, who attracted my attention to this source and provided me with the translation of the passages dealing with the Sursocks, and to Lubomyr Hadja, who translated from Russian the information needed from the title page for a full reference to this source. Some information on the Sursock family is also available in 'Isa Iskandar al-Ma'luf, *Diwan al-qutuf fi ta'rikh bani al-Ma'luf* (Ba'abda, Lebanon: al-Matba'at al-Uthmaniyya, 1907–1908), p. 391, n. 2.

22. Sursock papers; F.O. 195/479, Moore-Redcliffe, No. 69, 21-12-1855, and enclosures: N. Sursock and Fratelli-Moore, 20-12-1855, and Lesseps-Ambassadeur, 11-12-1855; F.O. 195/727, Moore-Bulwer, No. 7, 21-2-1862, and enclosure; C. P. Lascaridi-Moore, 18-2-1862; F.O. 195/787, Eldridge-Stuart, No. 22, 31-3-1865, and enclosures: Eldridge-Khourshid Pasha, 3-3-1865; and N. Sursock Fratelli-Canaris, 18 Feb./1 March 1860; Khourshid Pasha-Eldridge, 13-3-1865.

23. Landes, *Bankers and Pashas*; P. M. Holt, *Egypt and the Fertile Crescent, 1516–1922: A Political History* (Ithaca: Cornell University Press, 1966).

24. Skalon, *Puteshestvie*, p. 112.

25. I am indebted to Feroz Ahmed for this information.

26. Bustros papers. I am indebted to Nicolas de Bustros for information and for access to the private papers of Musa Bustros and family.

27. N.A.E., 234/93, 21 Dhu-l-Hijja 1247/1831; ibid., 236/161, 26 Safar 1248/1831; ibid., 237/188, 21 Rabi I 1248/1832; Asad Rustum, "Bayrut fi 'ahd Ibrahim Pasha al-misri," p. 130; A.D.A., MSS 31923; F.O. 195/251, 1845, p. 85; Farley, *Two Years in Syria*, p. 28; interviews in Beirut. Sa'id Pasha of Egypt visited Beirut in 1859 and stayed with the Bustros family: Albert Hourani, "The Syrians in Egypt in the Eighteenth and Nineteenth Centuries," *Colloque international sur l'histoire du Caire, 27 Mars–5 Avril 1969* (German Democratic Republic, n.d.), p. 227. Nicolas de Bustros told me about some of the visits to the Bustros by royalty—for example, the German Emperor William II was received by his father.

28. Bustros papers; F.O. 195/557, Moore-Redcliffe, No. 36, 21-5-1857; ibid., Moore-Redcliffe, No. 44, 18-6-1857; F.O. 195/760, H. Heald and Company, M. Bustros and Nephews, P. Pon. M. Schmeil and Company, F. Zalsal and Sons-Eldridge, 17-2-1863; Sursock papers, Nagib Habib Bostros, 1888–1889.

29. Ratib al-Husami, "Tijarat Bayrut"; A.D.A., correspondence of

merchants from Beirut; *al-Mahkama al-Shar'iyya al-Sunniyya*, 1236H/1846; 1288 and 1289H/1871–72, and other years.

30. Husami, "Tijarat Bayrut," p. 57; Urquhart, *The Lebanon*, II 190, F.O. 226/130, Allegations in the Memorial of British Merchants of 23–7–1859; F.O. 195/725, "Traduction d'une lettre officielle au Gouverneur," 8 Silkade 1277, in Moore-Bulwer, No. 7, 21–2–1862; F.O. 195/1153, Eldridge-Jocelyn, No. 36, 13–4–1877; Labaki, "Sericiculture," pp. 82, 106; Chevallier, *La société du Mont Liban*, p. 219; F.O. 195/1153, Eldridge-Layard, No. 48, 10–5–1877; F.O. 195/1843, Telegram from Eyres, 5–6–1894; ibid., Eyres-Currie, No. 22, 9–6–1894.

31. A.D.A., correspondence of various merchants from Beirut.

32. Bayhum papers. I am indebted to Afif and Jamil Bayhum for information on the Bayhum family and for access to their private family papers.

33. Ibid., F.O. 195/271, Rose-Stratford Canning, 15–10–1845; F.O. 195/437, 1854; F.O. 195/1153, Eldridge-Jocelyn, No. 20, 3–3–1877, and other reports; *Lisan al-Hal*, 12 Nov. 1877, No. 8, p. 4.

34. Bayhum papers; A.D.A. I am also grateful to Dominique Chevallier for putting at my disposal additional documents on the Bayhum family which he acquired from Louis Massignon.

35. A.D.A., Bayhum correspondence; Chevallier, *La société du Mont Liban*, p. 204; Husami, "Tijarat Bayrut"; Issawi, "British Trade and the Rise of Beirut," p. 98; *Economic History of the Middle East*, p. 207; n. 3; Labaki, "Sericiculture," pp. 39–43, 116; Ducousso, *L'industrie de la soie*, 133–135, 156.

36. *Mudhakkirat Jurji Zaydan*, ed. Salah al-Din al-Munajjid (Beirut: Dar al-Kutub al-Jadid, 1968), p. 4.

37. Debbas papers.

38. Kamal S. Salibi, "The Two Worlds of Assaad Y. Kayat," *Christians and Jews in the Ottoman Empire*, ed. B. Braude and B. Lewis (New York: Holmes and Meier, 1982), II, 135–158; Kayat, *A Voice from Lebanon*.

39. *Mudhakkirat Jurji Zaydan*.

40. Velde, *Narrative of a Journey*, p. 70; Porter, *Five Years in Damascus*, pp. 2–3; Eugene Melchior de Vogüe, *Syrie, Palestine, Mont Athos: Voyage aux pays de passé* (Paris: Librairie Plon, 1924), p. 28.

41. Van de Velde, *Narrative of a Journey*, I, 61–62; Thomson, *The Land and the Book*, 1913 ed., p. 20; Leary, *Syria*, pp. 36–37; L. F. Caignard de Saulcy, *Carnets de voyage en Orient (1815–1869)*, (Paris: Presses Universitaires de France, 1955), p. 177; Lortet, *La Syrie d'aujourd'hui*, p. 70; Vaux, *La Palestine*, p. 484; L'Abbé F. Bonnelière, *Souvenirs de mon pèlerinage en terre sainte* (Paris: Perisse Frères, n.d.), p. 375; *Da'irat al-ma'arif*, V, 750; al-Shidyaq, *Akhbar al-a'yan*, p. 14; Cuinet, *Syrie*, pp. 56–63; Vogüe, *Syrie*, p. 27; Kelman, *From Damascus to Palmyra*, p. 9; Barrès, *Une enquête aux Pays du Levant*, p. 32; Dodge, *The American University of Beirut*, p. 16; Princesse de Belgiogoso, *Asie Mineure et Syrie: Souvenirs de voyage* (Paris: Michel Levy, 1858), p. 176; Burton, *The Inner Life of Syria*, p. 16; *Palestine and Syria*, 1876 ed., p. 442; Ruppert, *Beirut*, I, B.

42. Atiyah, *An Arab Tells His Story*.

8. Sectarian Relations

1. *Mémoires du Chevalier d'Arvieux,* pp. 348–349; Browne, *Travels in Africa, Egypt, and Syria,* p. 377; Haydar al-Shihabi, *al-Ghurar al-hisan fi tawarikh al-azman,* ed. Na'um Mughabghab (Cairo, 1900), pp. 47–48, quoted by Hitti, *Lebanon in History,* 3rd ed., p. 392; Haydar Ahmad al-Shihabi, *Tarikh al-amir Bashir al-kabir,* ed. Bulus Qara'li (Bayt Shabab, Lubnan: Matba'at Jaridat al-'Ilm, 1933), II, 18–19; Haydar, *Lubnan,* new ed., III, 825–26; Mikha'il al-Dimashqi, *Tarikh,* p. 48; Mishaqa, *Mashad al-'iyan,* p. 125; Asad Rustum, *Bashir bayna al-sultan wa-l-'aziz* (Bayrut: al-Matba'a al-Kathulikiyya, 1956), I, 99–100.

2. Carne, *Syria,* II, 9; Blondel, *Deux ans,* pp. 20–21; Guys, *Voyage en Syrie,* pp. 21–23; Guys, *Beyrout et le Liban,* I, 74. Guys noted also Christian fanaticism.

3. Samir Khalaf, "Basic Social Trends in Lebanon," *Cultural Resources in Lebanon* (Beirut: Librairie du Liban, 1969), p. 153.

4. Guys, *Beyrout et le Liban,* I, 3, 64–65, 67, 72–73. Another sign of the simplicity of the way of life in the first half of the nineteenth century was the modesty, even humbleness, of the houses and furniture: Blondel, *Deux ans,* p. 16; Lamartine, *Voyage en Orient,* I, 116, 123; Delaroière, *Voyage en Orient,* p. 45; Clement Pelle et Leon Galibert, *Voyage en Syrie et dans l'Asie Mineure* (London: Fisher, n.d.), I, 90; Van de Velde, *Narrative of a Journey,* II, 50; Raoul de Malherbe, *L'Orient, 1718–1845* (Paris: Gide, 1846), p. 6. The modesty of the houses of the rich and the low cost of living in the 1830s is described also by Asad Bustum, "Bayrut fi 'ahd Ibrahim Pasha al-masri," pp. 126–127.

5. Ma'oz, *Ottoman Reform in Syria and Palestine,* p. 10.

6. Guys, *Beyrout et le Liban,* I, chaps. 8–11.

7. Lamartine, *Voyage en Orient,* I, 139, 385–87, 393–97, 420; Delaroière, *Voyage en Orient,* p. 46; Kayat, *A Voice from Lebanon,* pp. 219–221, 255–256; Guys, *Beyrout et le Liban,* I, 72, 83, 107, 129.

8. Guys, *Beyrout et le Liban,* I, 67, 133, etc.; Kayat, *A Voice from Lebanon; Mudhakkirat Jirji Zaydan,* p. 27.

9. Bustros papers; N.A.E., 233/40, 16 Dhu l-Qa'da, 1247/1831; ibid., 234/72, 16 Dhu l-Hijja, 1247/1831; *ibid.,* 234/93, 21 Dhu l-Hijja 1247/1831; ibid., 235/121, 18 Muharram 1248/1832; ibid., 236/11, 6 Safar 1248/1832; ibid., 236/160, 28 Safar 1248/1832; ibid., 236/131, 26 Safar 1248/1832; ibid., 237/36, 5 Rabi' I 1248/1832; ibid., 237/64, 9 Rabi' I 1248/1832; ibid., 236/85, 15 Safar 1248/1832; ibid., 236/96, 17 Safar 1248/1832; F.P. 195/127, Moore-Ponsonby, No. 1, 26-8-1835; ibid., Moore-Ponsonby, 1-9-1835; ibid., Moore-Ponsonby, No. 3, 13-2-1836; ibid., Moore-Ponsonby, No. 8, 7-4-1836.

10. Guys, *Esquisse,* p. 19.

11. A.D.A., Bayhum correspondence; Bustros papers.

12. Kayat, *A Voice from Lebanon,* pp. 50, 202ff.

13. F.O. 195/171, Moore-Stopford, 1-6-1840; Guys, *Beyrout et le*

Liban, I, 27. Clashes between people from Beirut and from Mount Lebanon are reported also in N.A.E., 231/124, 20 Sha'ban 1247/1831.

14. Samir Khalaf and Per Kongstad, "Urbanization and Urbanism in Beirut: Some Preliminary Results," *From Madina to Metropolis: Heritage and Change in the Near Eastern City*, ed. L. Carl Brown (Princeton: Darwin Press, 1973), p. 118. Poujoulat referred to Muslim quarters: Michaud and Poujoulat, *Correspondance d'Orient*, VII, 69; Nerval to a Greek quarter in Beirut: Nerval, *Voyage en Orient*, I, 396.

15. Guys, *Beyrout et le Liban*, I, 28; *al-Mahkama al-Shar'iyya al-Sunniyya* 1236H/1846 and after; Blondel, *Deux ans*, p. 21.

16. Michaud and Poujoulat, *Correspondance d'Orient*, VII, 69.

17. Ma'oz, *Ottoman Reform in Syria and Palestine; Tibawi, A Modern History of Syria*, part I; Chevallier, *La société du Mont Liban*.

18. Hourani, "Ideologies of the Mountain and the City," *Essays on the Crisis in Lebanon*, p. 34.

19. Hatred of Greek Orthodox and Catholics: Haydar, *Lubnan*, new ed., III, 585. Protestant missionaries were at first welcomed by priests and people of all sects, but after that, "It was evident that the chief priests and rulers of church, mosque, and synagogue in Bible lands, did not want the Bible": Jessup, *Fifty-Three Years in Syria*, I, 38. See also *Lebanon in the Last Years of Feudalism, 1840–1868*, p. 74. The one Protestant martyr of Lebanon — As'ad Shidyaq — was persecuted by Christians: Jessup, *Fifty-Three Years in Syria*, I, 29, 49, 183; Kamal Salibi, *Maronite Historians of Mediaeval Lebanon* (Beirut: Catholic Press, 1959), p. 163. Muslim sympathy for Protestants: Jessup, *Fifty-Three Years in Syria*, I, 92, 149, and Protestant severity about "nominal" Christians of other sects: ibid., I, 91–92, 133. Christians versus Christians: Mikha'il Mishaqa, *Mashhad al-'iyan*, pp. 76–77. Orthodox in Beirut not favorable to Maronite Shibabs: F.O. 226/74, probably Rose-Stratford Canning, No. 52, 29-7-1842. "With respect to the Greek Antiochean, of whom there are 2000 in the Lebanon . . . they have suffered both in their spiritual and their worldly interests from the jealousy and intolerance of the Maronite interest," ibid.; meetings of the Christian churches of Mount Lebanon, except for the Greek Antiocheans, the text does not make it clear whether the "Greek Antiocheans" were Greek Orthodox or Greek Catholics, the fact they were only 2,000 seems to indicate they were Greek Catholics: Albert Hourani; F.O. 195/195, September-December 1842; in Damascus, Jews feared Christians more than Turks; F.O. 226/72, Churchill, No. 2, Damascus, 3-5-1841.

20. F.O. 195/234, "Translation of Assaad Pacha's letter to Col. Rose dated 26th Safar 1260 and received 16 March 1844," in Rose-Stratford-Canning, No. 18, 2-4-1844; ibid., Whiting-Rose, Hasbaya, 13-5-1844, in Rose-Aberdeen, No. 25, 10-6-1844.

21. Khuri, "Sectarian Loyalty among Rural Migrants in two Lebanese Suburbs," p. 198–213, esp. p. 210. See also Khuri, *From Village to Suburb*; Hourani, "Ideologies of the Mountain and the City," p. 40.

22. al-Wali, *Ta'rikh al-masajid*, p. 21; *Mémoires du Baron de Tott*, part

3, p. 89; Haydar, *Lubnan*, new ed., II, 409, ibid., III, 779–780ff.; F.O. 195/171, Wood-Ponsonby, No. 19, 28-11-1840; Shidyaq, *Akhbar al-a'yan*, new ed., pp. 438–39; Frankland, *Travels to and from Constantinople*, 2nd ed., I, 351–53; N.A.E., 255/199: 25, 2 Rajab 1253/1837; ibid., 255/213, 14 Sha'ban 1253/1837; Volney, *Voyage en Egypte et en Syrie*, 241, 290; Mikha'il Mishaqa, *Mashhad al-'iyan*, pp. 31–32.

23. F.O. 195/519, Churchill-Moore in Moore-Redcliffe, No. 21, 12-4-1856; Michaud and Poujoulat, *Correspondance d'Orient*, p. 69; Jessup, *Fifty-Three Years in Syria*, I, 28, 194; Nerval, *Voyage en Orient*, I, 377; Ma'oz, *Ottoman Reform in Syria and Palestine*, p. 203; F.O. 195/351, Rose-Palmerston, No. 60, 13-12-1850, in Rose-Stratford Canning, No. 2, 8-1-1851; F.O. 195/479, Moore-Redcliffe, No. 12, 8-3-1855; F.O. 195/390, Calvert-Redcliffe, 24-6-1853; F.O. 195/194, Rose-Bankhead, No. 81, 21-2-1842.

24. F.O. 195/390; F.O. 195/479, Moore-Clarendon, No. 51, 24-8-1855.

25. F.O. 195/195, Moore-Aberdeen, 22-8-1842; ibid., Moore-Aberdeen, 1-9-1842; F.O. 195/194.

26. F.O. 195/519, Moore-Redcliffe, No. 69, 3-12-1856; ibid., Moore-Redcliffe, No. 68, 3-12-1856 and enclosure; F.O. 195/557, Moore-Redcliffe, No. 11, 17-2-1857, and enclosure; ibid., Moore-Redcliffe, No. 24, 28-3-1857, and enclosure; ibid., Moore-Redcliffe, No. 25, 4-4-1857; ibid., Moore-Redcliffe, No. 34, 4-5-1857; ibid., Moore-Redcliffe, No. 38, 29-5-1857, and enclosure; F.O. 195/648; Salibi, *The Modern History of Lebanon*, p. 89; Hourani, "Lebanon from Feudalism to Modern State," p. 258; Jessup, *Fifty-Three Years*, I, 160–161, 165–166. 193. Bishop Tubiyya was mentioned in numerous consular reports: F.O. 195/351, Moore-Stratford-Canning, No. 28, 25-6-1850; F.O. 195/657, Dufferin-Russell, No. 41, 19-21-1860, in Dufferin-Bulwer, No. 84, 21-12-1860, and other reports; F.O. 195/727, Moore-Bulwer, No. 16, 24-5-1862; F.O. 195/976, Eldridge-Elliot, No. 20, 8-4-1871.

27. F.O. 195/351, Rose-Palmerston, No. 60, 13-12-1850. Use of the term fanatical in the following reports: F.O. 195/351, Rose-Stratford Canning, 28-2-1851; ibid., Moore-Stratford Canning, No. 26, 14-10-1851; F.O. 195/390, p. 496; F.O. 195/519, No. 73, Moore-Redcliffe, No. 72, 19-12-1856; F.O. 195/557, Moore-Redcliffe, No. 67, 4-12-1857; F.O. 195/657, Dufferin-Bulwer, No. 68, 28-11-1860; F.O. 195/1113, Eldridge-Elliot, No. 29, 30-5-1876; F.O. 195/1410, Eldridge-Dufferin, No. 44, 2-7-1882; ibid., Eldridge-Dufferin, No. 53, 29-7-1882; ibid., Eldridge-Dufferin, No. 64, 27-8-1882; F.O. 195/1510, Eldridge-White, No. 11, 14-11-1885; F.O. 195/1581, Eyres-White, No. 17, 25-4-1761, Hallward-Clare Ford, No. 49, 2-8-1892; F.O. 195/1937, Drummond Hay-Currie, No. 19, 1-3-1896; F.O. 226/130, 1859, "Explanation to the allegation contained in the memorial of British merchants of July 23, 1959."

28. F.O. 195/171, Wood-Ponsonby, No. 19, 28-11-1840; F.O. 226/78, 29-2-1842; F.O. 195/320, 1848. F.O. 195/195, Moore-Stratford Canning, 3-6-1842; ibid., Moore-Stratford Canning, No. 31, 26-10-1842; F.O. 195/351, Rose-Stratford Canning, 15-2-1851; ibid., Rose-Stratford Canning, 28-2-1851; F.O. 195/171, Wood-Ponsonby, No. 19, 28-11-1840; F.O.

195/195, Moore-Stratford Canning, No. 5, 24–3–1842; ibid., Moore-Stratford Canning, No. 31, 26–10–1842; F.O. 195/557, Rogers-Redcliffe, 15–9–1857.

29. F.O. 226/72, Churchill-Rose, No. 2, 31–5–1841; F.O. 195/519, Moore-Redcliffe, No. 27, 28–4–1856; F.O. 195/351, Rose-Stratford Canning, No. 5, 15–1–1851; F.O. 195/557, W. H. Meshaka's report to Moore, 20–1–1857, in Moore-Redcliffe, No. 3, 20–1–1857. Even in the early 1850s, when complaints were filed about legal discrimination against Christians in the majlis at Beirut (for example, F.O. 195/351, Rose-Stratford Canning, 15–2–1851), cases involving Christians and Jews of other areas were referred to Beirut where they were more likely to obtain satisfaction: for example, F.O. 195/351, Rose-Stratford Canning, No. 5, 15–1–1851.

30. F.O. 195/351, Moore-Stratford Canning, No. 26, 14–10–1851.

31. Ibid., Rose-Stratford-Canning, No. 4, 9–1–1851; F.O. 195/479, Moore-Redcliffe, June 1855; F.O. 195/390; F.O. 195/437.

32. Greek Catholic differences became so acute at one point, in 1851, that the Greek Catholic bishop was assaulted by his opponents as he was officiating in the church at Beirut. The sacred vessels of the church were overturned, and Turkish police had to intervene to protect the bishop: F.O. 195/351, Moore-Stratford-Canning, No. 33, 20–12–1851. On differences between the Christian sects, see for example F.O. 195/260, Rose-Stratford-Canning, No. 21, 8–5–1856; F.O. 266/74, probably Rose-Stratford-Canning, No. 52, 29–7–1842; F.O. 195/251, Rose-Stratford-Canning, No. 57, 3–7–1845; F.O. 195/519, Moore-Redcliffe, No. 69, 3–12–1856; F.O. 195/557, Moore-Redcliffe, No. 24, 28–3–1857, and enclosures; F.O. 195/648, Stratford-Moore, No. 2, 18–2–1857, and enclosure. The Ottomans, as well as local people and foreign consuls in Beirut, drew distinctions between the various Christian sects. Thus the Ottomans were reported to prefer Greek Orthodox over Greek Catholics: F.O. 195/251, Rose-Stratford-Canning, No. 79, 4–9–1845.

33. Jessup, *Fifty-Three Years in Syria*, I, 91–92, 133, 149, etc.

34. F.O. 195/677, Moore-Russell, No. 11, 21–6–1861; U.S./3, Johnson-Cass, 27–6–1860.

35. F.O. 195/655, Moore-Bulwer, No. 33, 9–6–1860. In the same way, a report on the work of the Relief Committee established in 1860 described the distribution of food and clothing by "many ladies and gentlemen" of the committee and added that: "Not a few native Christians, *and even some Moslems*, have received refugees, and to the extent of their means fed, sheltered and clothed them" (italics mine); F.O. 406/10, Report of 22–8–1860 in Moore-Russell, No. 38, 31–8–1860. In Damascus also, "many Christians have been sheltered in Mussulman houses": ibid., Bulwer-Russell, No. 447, Therapia, 25–7–1860. This is confirmed in the memoirs of Dimitri Debbas.

36. F.O. 195/677, Moore-Russell, No. 17, 18–7–1861, in Moore-Bulwer, No. 35, 19–7–1861; ibid., Moore-Russell, No. 8, 1–6–1861; F.O. 195/656, Dufferin-Bulwer, No. 10, 21–9–1860; Jessup, *Fifty-Three Years in Syria*, I, 182, n. 1; F.O. 406/10, Moore-Russell, No. 35, 22–8–1860; ibid., Moore-Russell, No. 40, 8–9–1860; F.O. 195/656, Dufferin-Bulwer, No. 10, 21–9–1860; Atiyah, *An Arab Tells His Story*, p. 10; Kelman, *From Damascus*

to Palmyra, p. 12.

37. Jessup, *Fifty-Three Years in Syria*, I, 208. Salibi, "The 1860 Upheaval in Damascus," pp. 199–201, describes the reaction of a Damascene notable to the punishment of Muslims for their involvement in the events in Damascus in 1860.

38. F.O. 406/10, Moore-Russell, No. 35, 22–8–1860; F.O. 195/677, Moore-Bulwer, No. 18, 1–6–1861; ibid., Moore-Russell, No. 11, 21–6–1861.

39. F.O. 195/1410, Eldridge-Dufferin, No. 56, 12–8–1882.

40. Atiyah, *An Arab Tells His Story*, p. 10.

41. *Mudhakkirat Jurgi Zaydan*, pp. 23–24; Jessup, *Fifty-Three Years in Syria*, I, 245; F.O. 195/1980, Drummond Hay-Currie, No. 49, 3–9–1897; F.O. 195/1368, Dickson-St. John, No. 10, 17–2–1881; F.O. 195/1937, Drummond Hay-Currie, No. 55, 19–8–1896; F.O. 195/2056, Drummond Hay-O'Connor, No. 46, 15–6–1899; Leary, *Syria*, p. 39.

42. F.O. 195/194, Rose-Bankhead, No. 81, 12–2–1842, referred to in note 23 above and text; F.O. 195/976, Eldridge-Elliot, 28–9–1871, and enclosure from Consuls-Governor, 26–9–1871; ibid., Eldridge-Elliot, No. 58, 8–10–1871; F.O. 195/1368, Dickson-St. John, No. 10, 17–2–1881; ibid., from Dickson, telegram, 27–2–1881; ibid., Dickson-Goshen, No. 11, 28–2–1881.

43. F.O. 195/1410, from Eldridge, telegram, 6–8–1882; ibid., Eldridge-Dufferin, No. 56, 12–8–1882 (the name of the Christian quarter on the outskirts of Beirut where the young Muslim was found dead is not given); F.O. 195/1613, from Eldridge, telegram, 13–2–1886; ibid., Eldridge-White, No. 2, 20–2–1888; F.O. 195/1937, Drummond Hay-Currie, No. 1, 1–3–1896; ibid., Drummond Hay-Currie, No. 55, 19–8–1896; F.O. 195/1980, Drummond Hay-Currie, No. 22, 8–4–1897; F.O. 195/2056, Drummond Hay-O'Connor, No. 20, 2–3–1899; Atiyah, *An Arab Tells His Story*, p. 12; Leary, *Syria*, p. 39.

44. F.O. 195/1937, Drummond Hay-Currie, No. 19, 1–3–1896, mentions that Osta Bawla (spelled "Kosta Pauli" in the report) was Orthodox. Atiyah, *An Arab Tells His Story*, p. 11, says that Osta Bawla was a corruption of the ringleader's original Greek name, Costa Paoli. But Albert Hourani points out correctly was that "osta" is commonly used for someone who is a master of his trade.

45. Atiyah, *An Arab Tells His Story*, p. 11. Atiyah says that Osta Bawla was stabbed in the back at night and comments "at last, the Moslems got him." F.O. 195/1937, Drummond Hay-Currie, No. 19, 1–3–1896, reports that Osta Bawla was shot in broad daylight when he and another victim, a Maronite friend of his by the name of Yusuf Hani, were strolling on the quay opposite his residence.

46. F.O. 195/976, Eldridge-Elliot, 28–9–1871, and enclosure; ibid., Eldridge-Elliot, No. 58, 8–10–1871; F.O. 195/1368, Dickson-St. John, No. 10, 17–2–1881; F.O. 195/1369, Eldridge-Dufferin, No. 59, 17–12–1881; F.O. 195/1410, Eldridge-Dufferin, No. 56, 12–8–1882; ibid., Eldridge-Dufferin, No. 64, 1882; F.O. 195/1613, Eldridge-White, No. 2, 20–2–1888; ibid., Eldridge-White, No. 8, 17–3–1888; ibid., Eldridge-White, No. 31, 1–9–1888; F.O.

195/1761, to Clare-Ford, No. 46, 22–7–1892; F.O. 195/1761, Hallward-Clare-Ford, No. 46, 22–7–1892; ibid., Hallward-Clare-Ford, No. 50, 22–8–1892; F.O. 195/2056, Drummond Hay-O'Connor, No. 20, 2–3–1899; ibid., Drummond Hay-O'Connor, No. 26, 29–3–1899; F.O. 195/2075, Drummond Hay's report 29–4–1900; Leary, *Syria*, p. 39; F.O. 195/2075, Drummond Hay's report, 29–4–1900, mentions that the number of night watchmen in the streets of Beirut had been increased to an estimated 150. Even 150 watchmen, however, seem few for a city of about 120,000, and in any case the same report adds that the number of watchmen was likely to be reduced again.

47. F.O. 195/994, 1872; F.O. 195/1610, Eldridge-Dufferin, No. 56, 12–8–1882; F.O. 195/1761, Hallward-Clare Ford, No. 46, 22–7–1892; ibid., Hallward-Clare Ford, No. 50, 22–8–1892; *Mudhakkirat Jirji Zaydan*, pp. 17–18, 24; Jessup, *Fifty-Three Years in Syria*, I, 245; F.O. 195/1410, Eldridge-Dufferin, No. 56, 12–8–1882; F.O. 195/1613, Eldridge-White, No. 2, 20–2–1888; F.O. 195/2056, Drummond Hay-O'Connor, No. 24, 23–3–1899; ibid., Drummond Hay-O'Connor, No. 26, 29–3–1899.

48. The history of this educational and social activity, as well as of other intellectual developments such as the press, is available in a number of books, articles, and theses. Among them are Khairallah, "La Syrie," 1–143; Albert Hourani, *Arabic Thought in the Liberal Age: 1798–1939* (London: Oxford University Press, 1967); Yusif As'ad Daghir, *al-Usul al-'arabiyya lil-dirasat al-lubnaniyya* (Beirut: Habib 'Id, 1972); Isma'il Haqqi, *Lubnan*, II, 551–93. See also George Antonius, *The Arab Awakening: The Story of the Arab National Movement* (New York: Capricorn Books, 1965), pp. 35–60; unpublished article by Samir Khalaf and Linda Schatkowski, "Islamic Reform in Lebanon: The Emergence of the Makased Benevolent Society" (August 1969); Jessup, *Fifty-Three Years in Syria*, I, 243; *Mudhakkirat Jirji Zaydan*, p. 44.

49. Debbas papers.

50. Maurice Barrès, *Une enquête au pays du Levant* (Paris: Plon, 1923), pp. 36–38.

51. F.O. 195/787, Eldridge-Bulwer, No. 34, 27–5–1865. The title of the play is not given.

52. F.O. 195/1113, Eldridge-Elliot, No. 7, 7–2–1876; Eldridge-Elliot, No. 31, 11–6–1876; Eldridge-Elliot, No. 52, 30–10–1876.

53. For example, it was decided that in every district an agricultural majlis composed of six members, three Muslims and three non-Muslims, shall be established: F.O. 195/903, "Resolutions Passed at the Syrian Mejlis held in Beirut under the Presidency of His Excellency Rashid Pasha," in Rogers-Elliot, No. 9, Damascus, 3–2–1868. Mixed councils are described in F.O. 195/903, Rogers-Elliot, No. 31, 14–5–1868. By 1900, Muslims and Christians were still equal in number in the tribunals: F.O. 195/2075, Drummond Hay's report, 29–4–1900.

54. The most important single committee was probably that of the municipality of Beirut. Information on it becomes available especially after newspapers were published in Beirut in the second half of the nineteenth century, and particularly its last quarter. Its Muslim and Christian composition

for 1878 is given, for example, in *Lisan al-hal*, July 18, 1878, No. 72, p. 2. On Beirut's representation in the Ottoman parliaments, see *Lisan al-hal*, November 12, 1877, No. 8, p. 4; *Kanz al-ragha'ib fi muntakhabat al-jawa'ib*, pp. vi, 102–105. Four deputies at the head of the poll for Syrian representation to the Parliament of 1877 (1294/H) were natives of Beirut, two of whom were Christians, and more particularly Maronites: F.O. 195/1154, No. 118, 9–11–1877. The names of the delegates to the Ottoman parliament for 1878 (1295/H) is given in *Kanz al-ragha'ib fi muntakhabat al-jaw'ib*, VI, 263–265. When the Ottoman parliament was reconvened in 1908, leading Muslims and Christians of Beirut were elected again.

55. Antonius, *The Arab Awakening*, pp. 53–54. The Syrian Scientific Society is reported to have been founded in 1857, but *al-jam'iyya al-suriyya* (The Syrian Society) published as early as February 1852 lists its members and their functions: Butrus al-Bustani, *a'mal al-jam'iyya al-suriyya* (Beirut: American Press, 1852). My attention was drawn to this point by Yussef Khuri. On the Masonic lodge see Butrus Abu-Manneh, "Some Aspects of Ottoman Rule in Syria in the Second Half of the Nineteenth Century: Reform, Islam and Caliphate" (Ph.D. dissertation, St. Antony's College, Oxford, 1971), p. 280; Nadia Farag, "*al-Muqtataf*, 1876–1900: A Study of the Influence of Victorian Thought on Modern Arabic Thought" (Ph.D. dissertation, St. Antony's College, Oxford, 1969), p. 78; Zeine N. Zeine, *Arabic-Turkish Relations and the Emergence of Arab Nationalism* (Beirut: Khayat, 1958), p. 57, mentions that there was a Masonic lodge in Beirut. In the early twentieth century, the Beiruti Greek Orthodox notable Alfred Sursock belonged to the Masonic lodge of Beirut: "Diplôme de grade de Maitre pour A. Sursock, Secrétaire de l'Ambassade Ottomane, 15 Avril 1905": Sursock papers.

56. F.O. 195/1368, Dickson-St. John, No. 1, 3–1–1881; ibid., Dickson-St. John, No. 2, 14–1–1881; the Arabic version of the revolutionary text and its French translation are enclosed in ibid. Reference to the revolutionary placards that were posted also in other Syrian towns are found in ibid., Dickson-St. John, No. 3, 17–1–1881. See also Antonius, *The Arab Awakening*, pp. 78–89; Zeine, *Arab-Turkish Relations*, pp. 57–58, p. 61; Farag, "*al-Muqtataf*," pp. 72–78; Abu-Manneh, "Some Aspects of Ottoman Rule in Syria," pp. 279–280.

57. Leary, *Syria*, pp. 40–41; Antonius, *The Arab Awakening*, pp. 112–113; Zeine, *Arab-Turkish Relations*, pp. 86–87. The latest information on the Beirut Reform Committee is in Rashid Ismail Khalidi, *British Policy towards Syria and Palestine 1906–1914: A Study of the Antecedents of the Hussein-McMahon Correspondence, the Sykes-Picot Agreement and the Balfour Declaration* (London: Ithaca Press, 1980), pp. 285ff.

Index

Harvard Middle Eastern Studies

Out-of-print titles are omitted

* Published jointly by the Center for International Affairs and the Center for Middle Eastern Studies.